DEFENDING
LONDON

DEFENDING LONDON

The Military Landscape from Prehistory to the Present

MIKE OSBORNE

First published 2012

The History Press
The Mill, Brimscombe Port
Stroud, Gloucestershire, GL5 2QG
www.thehistorypress.co.uk

British Library Cataloguing in Publication Data.
A catalogue record for this book is available from the British Library.

ISBN 978 0 7524 6465 7

Typesetting and origination by The History Press
Printed in Great Britain

Contents

	Acknowledgements	7
	Abbreviations	8
	Introduction	11
One	Prehistoric, Roman and Saxon London	13
Two	London 1066–1300	24
Three	London in the Later Mediaeval Period 1300–1600	38
Four	Stuart and Georgian London 1600–1815	67
Five	The Victorian Period c.1815–1914	90
Six	London in the First World War	119
Seven	The Interwar Years 1919–39	140
Eight	London in the Second World War	154
Nine	London in the Cold War 1946–90	203
Appendix 1	Prehistoric Camps	214
Appendix 2	Mediaeval Fortifications and Defensible Sites	215
Appendix 3	Barracks, Camps and Depots	219
Appendix 4	Some Drill Halls and TACs of the Volunteer Forces	223
Appendix 5	Command and Control	225
Appendix 6	Military Airfields and Aviation Sites	229
Appendix 7	The Militia in 1850	236
Appendix 8	Intelligence and Communications 1939–45	237
Appendix 9	Site Gazetteer	240
Appendix 10	Munitions Production and Logistical Support	243
Appendix 11	Military Hospitals and Welfare 1642–2000	247
	Bibliography	250
	Index	254

Acknowledgements

Adrian Armishaw, Anneli at Stapleford Tawney, Alec Beanse, Jeff Dorman, John Guy, Lisa Harris and staff at Wickham Court School, Jeff Hogg, John Kenyon, Fred Nash, Eric Pearce, Mike Shackel, Richard Stewart of Funny Neuk, and Keith Ward.

Abbreviations

AA	anti-aircraft
AAOR	Anti-Aircraft Operations Room (ROTOR system)
AAP	Aircraft Acceptance Park
ADGB	Air Defence of Great Britain (1924 scheme)
AFV	armoured fighting vehicle
AMWD	Air Ministry Works Department
ARP	Air Raid Precautions
AT	anti-tank
ATA	Air Transport Auxiliary (ferry pilots)
BD	bomb disposal
BEF	British Expeditionary Force
BFPO	British Forces Post Office
BL	breech loading (gun)
CAA	Civil Aviation Authority
CASL	Coast Artillery Searchlight (Second World War)
CBA	Council for British Archaeology
CD	Civil Defence
CH	Chain Home (radar)
CO	commanding officer
COSSAC	Chief of Staff Strategic Allied Commander
DEL	Defence Electric Light (coast defence searchlight to First World War)
DEMS	Defensive Equipping of Merchant Ships (Second World War)
(E)(R)FTS	(Elementary)(Reserve) Flying Training School
EH	English Heritage
EOD	explosive ordnance disposal
ETO(USA)	European Theatre of Operations (United States Army)
GCI	ground-controlled interception (radar/fighter system)
GC&CS	Government Code and Cipher School
GDA	gun-defended area
GHQ	General Headquarters (as in GHQ Line)
GL	gun laying (as in radar for AA artillery)
GS	General Service (as in First World War Belfast Truss hangar)
HAA	heavy anti-aircraft
HAC	Honourable Artillery Company
HT	horse transport
IAZ	Inner Artillery Zone (London Second World War AA defences)

KRRC	King's Royal Rifle Corps
LAA	light anti-aircraft
LADA	London Air Defence Area
LDV	Local Defence Volunteers, later Home Guard (HG)
lmg	light machine gun
LNER	London & North Eastern Railway
L(P)TB/E	London (Passenger) Transport Board/Executive
LRC	London Reception Centre
LST	landing ship (tank)
MAP	Ministry of Aircraft Production
MI5/6/8/9 etc.	Military Intelligence (numbered departments)
MGB/L/TB	motor gun boat/launch/torpedo boat (RN)
MOD	Ministry of Defence
MOPW	Ministry of Public Buildings and Works
MOW	Ministry of Works
MOWP	Ministry of War Production
mph	miles per hour (5mph = 8km/h)
MU	maintenance unit (RAF)
OP	observation post
OSS	Office of Strategic Services (US version of SOE)
pdr	pounder (as in weight of projectile) 1lb = 454grams
PH	public house
PLA	Port of London Authority
PR	photographic reconnaissance
QF	quick firing (gun)
RAEC	Royal Army Education Corps
RAF	Royal Air Force (from 1 April 1918)
RAMC	Royal Army Medical Corps
RAOC	Royal Army Ordnance Corps
(R)ASC	(Royal from 1918) Army Service Corps
RCHME	Royal Commission on the Historical Monuments of England
RCM	radio counter measures (Meacon, Bromide, beam-bending etc.)
RE	Royal Engineers
REME	Royal Electrical and Mechanical Engineers (from 1942)
RF	Free French-controlled element of SOE
RFC	Royal Flying Corps (up to 31 March 1918)
RHA	Royal Horse Artillery
RM	Royal Marines
RMA	Royal Military Academy
RML	rifled muzzle loader (Victorian cannon)
RMP	Royal Military Police
RN	Royal Navy
RNAS	Royal Naval Air Service (later Fleet Air Arm)
RN(V)R	Royal Naval (Volunteer) Reserve
(R)OC	(Royal from 1941) Observer Corps
ROF	Royal Ordnance Factory

SAC/SAF	Strategic Air Command/Strategic Air Force (US)
SHAEF	Supreme Headquarters Allied Expeditionary Force
SIS	Secret Intelligence Service (aka MI6)
S/L	searchlight
(S)MLE	(short) magazine Lee-Enfield (rifle)
SOE	Special Operations Executive
TA	Territorial Army (from 1920)
TAC	Territorial Army Centre (drill hall post-1947)
TAF	Tactical Air Force (to support ground operations)
tb	temporary brick (single brick with buttresses in RAF buildings)
TF	Territorial Force (from 1908–18)
TVCB	Temporary Vehicle Control Barriers
UKWMO	United Kingdom Warning and Monitoring Organisation
UP	unrotated projectile (as in Z battery, AA rockets)
USAAF	United States Army Air Force (Second World War)
USAF(E)	United States Air Force (Europe) (post-Second World War)
VAD	Voluntary Aid Detachment
VD	Venereal disease
VTC	Volunteer Training Corps (First World War Home Guard)
WAAF	Women's Auxiliary Air Force
WAC	Women's Army Corps (US)
WRAC	Women's Royal Army Corps
WRNS	Women's Royal Naval Service (Wrens)

Introduction

Over the centuries, London, as the political, commercial, financial and cultural centre of an expanding nation, and then an empire, has attracted intended invasion by land, sea and, latterly, by air. Britain's island fastness insulated her from many of the wars that ravaged the continent of Europe, obviating the need for the vast fortifications that for so long characterised other great capital cities such as Paris, Vienna or Rome. Nevertheless, London was made defensible from Roman times, and there were times when insurrection, dynastic competition, civil strife or general social or political instability required individuals to fortify their homes just as the city chose to keep its walls in reasonable order. As Stuart kings raised royal household troops, perpetuating the pretence that Britain had no need for a standing army, these forces had to be housed, provided for and inspected. Over time, London became a garrison town, with barracks, ordnance stores and parades, and the application of industrial methods to warfare, with dockyards, gunpowder works and arsenals. If the Tower of London stood as the obvious and very visible symbol of military power, retaining a more than merely ceremonial significance into the 1950s, then many other public buildings such as Somerset House concealed their military associations. Burlington House in Piccadilly, built *c.*1664, taken over by the government in 1854 and nowadays home to the Royal Academy, is another example. In 1859 it became HQ of the 38th Corps Middlesex Rifle Volunteers, drawn from London's artistic community, who remained there until an amalgamation with another corps took them to Duke Street, Euston as the 20th Corps (Artists' Rifles). Another professional connection prompted the Dazzle Section of the Camouflage Workshop to be set up at Burlington House around the beginning of the First World War. Some years on, it became a focus for recruitment into various departments of Military Intelligence. Much former military activity, however, is now memorialised only in names: Tower Hamlets was the ancient district owing military service to the Tower of London; public houses such as The Volunteer (Epping), or The Artillery Arms (Finsbury); Brentford or Stoke Newington Butts, where archery was practised; and Artillery Lane and Gun Street in Spitalfields. At various times during the two world wars, the Crystal Palace, Lord's Cricket Ground, Sandown and Kempton Park racecourses, Olympia and Alexandra Palace have all fulfilled a range of overtly military functions.

With the expansion of its military infrastructure, London became an ever more attractive target, suffering hitherto unimagined aerial bombardment in the First World War and witnessing at first hand the measures being taken to prosecute the war, with armies being assembled, munitions being manufactured and despatched to the front, and the provision of anti-aircraft and anti-invasion defences. During the Second World War, the military imposed itself on the landscape to an even greater extent, and Londoners grew accustomed to being surrounded by AA sites, camps and depots, training grounds, anti-invasion defences and munitions plants. This military colonisation was typical of every part of London and, allied to the effects of bombing, the vast numbers of men and women in uniform, and the ever-visible presence of ARP, the whole of the London area must have at best seemed like an enormous armed camp, and at worst a city under siege. While threatened invasion in 1940–41 failed to materialise, Londoners would still have regarded the takeover of the central districts by foreign governments, agencies and armed forces, as a virtual invasion, however benign. There was hardly a public or commercial office building in the City or the West End that was not given over to one form of martial activity or another. The permanent state of confusion caused by the presence of a bewildering array of Allied troops, many of them in a state of culture shock, was one of the factors that encouraged German POWs to plan a breakout and march on London, coinciding with the Ardennes offensive of late 1944. The V1 and V2 onslaught must have seemed like the final straw. During the Cold War, London remained the most obvious target for anticipated Soviet aggression. Despite attempts to decentralise both government functions and defence assets, in the event of a nuclear exchange London would inevitably have been obliterated, almost certainly precipitating the defeat of the West. Londoners failed to be convinced by government encouragement to 'protect and survive', a farcical delusion maintained until a mere twenty years ago. Since the early 1970s, threats have intermittently been posed by terrorist activity, eliciting further defensive responses.

Land is at such a premium in densely populated London that it is unsurprising that continual redevelopments have swept away much of the evidence of those defensive precautions. This book attempts to describe the works that were constructed and the rationale behind them. Survivals make up in quality what they lack in quantity. They include stretches of the outer defence lines of 1940, First World War anti-aircraft gun emplacements at Honor Oak Park and Cheshunt, the 1907 Vickers/Maxim machine-gun factory at Erith, and a Second World War pillbox and roadblock in the shadow of the Olympic Stadium at Bow. Amazingly, one can be fairly confident that further survivals are still awaiting rediscovery, and readers who might be so lucky are asked to observe three principles: to respect private property and privacy; to take appropriate care in potentially hazardous locations; and to report discoveries to local authority historic environment officers or museum staff.

Even as I write these words, a HAA site on the Olympic site at Hackney Marshes has come to light. Gun emplacements linked by a magazine, the GL radar ramp and a close-defence blockhouse remain from what was presumably ZE21.

I know, having spent the first twenty-five years of my life there, that London as a geographical entity means different things to different people, and the area covered by this book is clearly arbitrary, roughly covering the area inside the M25 London Orbital motorway. This of course overlaps the surrounding counties, out of which the outer London boroughs have been carved since 1974. In 1939 seventeen of Surrey's thirty-two local authorities, forming London's Civil Defence Region Number 9, lay within the area now regarded as Greater London. Many units of volunteers and Home Guard had affiliations with Essex, Kent or Surrey. Additionally, all of Middlesex and parts of Hertfordshire have been swallowed up by the metropolis, and these links and historic associations have been recognised in the text.

Mike Osborne
January 2012

one

Prehistoric, Roman and Saxon London

Prehistoric London

Until a good while after the second Roman invasion, the site of what we now know as the City of London, if it existed at all, had little significance. It was not a tribal centre as Colchester was, it was not a centre of trade as St Albans may have been, and it was not a communications hub despite the fact that there is likely to have been a ford around Westminster, accompanied by a small settlement on one of the islands nearby.

The invasion of the Belgae around 100BC led to a greater density of population in the south-east, although not generally along the lower reaches of the Thames, however there was an increase in movement if not settlement in this area, with the ford and trackways opening the area up to traders. It is possible that the Old North Road was in use in pre-Roman times and this may have forded the Thames near Southwark where there have been finds of contemporary pottery. Another track may have run eastwards from around Windsor to cross the Lea at Walthamstow. The most likely centre of population in the London area at this time was in the south-west around Kew, Kingston and Richmond. Although signs of warlike activity have been found in the Thames, notably the magnificent Battersea Shield, dated to 300BC, these may simply indicate ceremonial sites where arms were deposited in the river as offerings to the spirits. Other finds however, which include a shield with a spear embedded in it, may be more tangible signs of actual conflict.

Iron Age settlements consisting of small clusters of roundhouses, perhaps enclosed by a ditch and a bank with a stockade as much to keep stock protected from wild animals as to keep the inhabitants safe from hostile tribes, tended to hug higher ground above river valleys. There were a number of larger settlements in the Greater London area, some of them meriting the status of what are generally known as hill forts. Caesars Camp at Holwood Park, Keston, is a large Iron Age hill fort, measuring 1 mile (1.6km) around its perimeter, and enclosing an area of 43 acres (17ha). It has a single bank and ditch (univallate) on the north side, but is bivallate on the west, its bank rising in places to 40ft (12m). The rest of its circuit of banks and ditches was destroyed by nineteenth-century landscaping. Uphall Camp in Ilford, another significant fortified enclosure in a strategic location, dominating Barking Creek and the Thames and possibly representing a high-status regional centre of the people who are remembered as the Trinovantes, is a large, univallate fort covering 60 acres (24ha). There is evidence for a double ditch along the side nearest to the River Roding, and in the interior, ring ditches signifying roundhouses and rectangular structures with post holes, dubbed 'four-posters' in the excavation report and interpreted as store houses, have been found. The rampart was up to 13ft (4m) in height, and the fort appears to date from the end of the Middle Iron Age. Loughton Camp was sited on a spur overlooking a tributary of the River Roding. Its oval univallate defences, with a ditch 45ft (14m) wide, enclose an area of 6.5 acres (3ha). Another small fort, also now in Epping Forest, was Amresbury Banks, a plateau camp with a ditch 10ft (3m) deep and 22ft (6.5m) wide. At the Woolwich Power Station site, roundhouses were found surrounded by massive ditches.

Roman London

Britain was subject to two Roman invasions nearly a century apart. The first was little more than a punitive reconnaissance in force, aimed at warning off the British tribes that were seen to be backing resistance to Rome across the Channel in Gaul. In 54BC, after an initial barely opposed landing, Julius Caesar met stiffer opposition from Cassivelaunus, who had been given command of the temporarily united tribes. His troops skirmished with the Romans, perhaps in the vicinity of Westminster or the future London Bridge site, defending a ford and a riverbank fortified with sharpened stakes. Having no more than interrupted the Roman advance, Cassivelaunus was defeated after the Roman army stormed his main hill fort, probably Wheathamstead on the River Lea near St Albans.

The second invasion was in AD43 when a Roman army of perhaps as many as 30–50,000 troops under Aulus Plautius landed at Richborough. The Roman army advanced through Kent defeating the Britons on the Medway in a battle lasting two days, pushing them back on London, where the Britons crossed the wide and shallow Thames by secret fords. The Romans camped south of the river, where they were joined by the Emperor Claudius. The army forced a crossing, defeating the Britons who retreated into the trackless wastes of Hackney Marshes and the boggy area around the mouth of the River Lea, possibly attempting to lure the Romans to follow. Further Roman successes resulted in the capture of Colchester and a speedy end to British resistance.

Morris suggests that a Roman army of 50,000 men would have had detachments guarding the 80-mile long (128km) lines of communication back to the coast, and also defending bridgeheads north of the Thames. While it was generally accepted that there had been no attempt to fortify the site in the early days, evidence has been unearthed of a double-ditched enclosure with characteristically military features on the eastern bank of the Walbrook with a corresponding northern section at Bishopsgate; defences that had been slighted by AD50. A further, apparently contemporary, but much smaller ditched enclosure found at Park Street in Southwark may represent a camp associated with the first arrival of the legions at the site, tying in with what appears to have been a marching camp on Blackheath on the Dover road. This, and other Roman roads, may have been laid down before a permanent bridge was built. The line of Watling Street clears the river via Marble Arch, apparently running north from a possibly temporary Westminster crossing near the present Houses of Parliament. This may have been on a long-established site of a ford or a pontoon bridge, and there might have been another bridge or a ferry upstream around Chelsea, Putney or Battersea. The level of the river was much lower than it is now, possibly only up to 40ft (14m) at its maximum depth. The island of Westminster is a likely place for a Roman pontoon bridge, enabling the army to cross in pursuit of the retreating Britons in AD43, and making it possible to establish a secure bridgehead.

Around AD47–55 London was established on a green-field site east of any previous settlement and the road alignments were altered accordingly. The first permanent bridge was built near the present London Bridge, and massive timbers forming the base for a bridge pier, dated to AD85–90, have been found on the north bank at Fish Street Hill. Roman London began life primarily as a supply depot but was already a large settlement by AD61, when it was sacked. Following the death of her husband, Boudicca the Iceni queen and her daughters were disinherited by the Romans and raised a rebellion. Most of the Roman troops under Suetonius were occupied in Anglesey putting down the Druids, so the Iceni, who had meanwhile destroyed the towns of St Albans and Colchester and defeated the Ninth Legion, had a clear run at London, their third major target. Suetonius hurriedly marched on London with not many more than 10,000 troops against possibly 120,000 tribesmen. Judging his forces too weak to resist the Iceni on ground not of his choosing, he evacuated as many as would leave. London, without walls, was virtually undefended and the Iceni slaughtered the inhabitants and fired the buildings. Evidence from this conflagration points to population clusters astride the Walbrook stream, around the Bank of England, along the Colchester road through Aldgate, and on the South Bank. Numbers of the dead at the three towns together are estimated at upwards of 70,000, as reported by Tacitus writing from eyewitness accounts. Suetonius then brought the Britons to battle, defeating them somewhere to the north of St Albans and, although some resistance continued, Boudicca chose suicide.

London had been obliterated and very little happened on the site for ten years while Roman efforts went into the conquest of the rest of Britannia. Evidence of a double-ditched enclosure at Plantation House to the east of the Monument, suggests a post-Boudiccan fort, built to protect urgent rebuilding works that were carried out on the port facilities. This fort itself had been built over within a generation, covering hundreds of skulls that may have been evidence of Roman retribution. By the end of the first century the main road network had been laid down with London not only as one of its major nodal points but also representing the most important port of the province. A period of peace and consolidation provided an opportunity for London to develop as the most impressive of Roman towns in Britain, a worthy home for the provincial government. The earliest Roman settlement appears to have been around Leadenhall. A V-shaped ditch found on the eastern side of the Baltic Exchange site in St Mary Axe was dated to the first century and was 7ft (2.1m) deep and 13ft (4m) wide. It may represent an early defensive ditch or boundary and had been in-filled between AD130 and AD150, at the time the settlement began to expand.

Early in the second century, a stone-walled fort was built at Cripplegate, covering an area of 12 acres (5ha), and over the years opportunities to explore surviving parts have presented themselves through bomb damage to surrounding buildings or redevelopment. The fort apparently escaped damage in the fire of the AD120s, soon after it was built. It was the usual playing-card shape with walls 4ft (1.2m) thick, a gate in the middle of each side and an internal turret at each corner. The wall was around 15ft (4.5m) high and had a rampart walk accessed by small, square turrets placed at intervals on the inside of the walls. The base of the northern part of the fort's west gate survives in the underground car park by the Museum of London. It consisted of twin arches in-between two-storey projecting towers containing guard chambers. Wood Street was the main north-south thoroughfare of the fort leading to the north gate, which became the mediaeval Cripplegate. Traces of Roman barrack rooms have been excavated either side of the road. The fort was large enough to accommodate around 1500 men, and this would have included a force acting as police commanded by the *legatus iuridicus*, an officer of the civil authority. They were probably auxiliaries but may have included detachments of legionaries. Additionally, the fort accommodated troops in transit on the road to or from Richborough, and soldiers who needed to be in London on official business. London's population variously peaked at 30,000 or 45–60,000 in around AD140–150.

1 A view of the external face of London Wall at Tower Hill, standing to a height of 35ft (10.6m). The lowest Roman courses are strengthened with layers of red tiles.

2 St Giles Cripplegate, a stretch of Roman wall with the lower courses of a mediaeval bastion, which was added in the thirteenth century.

During the rebellion of Clodius Albinus and the reign of his nemesis Septimius Severus (190–210), London's strategic importance increased over its commercial significance, and it needed some proper defences beyond the existing isolated fort. London Wall was built by AD225, using some 85,000 tons of Kentish rag stone, brought from the Maidstone area in, it has been estimated, around 1300 barge loads. Running in six straight lengths, two of which were formed by the western and northern walls of the pre-existing fort, London's Roman walls did not initially extend along the waterfront. The wall was 21ft (6.5m) high and 9ft (2.7m) thick, with a sentry walk on top and a V-shaped ditch 14ft (4.2m) wide and 5ft 6in (1.6m) deep. It has been suggested that the ditch, an obstacle of no great consequence, may have been water-filled from the various streams and rivers. The wall enclosed 240 acres (96ha), and was 3 miles (4.8km) long, making London the largest walled town in Roman Britain. At its north-west angle, these walls took in the fort whose wall, being thinner than the new wall, had to be doubled in thickness on the west and north. Four gates were built in the new walls – Ludgate, Aldgate, Bishopsgate and Newgate – the last, excavated in 1909, was shown to have had a double roadway running between two projecting towers containing guard chambers. That to the north projected 18ft (5.5m), but the southerly one projected only 8ft (2.5m). Aldersgate, to the west of the fort, was cut through the wall a little later than the rest, perhaps when the fort's West Gate was blocked up, and the existing north gate of the fort became Cripplegate. The projecting towers of these Roman gates may have been adapted to carry artillery at the same time that bastions were added to the walls. As well as the massive catapults, siege towers and battering rams used by the Roman army in the field, a range of lighter catapults firing bolts, stones or fire pots was available for mounting on the towers of forts and towns in a defensive role. Roman town defences in their final form were often the result of many decades, if not centuries of piecemeal development. An earthen bank and ditch with perhaps a palisade might have had stone gateways substituted for timber ones. Then the bank could have been cut back for a stone wall to be inserted, and then thickened to take a fighting platform. A final addition may have been the addition of external bastions to the face of the wall, which were sometimes bonded into the existing masonry

The end of the second century and the first decades of the third saw raids from the sea for slaves and portable treasure carried out by bands of deserters that were ultimately defeated by imperial power on land and sea. The danger from raiders sailing up-river was clearly anticipated, as a late third-century signal tower has been found at Shadwell. This may have been one of a chain, built to warn of approaching raiders. It was a square, stone tower within a ditched enclosure, a fairly common late-Roman structure. There is a suggestion that Uphall Camp at Ilford had later Roman occupation, possibly of a military nature, as the corner of a ditch has been discovered, possibly suggesting another signal tower, but there is nothing conclusive. London's later defences were built in the context of further imperial power struggles. Carausius ruled Britannia outside the Roman Empire in 286–293, and was then assassinated by Allectus who ruled until 296, when he was killed by his own troops, Frankish mercenaries who, on fleeing to London after their defeat near Silchester (Hampshire), were narrowly prevented from sacking the city by Constantius Chlorus, who arrived by ship in the nick of time and slaughtered them. Constantius then restored Britannia to imperial rule, and Londoners would have witnessed part of this denouement when a battle was fought in the Thames. A small sailing vessel has been discovered near Westminster Bridge, and it appears to have been sunk by heavy stones being thrown or fired into it, possibly by catapult. The signal towers were part of a wider system of coast defence based on a chain of forts such as Walton-on-the-Naze (Essex) and Reculver (Kent), which protected the coast and the approaches to the Thames Estuary.

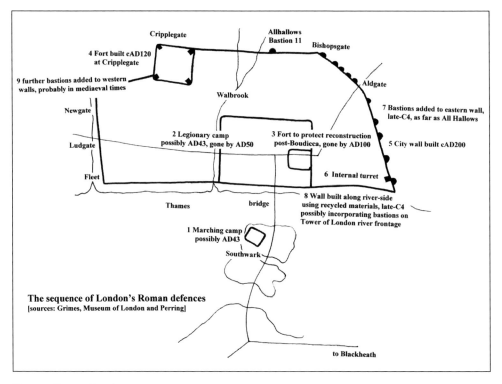

Figure 1 Roman London.

Continual raids by Irish, Picts, Franks and Saxons caused chaos, culminating in the disastrous events of 367 when Nectaridus, count of the Saxon Shore and responsible for coast defences and the Roman fleet, was killed by raiders, and a Roman army was badly mauled in an ambush. Count Theodosius was despatched with an army from Spain in time to restore order and to expel the invaders, and it was probably this episode that prompted an urgent attempt to strengthen London Wall. As happened at other places throughout the empire, this was achieved, under Valentinian, by the addition to the eastern walls of solid D-shaped bastions, roughly 180ft (55m) apart. These were up to 30ft (9m) in height, and probably capable of mounting light artillery. Possibly symptomatic of the urgency of this operation, attempts had been made to bond only two of the new bastions into the existing wall. The most westerly was Bastion 11, under All Hallows church, and there appears to have been some reliance placed on the marshy valley of the Walbrook as a natural obstacle. Fields of fire seem to have been cleared for the artillery, and the original ditch was filled in, with a wider and deeper one being dug in its stead. In addition to these new bastions, excavations in 1976–77 found that a riverside wall had finally been built of small blocks of rag stone held together by internal timber lacing, the whole built on piles on the unstable riverbank. Once again, such was the urgency here that any available materials, including an early third-century commemorative arch and tombstones, were all used. Where the line of the Roman wall now runs to the east of the White Tower, there is evidence for an internal turret, and this may be much earlier than the bastions, one of which formed the basis for the twelfth-century Wardrobe Tower. A strongpoint may have been formed in this southeast angle of the Roman defences, protecting the riverside approaches. It has been suggested, partly on the basis of the intervals between them, and partly from excavation, that the mediaeval towers along the waterfront – the Lanthorn, Wakefield and Bell Towers – may have been built on top of Roman bastions. To the west of the Lanthorn Tower there is evidence for a postern or sally port, set in a re-entrant angle of the Roman wall and opening onto the quayside, and stone floors, possibly dating from the fifth century, have been uncovered nearby.

As the empire lost its grip on its northern provinces in Germany and Holland it became less easy to export wheat from Britain to those places via London, and Southampton took over some of this trade using the French Channel ports. In AD410 the Romans announced that Britain could expect no further help from Rome and would have to look after itself. London, a Romano-British town living a Roman lifestyle, attempted to remain the seat of civil power but the general fragmentation of the established order, coupled with an increase in hostile incursions, steadily eroded the importance of what had proudly become *Londinium Augusta*. It retained the role of fortress for a while longer, being used by the succession of short-lived rulers trying, mainly unsuccessfully, to fill the vacuum following the end of Roman rule.

Saxon London

Archaeological evidence and artefacts all point to the fact that trade between London and the continent of Europe continued throughout the fifth century. After the defeat of the Britons by Hengest and Horsa at Crayford in 457, London and the Thames formed a physical barrier that prevented the Saxons of Kent and those of East Anglia from joining together as one cohesive territory under Hengest. In London, any organised settlement was likely to have been either in the fort or in the south-east corner where the Tower of London would eventually stand. There was an ecclesiastical centre at the west end of the walled area, and the riverside wall was remodelled early in the fifth century. It is also possible that the Saxon settlement at Mucking, downriver from London, was part of an early-warning system. After 592, control of London passed to the East Saxons under Aethelbert of Kent, with the Thames representing the boundary between Wessex and Mercia, and dominance oscillating between the two kingdoms. By the seventh century, the economy had begun to recover, with coins being minted in London. Within the city, the centre of gravity switched from the old Roman town to a new settlement, Lundenwic, now occupied by Fleet Street and Charing Cross; this area was a good deal safer than the decaying Roman waterfront with its dangers both real and imagined. There was a possible fortified royal centre at Aldermanbury within the old walls, lasting until the mid-ninth century. Offa of Mercia is reputed to have maintained a palace in Wood Street near St Albans church within the Roman fort, with a court or moot utilising the old Roman amphitheatre now buried under the Guildhall. Alfred used a palace or hall at Chelsea for a council late in his reign. Further upriver, at a convenient bridging point, Kingston-upon-Thames represented an important royal palace in the tenth century with seven kings of Wessex being crowned there. Grims Ditch or Dyke, a massive earth bank and ditch, 100ft (30m) in width and 9ft (2.75m) high, can still be seen at Bushey, Harrow and Pinner, and in other places, farther afield, including the Goring Gap west of Reading and the Chilterns between Tring and Wendover (Buckinghamshire). The ditch is consistently on the London side so it may be inferred that the dyke was dug in order to contain London rather than to defend it, perhaps as much to underline the limits of the city's influence as to threaten its security. But as the years rolled by and successive waves of invaders, some relatively peaceful, others less so, were assimilated, accommodated or annihilated, everyone's security was to be threatened by a new external force.

In 842 a Danish or Viking force (the names were usually interchangeable at the time) invaded, sailing up the river to plunder London. They returned in 850 with 350 ships, wintering on the

Isle of Thanet, and defeating Burgred, King of Mercia, leaving London with little choice but to capitulate to Ragnar Lodbrok and his son Ivar the Boneless. The Danish army moved on into Surrey and was eventually defeated at the Battle of Acleah, possibly Ockley, near Dorking, but equally plausible is Oakleigh near Gravesend, tying in with a movement back to their ships. The army that accomplished this rare feat consisted of the men of Wessex under Aethelwulf. In 853 the Vikings inevitably returned, wintering on the Isle of Sheppey in 855. In 871 they sacked London, and in 878 the Viking fleet sailed upriver, establishing their winter camp at Fulham, surrounded by earthworks 1 mile (1.6 km) round, which later became the site of Fulham Palace.

Alfred acceded to the throne of Wessex in 871, inheriting with it the challenge from the Danes. By 878 he had gained the upper hand, concluding the Peace of Wedmore, which brought Guthrum, the Danish leader, into the Christian fold, but divided the country between Saxon Wessex and the Danelaw. The rivers Thames and Lea were to form the boundary, placing London right on the frontier in a key strategic location. Alfred found a city occupying an area within the Roman walls, much of which had remained derelict for four centuries. People had been reluctant to occupy the ruins of the monumental stone buildings that were so alien to them and often characterised as the work of giants, and preferred to live outside the western walls in Lundenwic. Under Alfred, the city began to recover its former identity, but still contained large areas of unpopulated wasteland. Apart from the minster church of St Paul and one or two other stone churches, the buildings were of wood and daub. There was the old royal palace in the north-west corner of the town, consisting of an aisled timber hall and assorted outbuildings, but the town was still too extensive for its population and large areas within the walls were empty of buildings, allowing animals to be raised and vegetables to be grown. It was this capacity for self-sufficiency that was to sustain the population through future sieges, the only real deficiency being in cereals.

Over the next few years Alfred rebuilt the city, paying particular attention to its defences, and placing Ethelred of Mercia, his son-in-law, in charge. In 883 the Roman city walls were returned to a defensible state using whatever materials were available on-site. There is a possibility that Bastion 14 at Cripplegate, next to the Museum of London, was actually added to the wall by Alfred, as a Saxon pendant was found at an appropriate level during excavations in 1949–50. Examples of precedents for Saxon refortification of Roman walled towns include Bath, Winchester and Exeter. Saxon *burhs* characteristically consisted of earthen banks topped by stockades with fighting platforms and surrounded by ditches. However, where alternative defences already existed, they were eagerly integrated into new works, so it is quite feasible that Alfred could have built additional bastions onto London's Roman walls. He may also have patched up the wall, as is visible in St Alphege's churchyard. Bearing in mind the Danes' preferred mode of attack, there was work to be done on the waterfront too. Queenhithe Quay, projecting out from the Roman riverside wall, with timber pilings and possibly a defensive palisade, may date from Alfred's time. A wooden bridge crossed the river on the line of the Roman one, connecting the city with Southwark. This refortification of the old walled area had left Lundenwic dangerously exposed and it was most probably abandoned after it was sacked by the Danes in the 860s. There have been no archaeological finds later than the tenth century from the area, and later references are to 'Aldwic' or 'Aldwych', as in a document of 1211. It was usual for Roman forts to have a roadway, called the *pomerium*, running round the interior for moving troops to a threatened sector. This feature was not normal in towns but such a lane, now Dukes Place, has been traced inside the Roman wall marking the precinct of the Augustinian Priory of Holy Trinity, Aldgate, and it has been suggested that this might represent another of Alfred's initiatives. Excavations at Cripplegate have confirmed that there was a Saxon ditch, pre-dating the later mediaeval one but from about 950, making it too late for Alfred. It was about 50ft (15m) across, but an equal distance from the base of the Roman wall, thus possibly creating an external platform for an earthen bank, shoring up the crumbling Roman wall. Inside the Tower of London, evidence of a 16ft (5m) deep ditch running diagonally under the Waterloo Barracks and the new Jewel House, and possibly dated to late-Saxon times, may indicate a pre-Norman defensive enclosure. All these are examples of communal defences and for the slightest hint of a private fortress from Saxon times we must travel out of town. At Eynsford, under the twelfth-century hall, were found the stone foundations of a tower, possibly dating from pre-Conquest times. It may represent an example of a *burhgeat*, a practical structure with a defensive function, but also a symbol of the lord's responsibility for the protection of his tenants against external threats and the administration of justice.

The *Burghal Hidage* was the document that laid down the arrangements for manning the defences of the Saxon *burhs*, or communal fortresses. Each length of wall was to be manned by men from a given number of hides, which were the customary units of land area at the time. Applying this formula to known *burh* dimensions, it equates to around 3ft of wall for each hide. It is not now known whether the defended area was built and then subsequently measured and assessed for its manning requirements, or if the size of the fortified enclosure was determined by the number of men available to defend it. London, being nominally in Mercia, was not actually included in the *Hidage*, but Southwark, lying south of the river and thus more justifiably under the jurisdiction of Wessex, was. Southwark was assigned 1800 hides, a figure that produces a notional 2000yds of defences. A rough estimate of the probable extent of Southwark's Saxon *burh*, a rectangular enclosure extending southwards from points either side of London Bridge, produces a perimeter of 1700 or 1800yds. This would have made it one of the larger *burhs*, comparable to Oxford or Buckingham. The idea of the possession of defences on both sides of the Thames would have been prompted by a wish to make it more difficult for the Viking long-ships to force a passage up the Thames above London. The possibility of ship-borne penetration upriver suggests that the Roman bridge may have been destroyed or broken down, but it is likely that Alfred, or one of his successors, would have restored the bridge, perhaps inserting a drawbridge. Certainly by Edgar's time, towards the end of the tenth century, it was serviceable again. Possibly in parallel with the manning system of the *Hidage* there appears to have existed a guild of *cnihts* (knights), dissolved only around 1120, which had responsibility for safeguarding the eastern, more vulnerable, side of the city with jurisdiction extending beyond the walls to the Portsoken, a strip of land running down to the river outside the walls.

Despite the hopes of a lasting peace engendered by the Treaty of Wedmore, conflict with the Danes continued throughout the 890s. In 893 the Danes established a temporary fort at Benfleet, near Hadleigh Castle, which was then stormed by a Saxon army. Having removed all the women and children plus booty to London, destroyed the camp, and captured any service-able ships, they burned the rest. For a while conflict was confined to desultory skirmishing, but trouble soon flared again in 994 when Olaf of Norway and Sweyn Forkbeard led a renewed Viking onslaught on London which, this time, her defenders managed to repulse, establishing a period of peace. In 1009 London held out against Thorkell the Tall who was in revolt against Aethelred, known to history as 'The Unready', although '*unrede*' actually meant 'ill-advised'.

In 1006, Sweyn again defeated the Saxon levies and was bought off by Aethelred with a pay-ment of 36,000 pounds of silver. Aethelred then used this respite to build a fleet of 100 ships to pre-empt future Viking invasions. However, one of his captains sailed off with twenty of them to engage in what would later be known as privateering, and many of the remaining ships that were sent to bring him back were destroyed in a storm; the remnants withdrew to London. In 1011, a Danish fleet lay at Greenwich, the first firm landing above the marshes of the Thames Estuary, and in 1013, Sweyn Forkbeard invaded the north of England, sweeping round London and approaching from the south. He was faced by defenders on the bridge that linked the town with the *burh* at Southwark. Hoping to outflank these defences, some of his troops tried to wade across the wide, apparently shallow river, but misjudged the depth of water and the speed of the current and were drowned. Attacks were then pressed home but the Londoners, stiffened by the presence of Aethelred's army and the troops of Thorkell who had by now changed sides, managed to resist. Despite London's success, Sweyn went on to assert his position as de facto ruler of England, and Aethelred was forced into exile with his wife's family in Normandy, leaving Sweyn to occupy the city. Aethelred returned with a new ally, Olaf of Norway, but found London's Danish garrison unwilling to yield the town, and fortifying the Southwark bridgehead with walls of wood, stone and turf. The thirteenth-century *St Olaf's Saga* tells how the Norwegian king found an ingenious solution. Under cover of darkness his troops attached strong ropes to the piles supporting the bridge and fastened them to some of his ships lying downstream. As the tide turned, these ships, protected by mantlets of woven branches, were vigorously rowed away, collapsing the bridge and allowing free passage upstream, thus forming a blockade preventing supplies and reinforcements reaching the city from upriver.

In May 1016, two years after Olaf's assault, Aethelred was dead and his widow Emma, and Edmund Ironside, the Anglo-Saxon claimant who had been elected king in London but not elsewhere in the kingdom, were shut up inside London's walls. The city was undergoing its third consecutive siege, this time by the forces of Cnut, Edmund's Danish rival for the throne. Once again the bridge over to Southwark was seen as the key to the defences but Cnut's solution was innovative. He had a deep ditch dug around the southern bridgehead, allowing his ships to be hauled upstream and thus effecting a total blockade of the town. Having stopped up the riverfront, Cnut then turned his attention to the land, digging banks and dykes to seal it off completely from the outside world. Edmund Ironside had taken advantage of these operations to make his escape, leaving his mother and the now-desperate Londoners trapped, their only remaining hope being that he would return speedily with a relief force. The walls that Alfred had refurbished, defended by the un-warlike Londoners and some of Edmund and Emma's troops, nevertheless proved sufficient to keep Cnut's forces at bay. Edmund did indeed ride to their rescue, keeping north of the Thames and appearing out of the woods in Tottenham, driving Cnut off after a siege of three long months. The main Danish camp was south of the river, and Edmund's troops forded the Thames at Brentford to put the enemy to flight but took excessive and unnecessary casualties when a section of his force, apparently going ahead of the main army in order to secure more booty, was drowned. Despite this victory however, the Londoners' elation was brief as Edmund took the garrison away, initially pressing home his advantage against the Danes, but ultimately being defeated in battle at *Assingdun* – possibly Ashingdon near Canewdon (Essex), but more likely to have been Ashdon near Saffron Walden (Essex). Cnut soon resumed the siege; food shortages and renewed savage assaults took their toll, but the Londoners were defiant for a further three months. Eventually, a compromise gave Cnut everywhere north of the Thames while Edmund held old Wessex. Only after Edmund's death and Emma's marriage to Cnut, the now undisputed King of England, did the Londoners recognise the new reality and focus on paying the enormous fine of 11,000 pounds of silver. This represented more than twenty times the normal tax burden that would be levied even a century later, and had a crippling effect on trade in the city. In the meantime, Cnut made London his military HQ into the 1030s, retaining a large fleet of warships in the Thames, paid for by the Londoners themselves. It has been suggested that in addition to this fleet, Cnut built eight sturdy stone churches dotted around London in strategic locations that provided strongpoints for his garrison. This is not necessarily as far-fetched as it might seem, for there are plenty of examples of churches enjoying secular as well as religious significance in Anglo-Saxon England, often supplying a multi-purpose tower to private fortresses. One mystery thrown up by the account of Cnut's assault is the status of Southwark at that time. If the *burh* that Alfred had built and that the Danes had apparently refortified in 1014 had still existed, then Cnut would have been unable to bypass the southern bridgehead as straightforwardly as apparently he did. Southwark was still a collection of islets at this time, one of which provided a secure base for the southern end of London Bridge. It is possible that Cnut simply widened, deepened and linked up the existing rivulets and the *burh's* ditches to provide a navigable channel along which his boats might be dragged.

In 1035 the Saxon line was restored under Edward the Confessor, but his sovereignty was challenged by the Godwinsons who sailed a fleet up to London in 1051, penning in Edward's own ships at Westminster; after his father's death Harold continued to domineer this unworldly monarch. Around this time, the royal court moved to Thorney Island, now Westminster, where the Confessor began his great abbey church of St Peter's as well as a palace, the two together forming a new royal complex that would shortly witness the coronation of a Norman king, and would remain in royal occupation into Tudor times.

two

London 1066–1300

Norman London

After the Battle of Hastings, William marched on London by a circuitous route and occupied Edward the Confessor's palace at Westminster, laying siege to London. In the face of William's overwhelming force backed up by siege engines, and following hurried negotiations held at Berkhampstead (Hertfordshire), the Londoners quickly capitulated, accepting William's sovereignty. During his coronation at Westminster on Christmas Day 1066, the sound of Londoners cheering their much-loved new king was misinterpreted by his nervy troops as the sound of rebellion, and they began to fire the city itself, an act which undermined the feel-good factor normally associated with the accession of a popular monarch. William then moved out to Barking while his new capital was made defensible, as much against the potential enemy within as against any recognised sources of rebellion. These first structures were temporary forts of earth and timber. The classic early Norman fortress type was either the motte or the ringwork. The motte was a mound of earth produced by heaping up the spoil from a circular ditch, sometimes utilising an existing hillock, appropriately scarped, or raised from scratch. On top of this flat-topped motte there might be a timber tower, and if there were sufficient space, a palisade with a fighting platform around the edge. A flying bridge might span the ditch, defended by a timber gate-tower at one or both ends. If the mound was unstable there were a number of options open to the builder: it could be terraced, or layered with clay or gravel, or the timber tower could be built on stilts embedded in the mound, giving it solid foundations. The ringwork was a lower structure, consisting either of a simple banked and ditched enclosure, usually circular or ovoid, or a large, low, ditched mound with a timber palisade around its edge and other features shared with the motte. As to which was chosen, there appears to be little in the way of rationale beyond individual preference, possibly influenced by environmental factors or local fashion. The motte delivered dominance, while the ringwork provided more space, and Norman builders were required to strike a balance between the two. Both models were usually accompanied by one or more outer courts, known as baileys. These enclosures, defended by their own banks, palisades and ditches, held much of the castle's accommodation for the household and garrison, usually comprising a hall and chapel, barns and stables, workshops and storerooms, all of which, initially at least, were built of timber.

The Early Defences of Norman London

There appear to have been three early Norman forts built to overawe newly occupied London. In the south-east corner of the Roman walls, the Normans laid out a small rectangular enclosure of a bit more than 1 acre (0.5ha) in area, utilising the Roman walls on the southern riverfront and on the east. Ditches were dug on the other two sides to complete this initial fortification. At the other end of town there were two more forts inside the Roman walls. Baynard's Castle stood roughly halfway between Ludgate and the Thames, and its first definitive mention is in 1111, although it is generally accepted as having been raised very soon after 1066, since Ralph Baynard, Sheriff of Essex was one of William I's closest allies. It is likely to have been little more than an earthwork enclosure anchored onto the inside face of the existing city wall. It would have provided a secure base for a section of the Norman garrison, and was possibly also the home of a Norman official, since the office of castellan survived in the city hierarchy for several centuries, in both military and judicial capacities. The other stronghold is described by chroniclers as Montfichet's Tower, which would suggest a timber structure elevated on a mound. Baynard's Castle is possibly referred to as the 'palatine tower' in 1087, and Montfichet's may date from the early years of the twelfth century. In the mediaeval period, a stream ran south from the Aldersgate area, entering the Thames at Puddle Dock and possibly forming the moat of Baynard's Castle to its east with Montfichet around 70yds to its north. A kink in the street alignment at the north end of St Andrews Hill may indicate the line of a motte ditch that shared a boundary with the precinct walls of the minster of St Paul's.

Norman Stone Castles

It was at the other end of town, however, safeguarding the approach by river, that London's premier fortress would evolve. The simple earthwork enclosure inserted into the south-east corner of the Roman city wall was soon strengthened by a massive stone tower. The White Tower was started in the late 1070s by Gundulf, Bishop of Rochester. This massive keep was designed to

3 The Tower of London showing the eleventh-century White Tower and later defences along the riverside.

4 Ruislip, Manor Farm, looking across the ditch and castle mound to the later buildings.

provide palatial accommodation on a secure site. The White Tower stands 90ft (27m) high and measures 118ft (35m) by 97ft (29m), with walls 15ft (4.5m) thick at the base. The tower is mainly constructed of imported Caen stone with some stone from the Isle of Wight. Only when the basement had been completed was the apsidal projection at the south-east corner added to the plan. The original entrance, now restored to use, was at the south-west corner, raised above the basement level. This first floor probably contained rooms used by royal officials, its larger rooms partitioned by screens, and the chapel crypt has what appears to be a strongroom in the thickness of its north wall. It was only by going through these first-floor rooms that the upper floors could be accessed. The double-height second floor held the king's hall, chapel and private chamber, though privacy as we know it was not yet a concept familiar to mediaeval monarchs. The north-east angle turret contained a spiral stair linking basement to gallery, while the two western turrets had stairs between only the upper two levels. The building works clearly proceeded apace and were probably complete by 1100 when the tower housed important prisoners, although not securely enough to prevent the occasional escape. By this time the walls encircling the tower had been completed in masonry by William Rufus in 1097, with at least three refurbished Roman towers on the east, and across a bridge over the ditch, a gatehouse facing the city to the west.

Another castle site dating from the eleventh century is the motte and bailey at Manor Farm, on Bury Street, Ruislip. Later mediaeval barns stand within the earthworks of the eleventh-century castle built by Ernulf de Hesdin. It was apparently occupied for only a short while, the manor being handed over to the Abbey of Bec soon after 1090. Eynsford on the River Darent in Kent started life as a low ovoid mound with a timber tower set near to its centre. During excavations in the late 1950s, a rectangular stone chamber measuring 36ft (11m) square, was discovered under the later hall, and this proved to have been built as the foundation for a tower. This mound had an outer bailey that probably contained a hall and other domestic buildings. Around 1100 a strong curtain wall, 19ft 6in (6m) high and 6ft (1.8m) thick at its base, was built up, possibly on earlier foundations, around the edge of the low mound. A hall was built early in

5 Eynsford Castle, a view across the inner bailey with the hall/solar block in the foreground and the curtain wall of the bailey behind.

the twelfth century and rebuilt after a fire in 1250. The hall and a solar chamber were built over an undercroft, and were accessed via a staircase, initially external, but later encased in a fore-building. At the time that the hall block was built, the curtain was raised by a further 10ft (3m). A turret on the north provided a lookout position, and on the south there are the sockets for the timbers, which supported a *hoard*, or fighting platform. At the same time that the wall was heightened, an internal gate-tower was added, its arches constructed of Roman brick, presum-ably recycled from the villa at Lullingstone. It may be significant that these improvements might have been carried out during the violent years of the Anarchy.

The Anarchy 1135–54

After the death of Henry I in 1135 the succession to the throne was contested. Henry's nephew, Stephen of Blois, seized the throne, ignoring the legitimate claim of Henry's daughter and designated heir, Matilda. Matilda was then married to Geoffrey of Anjou, but had previously been married to the Holy Roman Emperor and been known as the 'Empress'. During the Anarchy, London backed King Stephen with treasure and service, on one occasion preventing the Empress from crowning herself during the period of Stephen's imprisonment by rising up to support the army of Stephen's queen, another Matilda, which secured the city. Londoners also fought for their king at the Siege of Winchester, helping Stephen to regain his freedom. However, any concessions the city gained in terms of exemptions or liberties were generally reversed once Henry II, a much stronger monarch, took control.

The Anarchy was a time when the mightier barons of the land sought advantage on the national stage by backing whichever contestant appeared most likely to succeed, while the lesser lords took the opportunity to feather their nests at a more parochial level. One of the means of achieving local power was to build a castle, garrison it with thugs, and prey on the local   and peasantry. These castles, sometimes referred to as 'adulterine' reflecting their apparent lack of planning consent, mainly took the form of the earthwork forts described earlier. It is possible that Baynard's Castle and Montfichet's Tower, both in the city itself, would have been brought back to combat readiness in those troubled times. A mention of a Ravenger's Castle in 1141 in connection with Geoffrey de Mandeville may simply be referring to the Tower whose constable he was, but it could refer to another temporary fort nearby.

There are a number of other castles around London with origins that almost certainly lie in the Anarchy. South Mimms was a de Mandeville castle actually licensed by Stephen in 1142. Although it shares many common characteristics with the myriad other earthwork castles of its time, it has some unique features. Prior to its excavation in the early 1960s it was thought that the site conformed to a conventional motte-and-bailey castle. However this was far from the case, since the motte had been heaped up around the tower. On a natural clay floor, levelled with rubble and with some flint footings, foundations measuring 35ft (10.7m) square had been constructed of horizontally laid timbers. These formed the basis for a tapering timber tower that acted as keep and lookout. The motte, 100ft (30m) in diameter, had been raised around this tower to a height of nearly 30ft (9m), and as much again could have extended above the motte top. Thus far, the arrangement was not too unlike a handful of other known examples, but in fact, it was still more unusual. A timber fence had been erected on a low clay bank, revetting the base of the motte, with the space between being filled with earth and rubble to provide a wide fighting platform. The motte, normally conical, was now drum shaped with an entrance at ground level via a tunnel through the motte, accessing the base of the tower, where there was a doorway through the foundation timbers. Finds from the site led the excavators to suppose that the tower had provided a degree of comfort to its occupiers. The motte was contained within a six-sided bailey, with a further outer enclosure to the south. Other earthwork castles include Cranford, listed in the RCHM Inventory as a small motte with traces of a bailey, at Cranford Bridge alongside the River Crane. Godstone Castle Hill is referred to as a partial ring-work by Alcock and King, because its 10ft (3m) high bank closes off the throat of a promontory above a brook. Castle Hill, Walton-on-the-Hill, is a small, low motte in the grounds of Walton Manor. It is ditched, 9–10ft (3m) high, 100ft (30m) in diameter at the top, and retains an earthen breastwork around the edge. Chessington Castle Hill, a platform measuring 100yds by 40yds and defended by a rampart on three sides and a stream on the fourth, may also represent a short-lived fortification from this time.

The Development of the Tower of London

After the completion of the White Tower in its cramped enclosure, it was almost 100 years before a serious expansion of this important fortress was begun. A new outer bailey was constructed to the west, anchored on the Bell Tower. This tower, which may have been superimposed on a Roman bastion, was unusual in that its lower stages were octagonal while its upper ones were circular, possibly in an attempt to make mining more difficult. The lowest level of the tower was solid, with a series of offsets forming a battered plinth. A new curtain ran north to a gatehouse with a drawbridge over a newly cut ditch, and then swung north-east at an angle to meet the eastern wall with its angle bastion. On the eastern side of the keep, the Wardrobe Tower was built on the existing reused Roman bastion. The Bell Tower was designed for domestic as well as military use, with chambers on two floors, garderobes, and easy access via a spiral stair in an attached turret. The key building years were 1189–90 when expenditure on works at the tower reached nearly £3000, a fifteen-fold increase on the previous two decades' total.

During the next 100 years, even more work was carried out to expand the Tower of London, consolidating its position as the foremost fortress in the kingdom. Henry III had transformed it into a true fortress palace by around 1270, and Edward I made it a truly contemporary concentric fortress between 1275 and 1285. Henry's improvements brought superior domestic arrangements to the complex that he built between the riverside curtain and the White Tower. The quadrangle that was formed, bounded on the south by the Wakefield and Lanthorn towers, took in a hall and adjacent kitchen, comfortable chambers in the Wakefield Tower, further chambers and a chapel. There was a twin-towered gatehouse, the Coldharbour Gate at the south-west corner of the White Tower, linked by a new curtain to the Wakefield Tower, a forebuilding to the keep, and a watergate, the Bloody Tower, to the river. Having completed the palace, Edward then more than doubled the area of the outer bailey, building a completely new circuit of walls with cylindrical towers at regular intervals and a twin-towered gatehouse in the middle of the western wall, more or less where the Beauchamp Tower now stands, and taking in the church of St Peter ad Vincula, which had stood outside the tower's precincts for over a century. The new southern walls were lapped by the waters of the river, and the other three sides were surrounded by a wet moat, filled from the Thames. Over £5000 was spent in 1238–41 with further significant expenditure twenty years later.

Edward I's new outer wall had the defensive benefits of keeping an attacker further away from the base of the inner walls and enabling defenders on the inner walls to command the outer ones, thus facilitating interlocking fields of fire. The gateway in the western curtain was rebuilt as the Beauchamp Tower, and in the south-west corner a very powerful new entrance was formed by constructing two entirely new gatehouses. The outer one, known as the Middle

6 The Tower of London, here the Byward Tower, built by Edward I, formed the inner gatehouse leading eventually to the keep and the state apartments.

Tower, was accessed by a bridge that crossed the outer moat onto a semi-circular platform and then by a further bridge to the gatehouse itself. Once through the Middle Tower, attackers had to cross a causeway to enter the inner gatehouse or Byward Tower, while cross walls blocked the narrow corridor between the outer and inner curtains, funnelling them into killing grounds overlooked on at least three sides. In order to gain the innermost enclosure, they then had to go through the Bloody Tower and skirt the inner curtain wall to the Coldharbour Gate. At the two northern corners were semi-circular bastions, very similar to those built at some of Edward's Welsh castles. The eastern curtain was built with three projecting platforms and heavily battered plinths, and on the evidence of the excavated remains of one of them they have been interpreted as platforms for catapults. At the river end of the curtain the moat was flanked by another projection, the Develin Tower, later reconstructed. Edward connected the Wardrobe Tower at the south-east corner of the keep to the Broad Arrow Tower, thus creating another discrete enclosure within the inner bailey, and a further impediment to free movement within it. Between 1275 and 1281, Edward spent over £21,000 on the Tower of London, an enormous sum at the time. Labour accounted for about 20 per cent of this, over half of which was spent on digging out the moats. As well as strengthening the fortifications, Edward also increased the living space available to his court by developing the complex that was begun with the chamber in his father's Wakefield Tower. In front of the original watergate he built a rectangular block containing an upstairs hall and larger chamber beside it, which became his own apartments, reached from both the Wakefield Tower and the new watergate. The queen had already been provided with separate quarters with hall and private chamber in the Lanthorn Tower and its adjoining annexe, now gone. His new block, St Thomas's Tower, had circular corner turrets and a boat dock to the Thames defended by a portcullis. Its traditional use as an entry for prisoners has left it better known as Traitors' Gate. Edward's works sought to consolidate the dimensions of comfort and defence, but after the waywardness of London's citizenry, which had character-ised at least the previous four reigns, the need to re-assert his authority must have been on his mind. The sheer size and magnificence of the buildings must have been mightily effective in restating William I's original message.

London in Times of Upheaval

In 1189, after the death of Henry II, the new king, Richard I, went on Crusade leaving his chancellor and justiciar, Bishop Longchamp of Ely, in charge and responsible for raising the enormous sums necessary to finance his king's adventures – a task guaranteed to maximise his unpopularity. A crisis was soon averted by deposing the hated Longchamp and appointing Richard's substitute, Walter of Coutances, Archbishop of Rouen, but the citizens of London only agreed to support the new chancellor and the king's brother, John, in return for the rec-ognition of London as a commune with some element of self-determination in the running of its own affairs. John subsequently used the city's privileged position as a way of keeping the Londoners on side when the Barons invited the French king to help them in their insurgency against John. He took the precaution of destroying the fortresses of Baynards and Montfichet, which were of as much potential use to rebels as they were to his own troops. However, the Barons were able to seize London by stealth, forcing John into a humiliating process of nego-tiation leading to his unwilling acceptance of the terms of Magna Carta, which he signed at Runnymede in 1215.

During the next reign, London's richest merchants supported Simon de Montfort against Henry III, provoking riotous behaviour in the streets and threats of violence to the person of Queen Eleanor as she tried to escape the troubles. De Montfort's army was admitted to the city in December 1263 after it had been bottled up in Southwark between two royal armies advancing from Croydon and Merton. Many Londoners served with de Montfort's army, perishing at the battles of Lewes and Evesham. During the troubles, the opportunity was seized to try and eradicate the commercial competition, and Jews and foreign merchants were attacked, suffering significant casualties. On de Montfort's defeat at Evesham in 1265, a large fine was placed on London for supporting his rebellion. Twenty years later Edward I suspended London's self-government for thirteen years after popular unrest. The city lost some of its liberties and trading advantages and its inhabitants were brought much more closely under royal control. Edward I made certain that the sites of Baynards and Montfichets were both neutralised for good by handing them both over to the Dominicans for the construction of their great Blackfriars community. It was recorded that in 1275 a ruinous tower was transferred to the Blackfriars, and this may have been the last vestige of Montfichets. During the reign of Edward II, London supported the Barons against the king, and was rewarded for its support by the granting of commercial privileges. Towards the end of the thirteenth century London had gained complete domination of the wool trade, with commerce from all over Europe being attracted to such a successful market place. London was thriving.

London's City Walls and Gates

It is difficult to determine with any certainty what sort of state the city walls were in at the time of the Conquest. It was six centuries since the Romans had left, and it is impossible to know how much actual refurbishment of the fabric Alfred had carried out. Danish armies had assaulted the defences on several occasions, and they generally held up, but Londoners appear to have readily accepted William's kingship in 1066, so the walls were not tested by him. The earliest evidence for a murage grant is in 1233: a specific allocation of money after more general allowances such as that granted in 1215. At least the foundations of the Roman walls and bastions around the tower site must have been visible, for the Normans utilised them for the eastern wall, Richard I used existing bastions in the construction of the Bell and Wardrobe towers, Henry III used two more as bases for the Wakefield and Lanthorn towers, and Edward I used another for the southernmost of the Middle Towers. There are several places where lengths of wall are visible, but it is difficult to differentiate between early- and later-mediaeval work. There are fine upstanding lengths at both Tower Hill and at Coopers Row, where mediaeval fabric, at least 20ft (6.5m) high over a Roman base 13ft (4m) high, and retaining discernible lengths of wall walk and loopholes for archers to shoot from, survives. A number of instances of work on the walls have been recorded. The ditch was re-dug in 1211–13, and repairs to the walls were made in 1215 using stone taken from Jews' houses, but Ludgate was doubling as a gaol by 1219, as was Newgate by the reign of Henry III, which must have detracted from their function as fortifications. As we have seen, the Romans added bastions to the eastern walls, and it would appear that a further ten open-backed hollow bastions were built onto the western walls from the north-west angle down to below Newgate by Henry III in around 1257. Four of these towers were soon inhabited by hermits.

7 Coopers Row, near Tower Hill, a length of London Wall with Roman courses below and mediaeval above, containing archers' loops. Socket holes for a timber fighting platform may be seen and only the battlements are missing.

8 Museum of London, a bastion added to London Wall around 1257, and subsequently turned into a house in the eighteenth century. However, it retains mediaeval features including arrow slits.

9 Tower Hill, the postern gate built on the edge of the moat of the Tower of London towards the end of the thirteenth century. It had three floors reached by a spiral stair. The entrance itself was to the left of the surviving tower, where the groove for the portcullis may just be seen on the extreme left of the stonework.

It would seem likely that since the sites of the pre-existing Roman gates continued in use into mediaeval times, those ancient gates were patched up and kept in use for as long as they could stand. Aldgate was actually rebuilt in 1108–47, and again in 1215. There was another rebuilding operation at Ludgate in 1260 when stone was sent from the works at Westminster for statues to be carved to adorn the gate, but some of the gates limped on for another century or more without refurbishment. The Barbican was a fortified projection extending out along the main road from Cripplegate, demolished by Henry III in 1267 after the Barons' War. Although there are no remains of the major gates, the lower courses of a postern gate near the tower can now be seen. This must have been built around 1270 when Edward I cut his new moat along the northern side of the castle, leaving a raw stump of city wall. The postern was equipped with arrow slits and a portcullis, and contained a guard chamber on the ground floor and maybe three more floors above. Built on the side of a newly dug moat, it always suffered from instability and had to be replaced following its partial collapse in 1440. There were also changes to the western walls. Blackfriars was allowed to straddle the wall between Ludgate and Puddle Dock, its new precinct following the line of the River Fleet. A commission met in 1277 to examine the consequences, and decided that the city wall should be re-routed to the west and then drop down to the river to enclose the entire Blackfriars site. This new wall was built with at least three square towers, one of which was uncovered in 1792, close to Ludgate. London Bridge had been rebuilt sometime post-1056, and was then rebuilt in stone between 1176 and 1209. It was 300yds long with nineteen stone arches and had a fortified gatehouse with drawbridge on the north bank of the river. This build, no doubt regularly patched up and repaired, lasted until the bridge's replacement in 1831. The city walls were probably not continuous along the riverbank, but there were a number of watergates giving access from commercial properties onto quays.

The City in the Early Mediaeval Period

Within the line of the Roman walls, apart from the out-and-out fortresses we have already examined, there were other defensible structures, a number of stronghouses generally built by wealthy merchants, but also by prominent nobles and prelates. In Cannon Street under Bracken House and Watling Court, excavation uncovered a number of stone cellars dating from the tenth and eleventh centuries. One had been used as the foundation for a twelfth-century tower, and the local name 'Tower Royal' commemorates a mediaeval mansion that stood in this area. Dowgate Hill now runs up the west side of Cannon Street station and was the site of the permanent warehouse and stronghouse of those traders from Cologne who were later to become the Hanseatic League. This plot, only formally granted by Henry III, had been occupied from 1157, and continued to develop over the next 100 years, gaining renewed royal approval from Edward I by 1275. St Paul's church was rebuilt between 1087 and 1136, and enclosed by a precinct wall with a gate at the west end of Cheapside. Very few remains of Norman stone houses survive, but two found in the city appear to suggest that a vaulted undercroft and a first-floor hall or chamber entered by external steps was probably the norm for houses of the wealthier merchants and other sections of the social elite. This arrangement gave protection against fire, and afforded a certain measure of security against either casual thieves or the mob.

Westminster in the Early Mediaeval Period

The Normans found the palace of Edward the Confessor, begun around 1050, on the banks of the Thames at Westminster to the north of his great church. It consisted of a stone hall as the centrepiece, with other domestic and service buildings around it. By the reign of Rufus, the Norman monarchy was confident enough to consolidate the existing palace as its own, and in 1097–99 the hall was rebuilt on an enormous scale, measuring 240ft (48m) in length and nearly 70ft (21m) wide, one of the largest such halls in Europe. It has been suggested that a slight bowing in the long sidewalls may indicate that the Confessor's hall was encased in new masonry and only demolished once the replacement envelope was in place. Building on the site continued through the next century when the White Hall was built with a great chamber at right angles to it, earmarked for the use of the king. Henry III completely rebuilt this great chamber, producing the Painted Chamber together with a chapel. Henry's second son, Edmund, had his own self-contained palace within the precinct. The whole palace complex, by now embracing offices of the evolving state such as the Exchequer and the Chancery, and the lodgings of the administrators who worked in them, was enclosed within a strong, buttressed wall pierced by a number of gates, the exact positions of most of which remain obscure. The main gate from King Street, built by Edward I, gave entry to the outer court, now New Palace Yard, and a watergate accessed a pier at the north-east corner of the site. An inner gate led into the Privy Palace, which was connected to the abbey by a postern gate north of the Jewel Tower. It would appear that this inner gate was originally built of timber, for in 1240 the wall connecting the Great Hall and the abbey wall was crenellated, and a few years later the gateway itself was rebuilt in stone, lasting until 1731. Henry clearly believed in recycling, as the timber gate was taken down, carried to Kempton and re-erected there. The Great Gate was rebuilt by Richard II.

To the north of the royal palace, between King Street and the Thames, another such complex of residential buildings surrounding a chapel was taking shape by 1220. It was bought by Walter de Grey in 1240 to become the London residence of the archbishops of York, and consequently named York Place. By the end of the thirteenth century, it was considered sufficiently grand to be loaned to Edward I.

The third great enclosed area in Westminster itself was, of course, the great monastic precinct of St Peter's. Edward the Confessor's church was largely completed by 1065 and lasted until its demolition by Henry III in 1245. After the Conquest, the Normans added extensive monastic buildings, all contained within precinct walls whose West Gate stood at the east end of Tothill Street, with the North Gate as far away from the abbey as Parliament Square, near the southern end of what is now Whitehall. At the south end of Great College Street was a large tower with crenellated parapet and battered base, which formed the south-east angle of the defended precinct, and would suggest that other similar towers punctuated the defences, particularly at the vulnerable angles.

Royal and Episcopal Palaces

On a far grander scale than stronghouses within the walls were the palaces that surrounded the centre of London. There were several royal palaces on the periphery of London at this time. A manor house had stood at Kennington from the twelfth century but only its boundary ditch and some post holes, possibly from a hall, were found when the site was excavated. The rest of the early period had been obliterated by the new buildings put up by the Black Prince. Henry III was evidently taken by the manor of Kempton, and obtained it in 1228 by exchanging lands elsewhere. Kempton consisted of a hall and chamber for the king, chambers for the queen and the household knights, a two-storey chapel and kitchens, all apparently free-standing within a walled enclosure entered through a timber-framed gatehouse, replaced in 1244 by the one from Westminster Palace. The manor enjoyed only sporadic use by Henry's successors, gradually deteriorating before being gifted to a local who sold the building materials for profit in 1374. Havering-atte-Bower was built by Henry II in 1164 and expanded by John in 1210 as an unfortified hunting lodge consisting of a loose grouping of stone buildings, including a hall, two chapels and the usual offices, surrounded by gardens. In 1253 Henry III ordered the buildings enclosed within a rag-stone wall, which was completed in 1263. Kingston-upon-Thames had had strong royal connections from Saxon times and a site on the corner of Kingston Hill Road has traditionally been known as King John's Palace. Richard II was staying in Kingston, possibly at this palace, when he was given the news of his father's death. A pillar outside the public library is reputedly a remnant of the house pulled down in 1805.

The archbishops of Canterbury had two palaces in London. Lambeth had been begun in the twelfth century but the only survival from that period is the undercroft below the later chapel of 1230, rebuilt following war damage. Croydon Palace, dating from before Domesday, was an administrative centre for the See of Canterbury's properties in the region. The audience chamber, currently known as the 'Guardroom', may have begun life as a twelfth-century hall positioned over an undercroft and measuring 51ft by 21ft (24m by 6.5m). The bishops of Winchester had two palaces in London; one of which, in Clink Street, Southwark, was built by Henry de Blois, brother of King Stephen and an enthusiastic builder of castles and palaces, in 1145. Some foundations dated to the first half of the twelfth century have been excavated, but the upstanding masonry is later. The other residence was near the river at Kingston-upon-Thames. It had been established by 955 and was still in use in 1392, but had disappeared by

1800. Like Croydon, its administrative function was probably as important as its ceremonial or domestic ones. Fulham Palace, the main residence of the bishops of London, also had its origins in Saxon times. It was constructed inside the largest mediaeval moat in Britain, first recorded in 1392. However, this moat, 1600yds (1.4 km) long, appears to have its origins in the winter laager of a ninth-century Danish fleet. Recent work on the moat has revealed timber beams dated to the middle years of the thirteenth century, discovered under a layer of silt containing pottery of no later than 1350. The timbers appear to have supported three vertical trestles of a timber bridge, superseded by the existing adjacent stone bridge.

King Street formed the southern section of the road linking Westminster and the city, while the Strand formed the northern section. Many nobles and bishops established their London mansions or palaces along these roads. In 1245, Peter of Savoy, uncle of Henry III's queen, was granted leave to build a grand palace on the Strand. He left England in 1263 to become Count of Savoy and on his death five years later he left the house to an alpine hospice. However, Queen Eleanor bought it back for her son Edmund of Lancaster, brother of Edward I, who received licence to crenellate his new property with a wall of stone and lime. Few of his neighbours will have sought licences but their houses would nevertheless have had defensible features, if only a wall and secure gatehouse. Arundel House on the Strand, a neighbour of the Savoy, was the town house of the bishops of Bath. A stone hall with timber-framed service rooms over stone undercrofts were ranged around a courtyard that was entered by a gateway.

The palace of the bishops of Ely, Ely Place in Hatton Garden, was built before 1290. It consisted of a Great Hall and apartments, ranged around courtyards. Its chapel of 1290 survives as St Etheldreda's church. The whole quadrangular palace, enclosed by walls, was entered through a gatehouse, latterly built by Bishop Arundel in the fourteenth century. The London Temple on Fleet Street was the HQ of the Order of Knights Templar in England from c.1160 when they moved there from Holborn. The order was savagely suppressed in 1308, and all their properties were handed over to the Order of St John of Jerusalem, the Hospitallers, in 1324. The characteristically circular nave of the Temple church survives.

Castles and Fortified Manor Houses of the Period

The dividing line between castles and fortified manor houses is a fine one, so, it being debateable into which of those categories they might fall, a number of sites will be dealt with together.

Farningham retains vestiges of a stone curtain wall, 5ft (1.8m) high and 7ft (2.1m) thick, within a moat, and dates from the thirteenth or fourteenth centuries. A brick manor house was built on top of this curtain some 200 years later. Neighbouring Shoreham, lying in the swampy Darenth Valley, was mentioned as changing hands in 1307 and retains three large chunks of flint masonry within a mediaeval moat. In 1429 Sir Rovert d'Aguillion received licence to crenellate his property known as Addington Castle Hill. In mediaeval times Kingston-upon-Thames was the next bridging point above London so tended to attract visitors to London who were put off by their hostile reception on London Bridge. Kingston's mediaeval bridge of 1219 was replaced in 1828 and its predecessor's site was excavated in 1972. The twelfth-century, three-arched Clattern Bridge over the Hogsmill River, a stream that flows into the Thames, survives but in a much-altered state. There are references to a castle, presumably guarding the bridge, built on common land, which would suggest some urgency in fortifying this strategically important crossing. It was apparently captured by Henry III during his march on London during the Barons' Wars in 1264. This castle may possibly have been a temporary construction erected hurriedly and standing for only a short time. Albury Manor, Merstham dates from about 1260 and consists of separate hall and chamber blocks within an inner moated courtyard. An outer moat had three sides, with a fourth formed by a stream, now in a conduit underground. The manor was occupied through the thirteenth and fourteenth centuries. Preston Hawe at Banstead comprised extensive earthworks of the twelfth to fourteenth centuries that incorporated small mounds dubbed 'mini mottes' by the excavator, but also known as guard points. The Moats at Leatherhead was a moated manor begun in the twelfth century but mainly built by Sir Eustace de la Hache in 1290–91, with a hall and chapel, and was in occupation until about 1350. These last three sites span the turn of the thirteenth century when the domestic arrangements of manor houses were undergoing quite a radical change. Hitherto, hall and chamber had been separate free-standing buildings, often built over undercrofts and entered at first-floor level, but around 1300, builders began to put the chamber block at the dais end of the hall, allowing the lord and his family access from one to the other. One interim solution was to use the refurbishment of a property to find some way of achieving as close a juxtapositioning as possible. Moor Hall, Harefield, was a cell of the Hospitallers from Clerkenwell, where, well into the twentieth century, there survived a mediaeval hall, later reworked as a farmhouse, and a stone building, dating from c.1220, with two chambers over an undercroft, most likely accessed at first-floor level and possibly representing the prior's lodging. The hall, dating from about 1300, had been built as close as could be managed up against the earlier chamber block.

Monastic Precincts

The last category of defensible structure to be looked at here is the monastery. Most monastic precincts were walled, with entrances through strong gatehouses, usually incorporating a room for the porter, the mediaeval equivalent of the security guard. The great monastic foundations of London, either within or without the city walls, were so protected. At St Bartholomew the Great, the present gate incorporates the thirteenth-century entrance to the original nave of the priory. The new Dominican friary of Blackfriars tucked itself inside a realignment of the city walls, and the Priory of Holy Trinity, Aldgate, encroached on the *pomerium*, inserting a postern gate in the city wall in 1122. The priors of St John's, Clerkenwell, the first Hospitaller house in England, lying outside the city wall, built the characteristic circular church in 1150 with a nave, enlarged to the east in 1185, within strong precinct walls.

three

London in the Later Mediaeval Period
1300–1600

The fourteenth century was a disastrous time for most of England's population. The early years saw the coming of the Little Ice Age, when extremely wet weather and a general lowering of the temperature caused crops to fail, wiped out livestock and resulted in extreme food shortages. As a result, the years 1315–22 saw acute social upheaval. As if that were not enough, there was the plague, which came particularly severely in 1348, 1361, 1369, 1374 and 1379. The population of London in 1300 probably numbered not many more than 40,000 people, with some small increase up to 1340, but a drastic reduction of population due to plague, with an estimated death rate of around 30–40 per cent, meant that it would take 150 years to regain its former levels. However, economic recovery came much more quickly than for the rest of the country as London continued to outstrip every other city in England, being ten times wealthier than the second city, Norwich, and increasing its wealth at a much faster rate than any other mercantile centre. There was some disruption of trade during periods of unrest, such as the Hundred Years War, but expectations of growth and progress were realised; successful trade was necessary to finance the wars. On the other hand, the war dislocated the social order, taking men away from families and then returning them, often damaged and with little hope of employment. The city of London was still mainly confined to the area within the city walls, and open, undeveloped areas remained. There was a straggle of big houses such as the Savoy on the strip that linked Ludgate and Westminster; the self-contained monastic communities such as Clerkenwell and the Charterhouse outside the northern walls; settlements on the Portsoken, the strip that ran down the eastern side outside the walls; and the large parish of Faringdon Without extending west to Temple Bar.

Developments at the Tower of London

The tower remained the premier fortress of London. While the major developments had already taken place, the castle continued to evolve both as a major fortification and as a palatial seat of kingship. Much of the work undertaken by Edward III had two major objectives. Firstly, there was a need, particularly during the wars with France, to ensure the security of the riverfront by raising and reinforcing the curtain walls, by creating a strong gatehouse between the Lanthorn and Salt towers, and by inserting the Cradle Tower as a watergate for the king's private use. At the southern end of the eastern moat, a screen wall was built to link the Develin Tower with a new iron gate on the outer bank. Edward's second objective was to develop new state apartments around the Lanthorn Tower, to which, it is surmised, the Cradle Tower was intended to provide discreet access. It is likely that Edward built the stone two-storey annexe housing the Royal Wardrobe against the eastern wall of the keep. Under Richard II the full-length quay was extended, giving ships better access. Sometime during the reign of Edward IV (1461–83) the tower received, in purely military terms, its most innovatory addition. This was the Bulwark, a screen wall that ran from in front of the Middle Tower with its semi-circular barbican, in an arc back to the outer lip of the moat at a point opposite the Beauchamp Tower where it terminated in a pair of squat bastions flanking a new outer gate. The whole work was built out of brick, and it seems likely that the bastions were designed to carry gunpowder artillery. There were penthouses built against the wall, one of which was designated for the Keeper of the Bulwark in 1484, who may have been initiated into the mystery of gunnery, after all there had been a Master of the Ordnance at the tower since 1414.

However strong the tower's fortifications might have been, they needed to be stoutly defended by a garrison. During the Peasants' Revolt these defences failed when the mob ran-sacked the Royal Wardrobe, prompting the construction of more secure accommodation for the royal regalia, robes, clothes, jewels, armour and weapons. In 1460 the garrison underwent an artillery bombardment, but managed successfully to hold out against the Yorkist besiegers, only capitulating after Henry VI's capture.

London Walls

The mediaeval city walls, serving a variety of functions, were periodically repaired but the city authorities were not under the same pressure to expand the walled area as in cities elsewhere on the Continent, which were continually threatened by territorial conflicts and marauding armies of mercenaries. This meant that undefended suburbs spread outside the walls, with build-ings encroaching on the city ditch or even on the walls themselves, and the citizens sometimes taking building materials for their own use. Richard II ordered a clean-up and general repair in 1387, but the city authorities had been attempting to tackle the problem for the previous ten years. Despite these criticisms, the walls were nevertheless not unimpressive. Where they can be seen at their full height at Tower Hill or Coopers Row their height can be gauged to have been nearly 40ft (12m) above ground level. Add in the depth of the ditch, probably at least a further 15–16ft (5m), and their defensive effect becomes evident. The bastions and corner towers had walls 7ft (2.1m) thick on substantial foundations, and that at the GPO building at St Martin-le-Grand projected some 26ft (8m) into the field. When the city moat at Houndsditch was excavated it was found to be 18ft (5.5m) wide. In 1415 a local mercer paid for a proper gate at Moorgate where there may have been an earlier postern for convenient access to the moors, where cloth was laid out on trestles in the sun. Bridgegate, where London Bridge entered the city, was built in 1426, and Newgate was rebuilt in 1423–32. The postern by the Tower of London was rebuilt in 1440 because it was sliding into the moat. Since about 1350 Temple Bar had marked the boundary of the City of London. We have seen how Ludgate and Newgate had become prisons and Aldgate a dwelling, tenanted by Geoffrey Chaucer from 1374–85, towers had their resident hermits, and others served as vicarages for some of the churches that nestled up to the walls. The gates presented sturdy stone towers with arrow slits and battlements to the outside, but were often backed by timber-framed extensions. At times of stress ordinances were issued detailing measures for the city's security. These usually included ensuring that the gates were secure with working drawbridges, portcullises, chains or draw bars, and barbicans, prob-

10 London Wall at St Alphege's churchyard showing the red-brick battlements added to the earlier wall during the Wars of the Roses by Mayor Joceline in 1477.

ably temporary constructions of timber, were emplaced. If there was a real emergency, then a retrenchment inside the gate would be assembled. This would basically be a barricade of carts and barrels and whatever else was available. In 1477, Mayor Jocelyn embarked on a rebuilding programme for London Walls. Brick arches were added to the interior of vulnerable lengths of the walls to make them stronger against artillery or to support a wider fighting top. Stretches were given new brick merlons, as can still be seen in St Alphege's churchyard above earlier patchings. Moorgate was rebuilt in 1472, Bishopsgate in 1479, and Cripplegate in 1491.

Stronghouses Within the City Walls

Readers may be familiar with those Tuscan hill towns such as San Gimignano that present a skyline filled with mediaeval towers, and it may be hard to accept that other than being on a much larger scale, London was very little different. Violent times breed a quest for security, especially in those with much to lose from civil disorder, riot, political gangsterism or everyday criminal activity. The early fourteenth century saw the development of a trend, particularly among wealthy merchants, of obtaining licences to crenellate their houses in the City of London. These stronghouses were built of stone, usually over a vaulted basement or undercroft, with a secure front door sealed by an iron grille or yett. These features were prompted largely by common sense in the context of having mainly timber buildings for neighbours. The Licence to Crenellate introduced a fortified dimension, usually achieved by the addition to the house of a tower, which would be tall, battlemented, equipped with arrow-loops, and capable of being isolated from the rest of the house by a stout, barred door, maybe with a further yett. A good example is the house in Pountney Lane, Candlewick Street, near the Thames waterfront. Here, the Manor of the Rose was built by Sir John Pultney, who had been Mayor of London in

1336 and also built Penshurst Place (Kent), and the Manor of Cheveley (Cambridgeshire), with all three properties being licensed by Edward III in 1341. Attached to the house was a four-storey battlemented tower that survived into the mid-sixteenth century. Pultney died of plague in 1348, by which time his house was occupied by the Black Prince. At least a dozen similar houses are recorded, some, such as that in Ave Maria Lane with tower and gatehouse, belonged to aristocrats like the Earl of Pembroke, from around 1350. Others were owned by princes of the Church, the Bishop of Hereford, for example, built on the corner of Lombard Street and Old Fish Street. Roles were often blurred in mediaeval London, and several men described as 'clerics' had put their monastic education to good effect by serving as lawyers with strong commercial interests. These included John de Pelham who held two stronghouses, in Distaff Lane near St Paul's, and in Silver Street on London Wall, both licensed in 1311, and Robert de Kelsey, citizen, lawyer and trader, who was licensed in West Cheapside in 1315.

It has been suggested that the grant of licences was sometimes a reward for services rendered to the Crown, and it is possible that John de Cologne was granted a licence for a house in Cornhill in 1337 in recognition of his services to Edward III in helping to finance the wars in Scotland and France. Some, holding large amounts of money on their premises, might have thought it a wise precaution, while for others, their general unpopularity may have been the motivation. La Tour, a property fronting the Thames in Coldharbour, possibly consisting of a hall with a crenellated tower attached, was owned by Alice Perrers, the mistress of Edward III in the 1370s. Royal mistresses and officers of state constantly ran the risk of attracting the attention of the mob. Sadly for John de Molyns, treasurer to Edward III, his house in Baynards Ward, licensed in 1338, could not save him from a public lynching. The City Livery companies also made sure that their valuables were safeguarded. The Merchant Taylors' Hall of 1375 in Threadneedle Street was built on an undercroft, later extended to support a chapel. There was a detached stone kitchen, and the Great Gate onto Cornhill. In a city of often poorly built timber structures, these longer-lasting and more secure stone stronghouses were highly prized, frequently changing hands and enjoying extended lives. The merchant for whom Servats or Serne's Tower, in Bucklesbury, was named, was granted a licence in 1305, allowing him to crenellate a turret above the gate of his house in Lombard Street, with the River Walbrook forming one boundary. The house was acquired by Queen Isabella in 1317 and later housed the Great Wardrobe, providing a convenient base for royal procurement in the heart of the city's mercantile district. These premises, however, proved inadequate and in 1361 the mansion of the late Sir John Beauchamp was bought for the purpose by Edward III. The Prince's Wardrobe, on a site off Old Jewry, had passed to the Black Prince from John of Eltham. The spacious premises included a great hall, chamber, chapel and kitchen, and later on an outer wall and a tower, making it defensible.

In addition to these compact stronghouses there were larger complexes of buildings within their own secure enclosures. The Steelyard of the merchants of Cologne expanded as the commercial power of the merchants of the Hanseatic League developed. By the end of the fourteenth century the site had grown to include a great hall, the master's house, a roofed gallery along the river frontage, a four-storey tower, a tall crane and warehouses, reaching its fullest extent by 1475. Bishopsgate's Crosby Place was an extension of an existing house, forming a large courtyard with parlour, hall and service buildings, and two further courtyards with extensive storage vaults. It had been built in 1466 by Sir John Crosby, a successful silk merchant and member of the Grocers' Company, and was later lived in by Sir Thomas More. The hall alone survived the Great Fire and, threatened with demolition in 1907, it was taken down and re-erected on the Chelsea Embankment. Other such imposing enclaves were built by the religious orders.

Monastic Precincts in the City

The English headquarters of the Knights Hospitaller or Priory of St John of Jerusalem was in Clerkenwell, just outside the city walls. The church had been consecrated in 1185 by Heraclitus, Patriarch of Jerusalem, at the same time as the London Temple, administrative centre of the Knights Templar in England. Their buildings were considered to be so secure that kings deposited their treasure there for safekeeping. In 1307, when Edward I suppressed the Templars as an order, their properties went to the Knights of St John, with the Temple being taken over in 1312 and leased to the Inns of Court by the mid-1300s. The round church can still be seen, with effigies of knights lying on their tombs. Both the Temple and the Priory of St John were sacked during the Peasants' Revolt, when the Hospitallers' master, Sir Robert Hales, as the king's treasurer, was seen to be responsible for the Poll Tax. His head ended up on a spike on London Bridge. The Priory of St John of Jerusalem in Clerkenwell was gradually rebuilt and made more secure against external threats. The present gatehouse was built in 1504, and much remodelled in Victorian times, built in brick and faced with stone. There is a gate hall over the arch, which is flanked by four-storey towers with a chamber on each floor. Beneath St John's church lies the original twelfth-century crypt. The precincts of the priory may be traced in the neighbouring street pattern, with Jerusalem Passage marking a former postern gate.

The London Charterhouse, a Carthusian priory founded in 1370, lies very close to the Priory of St John, also just outside the city walls. It lies within a strong boundary wall built in 1405 to ensure the integrity of the monastic enclosure, and retains an early fifteenth-century arch and the doors of the Outer Gatehouse, whose lower parts, mainly built of stone, are original, with a carriage arch and a slightly later pedestrian arch in brick. The adjacent later house of two

storeys extends over the top. The priory was redeveloped in the sixteenth century by Lord North and in the seventeenth by Thomas Sutton, whose badge of cannons and gunpowder kegs signify his holding of the office of Master of the Ordnance of the North. The buildings, subsequently much rebuilt following bomb damage during the Second World War, include the brick inner gateway of the early sixteenth century, basically original but with some reconstruction. Next to the monks' chapter house, now the chapel, stands the Chapel Tower, on its first floor containing the priory strongroom, which housed its treasury.

11 Clerkenwell, the gate of the priory of the Hospital of St John, destroyed by the mob in the Peasants' Revolt. The gate was rebuilt in 1504 and still houses the headquarters of the Order of St John, now better known as St John's Ambulance.

The Priory of Our Lady of Mount Carmel, the Whitefriars, lay between Fleet Street and the Thames next to the Temple, with two gates onto Fleet Street. In 1385 Matilda de Well was granted a licence to crenellate a house within the Carmelite property. It may have been a small tower house reflecting her status as the widow of Lord Welles, a prominent Lincolnshire land-owner. The only relic of the buildings on the priory site is a small, stone, vaulted cellar, thought to represent the prior's lodging, now under Britton's Court. Other houses, including that of the Courtenay earls of Devon, the priory's benefactor, lay on the eastern side, fronting onto Whitefriars Street, and this may have been where Lady Welles had her house. Most conventual houses had some form of secure entrance, usually a full gatehouse, attended by a lay porter. Blackfriars, on the site of Baynard's Castle, where the line of the city walls had been diverted in 1276, provided a well-defended neutral venue for State business managed by the Dominicans, accommodating parliament, for instance, in 1311.

Westminster in the Later Mediaeval Period

Westminster was very much a separate settlement, a couple of miles removed from the city, with a population of around 3000 in 1300, but falling through the plague years to not many more than a hundred years later. Much of this population was dependent on the several institu-tions that constituted Westminster's raison d'être: the royal palace, the great abbey, and the town houses of the officers of state, the rich courtiers and even richer prelates, and the royal house-hold, which is estimated to have employed around 1000 servants of differing degree.

Westminster Palace continued in use as the major royal palace in London, and from the mid-fourteenth century the administra-tive hub of the kingdom, until much of it was destroyed by fire in 1512. The Great Hall had been remodelled by Richard II in 1394–1402, using much of the existing masonry but incorporating a magnificent new hammer-beam roof structure designed by the carpenter Hugh Herland; its extremely wide span and 600-ton weight are now reckoned to be largely sup-ported by the corbels and walls. Started by Edward I 1292–97, and continued in 1320–50, the two-storey chapel of St Stephen was built as a rectangular block with corner turrets. The lower part, or crypt, survives as

12 Westminster Palace, the Jewel Tower built in 1366 as the corner tower of the moated enclosure within which stood the royal palace.

St Mary Undercroft in the Houses of Parliament. Edward I had also improved the private lodgings, particularly the queen's chamber. The palace was surrounded by a stone wall and moat, and the south-west corner tower survives as the Jewel Tower, built in 1365–66 by Edward III as a secure store for his personal treasure. The L-shaped stone tower of three storeys has a polygonal stair-turret on its north-east side, and was built on elm piles, reflecting the marshy nature of the site. Traces of the adjoining curtain walls can be seen on the north and east. The moat, a small stretch of which has been reconstructed, was fed by the Thames. The building of the Jewel Tower necessitated the re-alignment of the abbey precinct wall, which was shifted to the west by Abbot Litlyngton, thus ceding a rectangle of land to the royal palace. The tower, which has been much altered over the centuries, appears to have replaced an earlier one. Excavations in 1964 revealed that to the north of the Jewel Tower, the foundations of a curtain wall, 5ft (1.5m) thick, terminated in a massive tower with walls 8ft (2.4m) thick. This may have been the original south-west corner tower of the palace or may have had greater significance as a defensive Great Tower. Contemporary with the Jewel Tower was the Clock Tower on the northern perimeter wall. Edward I's Great Gate from King Street was rebuilt by Richard II in 1397 with polygonal angle turrets and lasted until 1706. The watergate was also replaced in the fifteenth century, and survived into the early 1800s. York Place was also enlarged over the years, with Archbishop Neville building a new great hall and a gatehouse facing onto King Street, now Whitehall, in the late fifteenth century.

The abbey was surrounded by a precinct wall with gatehouses and towers that stood well into the sixteenth century. The Abbot's House at Westminster Abbey was built around a courtyard with a gatehouse by Henry Yevele and was completed in 1385 and restored during the nineteenth century. The Jerusalem Chamber, College Hall, and the other buildings in the angle formed by the cloisters and the southern tower of the abbey's west front, were all part of this residential block now known as the Deanery.

In 1379, a pardon was issued to Thomas Orgrave for crenellating a tower without prior permission at the Hospital of St James, Westminster. This structure was no doubt intended for the safekeeping of valuables; a strongroom similar to those built by other monastic houses for the storage of their own treasure and reliquaries and acting as a safe-deposit for wealthy patrons. At the property known as Rosemont, at Eye next to Westminster, a licence to crenellate was granted in 1308 to John de Benstede, a cleric holding a succession of royal appointments. This may represent one of those instances where a loyal servant was being publicly recognised for his services, the mediaeval equivalent of an OBE. Robert, Bishop of Salisbury received licence to crenellate Salisbury Court in Fleet Street in 1337, a licence renewed for Bishop Radiphus forty years later. Walter Langton of Coventry and Lichfield was granted a licence to crenellate a house in the parish of St Mary at Strand in 1305, one of four licences granted to Langton, another of which was open, allowing him to apply it to any property he chose. By 1345, the Savoy Palace had passed to Henry, Duke of Lancaster. Having captured enough loot while campaigning in France that season, he rebuilt the entire palace, surrounding it with high walls and securing access with gatehouses onto the Strand and the waterfront. His heiress, Blanche, married John of Gaunt, son of Edward III, who made himself unpopular with just about everybody. His magnificent palace with hall, chapel and cloister, and used for great state and diplomatic occasions, was a tempting target for the mob, situated as it was in the no-man's-land between the city and Westminster. In 1377 rioters were narrowly diverted from sacking the Savoy at the time of Wycliffe's trial, Gaunt's liveried retainers being intimidated by the mob, and threats made against their master's life. Fortunately for Gaunt, he was able to flee across the river while the Bishop of London calmed the angry rioters. Only four years later, however, he was not so lucky. The Peasants' Revolt had a range of targets, and Gaunt, widely believed to be coveting his nephew's throne, and having the unfortunate (regnal) forename 'John' was one of them. In his absence, his household was attacked and the Savoy was burned to the ground by Kentish rebels under Wat Tyler, joined by the citizens of London who had their own reasons for hating him. Although the palace was uninhabitable, parts of the chapel and walls, gates and Simeon's Tower survived, and in 1404 attempts at rehabilitation were made. After a spell as a prison with the gaoler living over the main gate, the site was chosen by Henry VII in 1509 as the site of a hospital, completed by Henry VIII in 1517. Apart from the chapel, which continues in use by the Duchy of Lancaster, these buildings were demolished in 1820. Among the proliferation of defensible town houses in the Strand/Whitehall area was The Mote in King Street, kept by Lord Lovell, who disappeared after the Battle of Stoke in 1487.

Southwark in the Later Mediaeval Period

Southwark, south of the Thames, was a small satellite settlement, with a tax assessment of less than 4 per cent of the city's. As well as the task of securing the southern end of London Bridge, it was home to a number of important manor houses. The Bishop of Winchester's palace in Clink Street had a hall that measured 80ft by 36ft (24m by 11m) over an undercroft. It was built, probably in the early fourteenth century, by the mason Yevele for Bishop William of Wykeham, and was adjacent to the footings of the earlier palace built by Henry de Blois. The rose window in the upstanding western gable wall of the hall appears stylistically to date from Yevele's build. The area was notorious for the brothels or stews in property rented from the bishops, and their Clink Street prison provided a generic name for jails. The palace lasted until 1630.

Copt Hall was a mediaeval house with a second building, possibly a chapel, within a moat and accessed by a gatehouse. By the time of Henry VIII it was ruinous but it was repaired as a public gaming house. In 1622 a new house was built and run as a brothel by Madam Holland into the 1630s. Paris Gardens was held by Bermondsey Abbey from 1113, then by the Templars, and from 1324, the Hospitallers. The manor house, which lay below the river level, was surrounded by ditches and embankments, as much for drainage as for defence, memorialised by the local name 'Broadwall'. It was held by the Duke of Bedford from 1420–35, when it reverted to a hospital.

13 Southwark, Clink Street, the palace of the bishops of Winchester. The rose window dates to the early fourteenth century when the palace was rebuilt. The bishops had their prison next to the palace, giving us the generic name 'clink' for any gaol.

Suffolk Place was Sir Thomas Brandon's house and stood opposite St George's church in Southwark's Borough High Street, which his nephew, Charles Brandon, newly created Duke of Suffolk in 1514, obtained around that time. The original house, which Suffolk extended, appears to have consisted of a courtyard, one of whose ranges was formed by a hall. The south range had two octagonal towers with crenellations, and possibly machicolations as well, and was very similar in appearance to the contemporary Thornbury (Gloucestershire). The whole sat within a moat, larger than the footprint of the house. This extra space allowed the Duke of Suffolk to add an eastern courtyard with an L-shaped northern range, corner turrets and a polygonal central tower, all topped with domes as at Nonsuch. The moat was crossed by a stone bridge, with an outer gatehouse onto the street, all backed by the imposing eastern range, which had oriel windows and a steeply pitched roof with dormers, presenting a very grand show front. He also established a deer park. Henry VIII was gracious enough to accept the house and park from Brandon in 1535 in settlement of a debt.

Licences to Crenellate

The problems of interpreting both the underlying principles and the application of royal policy with regard to the granting of licences to crenellate, have prompted a number of suggestions. Taking into account that the numbers of actual fortified, especially moated, sites on the ground far exceed those for which licences were either sought or granted, and the discrepancies between the numbers of licences granted in one monarch's reign compared with those in another, it might be reasonable to infer that the process was completely serendipitous. The acquisition of a licence might have been driven by fashion, by a desire to emulate one's neighbours, peers and betters, by aspirations to advance a rung or two up the social ladder, or by the need to be recognised as a person of substance and property. It was also a good way of demonstrating newfound wealth or promoted status. Licences might have been granted by grateful monarchs seeking to reward a loyal servant, affording the recipient tangible evidence of his king's approbation. Alternatively, in the case of moats particularly, the explanation may be more prosaic. A purely utilitarian approach to land drainage, or to the provision of a constant supply of fish for all the non-meat days, or a response to localised violence and disorder, are all perfectly practical and plausible justifications. However, alongside all these quite rational explanations, most of which would undoubtedly have applied in one specific instance or another, recent work by John Dean has sought to show that there was nothing random about the distribution of licences from either a spatial or a temporal perspective, and that fashion can only have had a minor influence. Based on detailed and comprehensive statistical analysis of the records, he argues that the majority of licences were granted in troublesome times, in conflicted locations, to men who considered themselves threatened in one way or another. And at the time there was plenty going on to feel anxious about.

Civil Unrest and Political Turmoil

London in the fourteenth century appears to have been involved in a constant power struggle with successive monarchs over the governance of the city with its long-established freedoms and practices, and its continuous quest for autonomy. In 1321, Edward II deprived the city of its liberties, thereby forfeiting the citizens' support, and hastening his own end. When his queen and her new consort drove Edward away, his chancellor, Bishop Stapledon of Exeter, was decapitated in the street with a butcher's knife, and the presence of an irate London mob helped persuade Parliament to depose Edward in 1327. The Londoners had their privileges restored by Edward III during his mother's regency. Richard II, however, imprisoned the mayor and sheriffs for failing to produce the loans he needed to pursue his ambitious wars with France. Commerce was affected by war in that markets literally opened and closed. The wool staple was subject to the military and political influences on the choice of Continental market, but the capture of Calais in 1347 provided a fixed venue until its loss in 1558.

Richard's eternal quest for money brought about the Poll Tax of 1380, which sparked the Peasants' Revolt. Under its leaders John Ball, Wat Tyler, Abel Ker and Robert Cave, the rebels, thought at the time to have been incited and tacitly supported by the citizens of London, converged on Mile End Green in June 1381 prior to marching on the city. They stormed the Bishop of Winchester's prison in Southwark, and the Archbishop of Canterbury's palace at Lambeth, returning to their camp on Blackheath. Richard II's ministers Hales and Sudbury knew they were unlikely to come out alive from a parley with the rebels, so aborted a planned meeting, and sympathisers admitted the rebels to the city over London Bridge. Meeting with the king on neutral ground at Mile End, agreement was apparently reached on all the rebels' demands, including bringing the royal ministers to justice. Interpreting this as a carte blanche, the rebels stormed into London, executed Sir Robert Hales and Archbishop Simon of Sudbury, and proceeded to slaughter foreign merchants (mainly Lombards and Flemings who had enjoyed favourable conditions of trade), killing around 150 people in all. The next day the king met with Wat Tyler again on Tower Hill but the peasants' familiarity with the anointed of God was too much for the Lord Mayor, who provoked the rebel leader to draw a weapon, giving him a pretext to kill him while protecting his monarch's sacred majesty. Without their leader the disorganised peasants drifted away to be defeated at Waltham Cross and returned to their bondage.

John of Gaunt was perceived as attempting to undermine the power of the city merchants and removing trade to other centres such as Southampton. He was also seen as a malign influence on the young King Richard II, so the mob burned his Savoy Palace. All of this was against the backdrop of a power struggle between the civic and the mercantile leaders, as well as within the guilds themselves. One mayor, John of Northampton, provoked riots after he had been voted out of office and was imprisoned in Tintagel Castle (Cornwall), being lucky to escape with his life. Another mayor, Nicholas Bembre, was less fortunate, arraigned before Parliament and sentenced to be hanged, drawn and quartered at Tyburn for his support of Richard in the face of the opposition of the Appellants in 1388. Within a few years Richard was strong enough to take revenge on Londoners for their support of his opponents, removing state offices to York, establishing foreign monopolies in cities such as Southampton, and revoking London's liberties. The imposition on the city of Mayor (Dick) Whittington was intended to underline the king's supremacy, and Londoners only regained their ancient rights through the payment of enormous indemnities. Despite their anger at Richard's arrogance, Londoners waited until he had been captured and safely imprisoned before throwing in their lot with Henry Bolingbroke.

Throughout the protracted struggles between the houses of York and Lancaster the city attempted to remain neutral, seeking thereby to avoid provoking either side into actions that might threaten the business of accumulating wealth. Despite apparently supporting the absent Lancastrian Henry VI in 1460, the Yorkists were admitted into the city to avoid its destruction and from then on maintained a hold over London until Richard III's death in 1485 at Bosworth

Field. The Lancastrians' only chance to retrieve the city had come in 1461 after their victory at St Albans, but they failed to press their advantage and the opportunity was lost. In 1460, Richard of York was killed at Wakefield but his son was made king the next year as Edward IV, in order to bring some order to a country that had suffered from Henry VI's mental instability for long enough. The remnants of the Lancastrian party were decisively defeated at the Battle of Barnet in 1471 and Margaret of Anjou was overcome at Tewkesbury. While Londoners had apparently opened their gates to more or less anyone who came knocking, they drew the line in 1471 at the Kentish rabble led by Thomas of Fauconberg, who was in revolt against Edward IV. Fauconberg gathered his forces on Blackheath and marched on the city, only to be repulsed by the defences of London Bridge and Aldgate, and then put to flight by a determined sally. After Bosworth Field, Henry Tudor arrived to receive a characteristically warm welcome in 1485. The city fathers escorted the new king to St Paul's to dedicate his standards and celebrate a mass of thanksgiving, followed by pageants and street parties, very much the way in which Richard III had been welcomed. Henry VII and his son Henry VIII were both paranoid over the threats, real or imagined, from the Yorkist succession, but they had some cause for real concern. In 1497 for instance, Lord Audley, with 6000 Cornish rebels, camped on Blackheath ready to march on London, but the Yorkist leadership failed properly to exploit this opportunity to topple Henry. Lacking cavalry, cannon and an effective general, the rebels were defeated with heavy losses.

Royal Palaces around London

By the fourteenth century, London was surrounded by a ring of royal manors, which included Eltham, Greenwich, Isleworth, Kennington and Sheen (later Richmond) as well as regular access to the hospitality of such monastic houses as Chertsey. Over a period of two centuries, these manor houses, palaces or fortified houses underwent enormous changes. At the very end of the thirteenth century, Bishop Anthony Bek of Durham built a manor house at Eltham. It consisted of a large moated platform with curtain walls, corner towers and a gatehouse. The corner towers are shown as being octagonal on plans including that produced by the RCHME in 1930, but this feature could be a later remodelling. In its original form it had the traditional layout of separate hall, chamber and offices. These would later become better integrated for the sake of comfort, family life, security, privacy, ceremony and hot dinners. In 1305 Bek presented the manor to the future Edward II. There was much building activity during the fourteenth century, including a strengthening of the walls ordered by Queen Isabella and more work – new kitchens, a new gate, chambers and an oratory – carried out for Edward III, who spent time here mounting a great tournament in the Tilt Yard in 1347. Most of the structures from this period have now gone. After the Battle of Poitiers, the captured French king, John II, was imprisoned at John of Gaunt's Savoy Palace, but when given his parole, he was allowed to hunt at Eltham. Further alterations were carried out by Henry VI while under virtual house arrest at Eltham after the Battle of Northampton in 1460, but the main mediaeval survival is the hall of 1479, built by Edward IV and designed by the king's mason, Thomas Jurdan and his master carpenter, Edmund Graveley. The hall measures 100ft by 36ft (30.5m by 11m) and has a magnificent timber roof to challenge Westminster's. This new hall, on a completely different alignment from the original one, was part of a radical redesign of Eltham, intended to introduce private royal apartments for the queen into the palace, with new lodgings with bay windows and a gallery, patently domestic features. Edward had enjoyed extended hospitality in the great Burgundian

14 Eltham Palace, the Great Hall begun by Edward IV in 1479, placed on a moated platform with walls and corner towers.

houses, particularly at the time of his sister's marriage to Duke Charles the Bold, and he was impressed by the novel domestic arrangements he had seen. Contemporary with the other improvements, the timber bridge with drawbridge that Richard II had built over the moat in 1368 was replaced with a permanent bridge of stone. Later additions included Henry VII's work on the royal apartments, the outline of which has been uncovered, revealing bays built of brick overlooking the moat. An older turret at the north-west corner of this range had been given gun ports, suggesting that at least a semblance of defence remained important. Henry VIII rebuilt the chapel, now only surviving at foundation level, and added a private bridge and tunnel through to a garden outside the moat. There were two outer courts containing all the household offices, along with lodgings. Much of the palace was demolished after the Civil War and the remnants became a farm, with the Great Hall being used as a barn. In the 1930s the Courtauld family erected an art deco mansion alongside the hall.

Greenwich, originally granted to Thomas Beaufort, Duke of Exeter, by Henry V, subsequently passed to Humphrey, Duke of Gloucester, who was Henry VI's uncle and regent during his nephew's minority from 1422. It was he who built at least two fortified structures for which he and his wife Eleanor received licence to crenellate in 1433 (Estgrenewich), and again in 1437 (Grenewych). Coulson suggests that the second, possibly confirmatory, licence was required to adjust the boundaries of the land in question. According to a local historian, W. Braxton Sinclair, presenting a paper to the London Society in 1955, Duke Humphrey, following the untimely death of his brother Henry V, under whom he had fought at Agincourt and in numerous other actions, was particularly concerned for the security of the nation. As a military man he was aware that the strategic location of Blackheath/Greenwich was vulnerable to attack, given the traditional role of Blackheath as a jumping-off point for assaults on London via the Dover Road and Greenwich's role as the earliest convenient landing stage for sea-borne incursions via the Thames. As regent, he saw himself as the country's champion, resisting the attempts of the majority peace party in the Council of Regency to sell off the navy and to cut back on military expenditure generally. He therefore set out to establish a fortified zone covering the present extent of Greenwich Park that could defend against both of these invasion possibilities. He identified the area of some 200 acres (80ha) that now forms Greenwich Park as his chosen citadel, surrounding it with double banks and ditches surmounted by high timber palisades. Sinclair may be giving us something of a romantic interpretation of this boundary, for the terms of the licence could point more towards the enclosure of a park, rather than to a serious work of defence. However, these (de) fences were only demolished by James I and their location and dimensions recorded when the present brick wall was built. The centrepiece of his estate was an authentic fortified tower on the edge of the plateau overlooking the river. A sketch by Wyngaerde in 1558 shows Duke Humphrey's tower, sometimes known as Mirefleur, to have been a rectangular structure of two storeys with a higher tower, itself of two levels, set centrally. Adjoining this main block, a small outer court contained a well, and Sinclair refers to recent research on the site determining this layout. He dates the fort to 1423, so the licence may have been retrospective, especially as Duke Humphrey as regent was granting it to himself in the name of Henry VI. By 1447, Duke Humphrey had been discredited, charged with treason, arrested and had died in prison, and the manor house of Bella Court, down by the river, came to Margaret of Anjou, Henry VI's queen, who renamed the manor 'Placentia'. Excavations at Greenwich Palace in 1970 uncovered the riverside foundations of Duke Humphrey's Bella Court manor house of c.1430, and it is likely that it is to this building that the second licence relates. The Tudor palace of Henry VII and then Henry VIII was built on the footprint of Duke Humphrey's fortified house and may have incorporated some standing remains, but it is equally likely that all was swept away. Henry VII's palace, begun in 1498, was a courtyard house, consisting of a range of lodgings for the king along the waterfront, with a five-storey brick donjon containing the king's private chambers attached at one end. A range at right angles to the river contained the queen's lodgings and the courtyard was closed with two further ranges of service rooms. Henry VIII added a watergate to his father's riverside range, converted the detached Friars' church into his armoury, and constructed a tiltyard with adjacent banqueting house and changing rooms for indulging his chivalric fantasies, much as Edward III had done 200 years previously at Windsor. It is also thought that Henry VIII enlarged Duke Humphrey's tower on the hill, taking advantage not only of the views of his birthplace and the river below, but also of the healthy breezes that helped to disperse some of the olfactory challenges of Tudor domestic life. It was this hilltop site that was chosen for Flamstead's observatory in 1675, utilising much of the earlier fabric in the new building that we see today.

The manor of Isleworth came to the Crown in 1312 and consisted of a courtyard with hall, chapel, chambers for the king and queen, kitchen and storerooms all ranged around a quadrangular courtyard within a moat. An outer courtyard was basically a farmyard with barns. In 1421, Henry V made it over to the nuns of Syon. On a site between Black Prince Road and Sancroft Road stood Kennington Palace, built in the 1100s but in 1337 given to the Black Prince, who, between 1340 and 1362, proceeded to transform the old buildings. Excavations in 1965–67 found evidence of a hall built in 1347, measuring 82ft by 50ft (25m by 15m) of stone with stone details and mouldings, over an undercroft with a stone vault supported by pillars. At the west end of the hall was a possibly two-storied solar block with parlour and perhaps a chapel. A tower on one corner later became a garderobe tower. A second hall of 1355 also stood over an undercroft, and within the compound were chamber blocks and a long stable block, all built on dwarf walls with half-timbering above. The palace was demolished in 1531 to be replaced by two small brick manor houses, which themselves had been demolished by the middle of the eighteenth century. Some of the mediaeval buildings had used locally produced yellow bricks, probably from Vauxhall.

Rotherhithe Palace was a moated manor of Edward III, incorporating earlier chambers and possibly the hall as well, and consisting of an inner court fronting onto the river, with another to the south. The inner court was surrounded by a stone wall within a moat, with a paling fence on the outside bank of the moat. The outer court had earth banks around it and a timber gate with a chamber over. The riverside wall contained a watergate leading to a wharf via a bridge. Work was carried out here in 1353–57, but before Edward's death it had been given to the Cistercians of nearby St Mary Graces.

Sheen, which he had enlarged around 1356 from an existing manor house, was one of Edward III's favourite palaces. It was demolished by Richard II after his consort, Anne of Bohemia, had died there, but was then rebuilt by Henry V from 1414, to what was a revolutionary design, apparently influenced by what he had seen of French châteaux. Although Henry V did not live to see his plans come to fruition, his vision was achieved during the reign of Henry VI, with work being resumed in 1429 and brought to completion in time for his marriage to Margaret of Anjou. The centrepiece, which was what made it so unusual, was the enormous rectangular stone donjon that stood within its own moat (fed by the Thames) and insulated the private royal lodgings from the rest of the establishment. There were a number of motivations for this arrangement. One was a desire for comfort and privacy in an age when barriers were being erected between the great and the rest. Another was an emphasis on the grandeur of the king, the magnificence of his surroundings, and his aloofness from those around him. A third was security, especially in those times of frequent regime change, when friends and relations, those wearing the royal livery, or those charged with safeguarding the king's person, could not always be relied on. Once the divinely appointed had been seen to be fallible, it was often politic for even (or especially) his nearest and dearest to at least contemplate throwing in their lot with the new power approaching the throne, so a strong door, a drawbridge and a moat between monarch and bodyguard might induce a sounder sleep at night. This inner enclave was adjacent to the river, so there was always the opportunity of a quick getaway through the watergate that conveniently adjoined the donjon. At Sheen, the great three-storey donjon was adorned with towers and turrets; stately rather than forbidding, but nevertheless an assertive statement of royal power. The rest of the royal household lived in the outer courts that contained the communal areas of hall and chapel, the service areas, and the lodgings. Sheen was largely destroyed by fire in 1497 but rebuilt by Henry VII who renamed it after his former title of Richmond. Henry VII gave *his* palace a decorative rather than a utilitarian appearance, refurbishing the fire-damaged donjon with its three main floors with twelve rooms on each, and its large numbers of turrets. In front of the donjon, the chapel and the great hall formed two sides of the inner court, with a porch closing it off. There were three courts enclosed within walls with interval towers. Parts of the base court with its two-storey ranges still survive in Old Palace Yard, as does the outer gateway of two stone arches set in a largely brick gatehouse block. Henry V had imported bricks from Calais, but materials for the later buildings were subsequently produced locally, particularly in nearby Petersham. An illustration of the palace in around 1500 shows some very fanciful onion domes crowning the towers and turrets, completely nullifying any defensive aspect it might once have presented.

Episcopal Palaces around London

As late as 1474, Laurence, Bishop of Durham, received a licence to crenellate his London house of Bridgecourt Manor, Battersea, probably reflecting the instability of the times, but maintaining a long-established pattern of prelates holding defensible properties. The palace of the archbishops of Canterbury at Croydon dates from the fourteenth and fifteenth centuries. Archbishop Courtney's Great Hall of *c.*1381–96, measuring 56ft by 38ft (17m by 11.5m), was remodelled by Archbishop Stafford in 1443–52. All the other buildings including the chapel were at first-floor level. The guardroom was remodelled as an audience chamber early in the fifteenth century and lies between the two inner courtyards. Originally, an outer court entered through a gatehouse was formed by three ranges of lodgings and barns, with the fourth side occupied by the hall block. The palace was relinquished in 1780 and subsequently became a school. Another palace of the archbishops' was Lambeth, rebuilt by Archbishop Morton in 1490. A four-bay first-floor hall of the early fourteenth century, now called the Guard Room, survives, but the main hall has gone. There is an imposing brick gatehouse with a stone vault over the gate passage. The earlier Water or Lollards' Tower of Archbishop Chichele in 1435 is chiefly of stone, of four storeys with a higher stair turret. Cranmer's Tower, of brick, was built onto the chapel in the mid-sixteenth century. Headstone Manor, Harrow, was built within a moat *c.*1344 for use as the principal Middlesex residence of the Archbishop of Canterbury, with a hall of conventional aisled construction. A later barn of 1506, originally one of four, exhibits more experimental ways of avoiding pillars in order to maximise unimpeded floor space.

In addition to the palaces of the archbishops of Canterbury and those of the bishops of London at Fulham and Highgate, the bishops of Winchester had palaces scattered about

their see at Kingston-upon-Thames, Rickmansworth, Southwark and Esher, where Wayneflete Tower is all that remains of the palace built by Bishop Waynflete of Winchester around 1478. It was never very large, probably consisting of a single courtyard. Waynflete was one of a coterie of bishops building in brick in the late fifteenth century, some of whom used John Cowper as their mason. The fabric is red brick with blue diaper work and stone mouldings. The remaining structure is a three-storey gatehouse with octagonal angle turrets extending a further storey. Inside, the present entrance chamber is rib vaulted. The palace was accessed by river so this watergate was in fact the main entrance. In 1529 it was in

15 Lambeth Palace, the Water or Lollards' Tower built by Archbishop Chichele in 1435, and forming the north-west angle of the palace.

16 Harrow, Headstone Manor, the moat of this house of the archbishops of Canterbury, built in *c*.1344. Later buildings occupy the moated platform, and picturesque barns stand in the adjacent outer courtyard.

17 Esher, Wayneflete Tower. Recently refurbished as a private home, this gatehouse is all that remains of the palace of the bishops of Winchester built by Bishop Waynflete in *c*.1460 and rebuilt in Gothick style by William Kent *c*.1730.

the possession of Wolsey, from whom it was acquired by Henry VIII. At the time of the Armada, the house was owned by a cousin of Sir Francis Drake, and three Spanish admirals were imprisoned here. The gatehouse was radically remodelled in 1729 by William Kent acting for Henry Pelham, later prime minister, who had commissioned an early Gothick house. In the early 1990s the house was renovated as a family home. Henry Beaufort, Bishop of Winchester and Henry VI's chancellor, along with others including Cardinal Langley, the Bishop of Durham, were granted a joint licence to crenellate the manor of the More, Rickmansworth, with turrets and curtain walls using stone, lime and brick, in 1426. On this low-lying site near the River Colne, they built a quadrangular house around a central courtyard. All this lay within an existing earlier moat, parts of which had to be filled in. However, these backfills were incapable of taking the weight of the structure envisaged by these builders, and pits needed to be dug down to the natural gravel and then filled with rammed chalk to afford a solid foundation. Relieving arches were built to link each pit, thus ensuring an equal distribution of weight onto the firmer ground. A large gatehouse with projecting semi-octagonal towers was reached by a bridge across the reworked moat. The site appears to have been quite marshy as there are streams criss-crossing it, and at least three distinct moats had been dug in earlier times, most likely with drainage as an important factor. The More was later licensed to Ralph Botiller, knight, in 1458. From 1460 a brick-and-tile conduit carried drinking water across the moat to a storage cistern, from where it was distributed through lead pipes with waste water going back into the moat.

Manor Houses and Moated Sites

As we have seen, the motivations behind giving one's home features of defensibility were complex – especially when it came to moats that had both symbolic and intensely practical rationales – and some of these structures challenged the splendour of the royal and episcopal residences. Others were quite sparse, and some moated platforms appear to have contained no structures at all, suggesting that they were built to protect orchards or livestock, or even simply as drainage or fishponds. However, the amount of labour involved, particularly when labour was becoming expensive, would suggest that moats were dug for better reasons than to satisfy an owner's whim.

   At Carew Manor, Beddington, the fifteenth-century hall of the manor house survives, measuring 60ft by 30ft (18m by 9m). It is noteworthy for its similarities to the near-contemporary roof at Eltham Palace, although structurally it differs in some respects, such as in the details of its braces. It was moated and entered across a drawbridge. Excavations at Northolt Manor in the 1960s revealed the remains of a late fourteenth-century manor house inside a roughly square moat. A hall measuring 30ft by 24ft (9m by 7.3m) stood over cellars with a solar block lying crosswise at its east end, the typical layout for this period. A horseshoe of ranges of outbuildings contained the detached kitchen, with ovens, and a hall in the open end. A moat surrounded the complex and a fourteenth-century bridge abutment was found on the north-east side, dating from the time when the original timber buildings were replaced in stone. Ditton Park at Datchet was licensed to John de Molyns in 1331. The later house, built around a small central courtyard, incorporates a fourteenth-century tower and sits on a moated platform, the whole surrounded by a fenced park and fishponds. Simpson's Moat or Place, Bromley, was owned by the Bankewell family in 1302, but in 1310 a licence to crenellate was granted to William de Bliburgh, described as a cleric, probably another lawyer. On the death of Thomas de Bankewell in 1352, the property passed to the Clarks. Possibly de Bliburgh's plans failed to materialise,

18 Wickham Court, a quadrangular tower house of 1469, built around a tiny central courtyard. The four corner towers are provided with cannon-loops but it was apparently never moated. It is now a school.

or never got past the moat stage, for now Thomas Clark sought licence to crenellate from Henry V in order to build a fortified house within a moat fed by a spring. In the reign of Henry VI the house then passed to John Simpson who carried out improvements. Some time in the sixteenth century, the house was rebuilt in brick and timber, probably by Sir Humphrey Style of Langley, Sheriff of Kent, who died in 1557; eventually it became the farmhouse of Jeremiah Ringer, after whom the road on which the moat now stands is named. Warren Farm, Romford, is the site of Marks, a moated house acquired by Sir Thomas Urswyck c.1461. Three centuries later it still consisted of four ranges around a quadrangular courtyard, and retained two battlemented towers. Two moated sites in Enfield were clearly important. Camlet, in Trent Park, reputed to have been a de Mandeville property, was probably a Forester's Lodge for Enfield Chase. Timbers from the bridge over the moat have been dated to c.1357. The second moat represents a fortified house of Humphrey de Bohun, Earl of Hereford, licensed in 1347 along with ten other of his properties. In Bromley-by-Bow, 43 Gillender Street may possibly be part of a gatehouse range, a relic of the South Bromley manor house, with tree-rings dated to c.1490 and Tudor brick, but much altered over the centuries.

   All of the above appear to be paying more than mere lip service to the provision of defensive features in quite substantial properties. On the other hand, Wickham Court, West Wickham, is more enigmatic. A square mass of brick with stone dressings was built in 1469 by Sir Henry Heydon, with octagonal corner turrets and four ranges of buildings around a tiny 16ft (5m) square courtyard, now roofed over. It has battlements and quatrefoil arrow/gun loops but neither moat nor gatehouse. Here, maybe, it was the image rather than the substance that was important. Of equal mystery is Tollsworth Manor, Chaldon, where a fifteenth-century timber-framed house with a hall and a cross-wing containing the solar has been found to have timbers dated to the previous century. About 130yds to the south is a quadrangular moat. The house also has blocks of high-quality stone that could have come from an earlier structure within the moat. It is also possible that there was no structure at all on the moated platform. Tower Place in Woolwich, owned by a Lord Mayor in 1538, but thought to have been built during the previous century, was of brick with battlements and a tall octagonal tower. Remodelled in 1682 by Bernard de Gomme, the chief military engineer, to provide accommodation for the Master Gunner of England and ordnance staff, it was again rebuilt by Vanburgh in 1719. The tower, demolished in 1786, had stood detached, next to a new building which housed the RMA, from 1741.

Other manor houses include King John's Palace, Bow, a mediaeval house demolished in the 1860s for a match factory; Worcester House, Stepney Green, built over in 1810 for Stepney College; and Walton Manor, containing the walls of a fourteenth-century stone house with a two-storey hall block with a chapel projecting at its east end. There are large numbers of moated sites around the outskirts of London, often with contemporary or later buildings, some sixty of which are listed in Appendix 2.

Monastic Precincts in the Outskirts of London

Both the monasteries themselves and their granges or manors outside London were provided with some defences, but few traces of anything remain. At Barking Abbey, the Curfew Tower, a two-storey gate tower with a higher, octagonal stair turret was built around 1460, and still gives access to the churchyard. The abbey, founded in the seventh century, was torn down in 1541 with much of the stone being taken away for Henry VIII's new house at Dartford. In 1319, the Abbess of Barking was licensed to cut timber from the royal Forest of Havering in order to build a manor house at Loxford. Opposite a mediaeval barn, a blocked archway in one corner of the former monastic enclosure at Chertsey may represent the remains of a gatehouse. Similarly, the only surviving relic of Bermondsey Abbey is the south wall of a mediaeval gatehouse at 5–7 Grange Walk, which may have been the abbey's exit to its grange.

Waltham Abbey was granted a licence to crenellate in 1369, and the existing portal and bridge appear to date from around then. Although there may have simply been two arches, one inside the other and connected by sidewalls, the existence of part of a turret on one side of the outer one may suggest that a substantial gatehouse had been built here. Highbury, a moated manor house of the Knights Hospitaller, was destroyed in 1381 at the same time as the parent house in Clerkenwell was attacked. It stood on the corner of Grove and Leigh roads in Highbury. The site of the moated manor house of the Canons of St Paul's is now marked by Barnsbury Square.

Tudor London

The reigns of Henry VII and VIII saw a move away from private fortresses to public fortifications, evidenced by an upsurge in the construction of grand houses. At the same time the Dissolution of the Monasteries brought many ex-conventual buildings onto the market. Some became houses and others sources of building materials. In London the uses to which these buildings were put was particularly varied, including industrial, military or commercial premises, and halls for the city livery companies.

The Development of Artillery Fortifications

The Tower of London was included in Henry VIII's systematic approach to the defence of the kingdom using fortifications designed for use by and against gunpowder artillery. The Office of Ordnance had already been established at the tower for a century and Edward IV added the Bulwark to carry guns, but Henry brought innovative architects and a fresh approach to the problem. Threatened by the possibility of foreign invaders, he set out on a building programme that was to girdle the coast, from Kingston-upon-Hull in the north to Milford Haven in the west, with forts designed to mount cannon. A number of modifications were made at the tower to ensure that cannon might be mounted effectively. It has long been thought that Brass and Legges bastions were built by Henry VIII, but they have been shown to have been integral to Edward I's outer curtain. Nevertheless, they were well adapted to carry cannon that could rake the moat, but it was only much later, around 1597, that Brass Mount was properly transformed into a solid artillery platform. Henry VIII *was* responsible, however, for the small pointed two-storey bastion next to the Byward Tower. There are loops at low level for small artillery pieces mounted on wooden blocks and, at a higher level, an elaborate double keyhole loop for hand-guns. Cannon had previously been mounted on the roof of the White Tower, damaging the fabric, which had to be repaired, but it was still found necessary to mount three guns on the roof of St Thomas's Tower, suitably strengthened with baulks of timber. In the reign of Elizabeth, wooden platforms to carry cannon were added to a number of towers, very much as a stopgap rather than being permanent fixtures. As the inventory of artillery increased, proper armouries and workshops became necessary and a range of gabled buildings filled the space between the Devereux and Martin towers.

As an extension of Duke Humphrey's defences, according to Sinclair, Henry VIII added three artillery blockhouses to command the road across Blackheath. One was apparently discovered in Eliot Vale during building works in 1953, with two more being found close by on the edge of the escarpment within twelve months. They appear to have been small cylindrical blockhouses for mounting cannon, similar to those of a contemporary date built at Gravesend, Tilbury, Dover and elsewhere.

London Walls had been allowed to decay since their last proper refurbishment by Mayor Jocelyn in 1477. The ditch had become so offensive that sections were covered over and the ground thus gained had been given over to gardens, with dwellings encroaching on the walls themselves. The

19 The Tower of London, Brass Mount, built by Edward I but adapted for artillery in the reign of Henry VIII.

20 The Tower of London, dating from the time of Henry VIII this early arrowhead-shaped tower was designed to carry small artillery pieces, for which a variety of loopholes were provided.

gates continued to serve as traffic-calming measures, and also retained their function in encouraging good behaviour; the dis-assembled corpses of the unlucky twelve apprentices, hanged, drawn and quartered after the May Day disturbances of 1517 being displayed for public enlightenment. Although Ludgate had been completely rebuilt in 1585, its future, along with those of the other city gates, was to serve only ceremonial or cus-todial functions. Owners of properties in Fleet Street and Ludgate Hill were neverthe-less ordered to ensure that signage did not obstruct views of the gate as it would thereby detract from its symbolic significance.

Tudor Great Houses

Henry VII's statutes of livery and maintenance, limiting the scope of his lords to keep private armies of liveried retainers and also discouraging the fortification of private houses, gradually diminished the military aspect of both royal and lordly residences. As he put down the various plots and rebellions against him, and executed their leaders and instigators, he was able to build palaces where security was of lesser importance. Perimeter walls were still employed to discour-age casual entry, and guarded gatehouses retained their traditional role of restricting access to legitimate visitors. While such structures were often given crenellations, machicolation and gun ports, and were frequently approached by a drawbridge across a moat, all these elements were intended more to emphasise the grandeur of the occupant than to keep murderous intruders or hostile assailants at bay. Features such as galleries, prospect towers and an increased use of stacked oriel windows all contributed to the peacetime aesthetic. This is demonstrated by the shift in the meaning of the term 'donjon', from the tall, windowless keep of the White Tower, to those at Richmond or Greenwich, which could have come from the illuminated manuscripts of the Limbourg brothers. It must not be forgotten however, that licences to crenellate were still being applied for, and granted, right through the reign of Henry VIII. This may have been anachronis-tic but there must have been some point to an otherwise meaningless exercise.

When occupied, the Tudor palace had the population of a small town, which made the control of individuals' comings and goings difficult. The solution to this problem of security lay with the Royal Guards, an institution of Henry VII in late 1501, which inhabited the Guard Chamber. The king and queen each had their own Guard Chamber, generally on the first floor, controlling access to their private apartments, and as they moved around the palace, guards lined their route. Being the largest space in the palace after the Great Hall, the Guard Chamber became a sort of mess

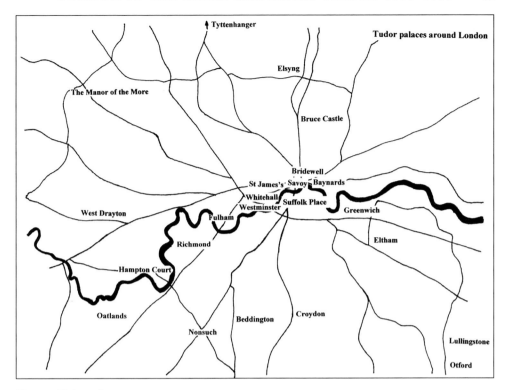

Figure 2 Tudor palaces.

room for some of the senior officials. Henry VII had established the Yeomen of the Guard back in 1485, first as a body of fifty archers, then as a larger force of 200 armoured men-at-arms. In 1509 another corps of household troops was established as the Band of Pensioners or Spears. Each of the fifty members was required to bring with him an archer, a pikeman and a swordsman, along with three suitable warhorses. This body was to evolve as the Honourable Corps of Gentlemen at Arms. The size of the Royal Guard fluctuated from this initial establishment early in the reign of Henry VIII, peaking at 600 a few years later when Henry was at war with France, then falling back to under 100 by the end of his reign. Besides providing royal bodyguards, they were expected, in the absence of a standing army, to fulfil the role of elite troops and to form the core of the field army.

It is worth reminding ourselves here of the sheer quantity of real estate held by Henry VIII by inheritance, purchase, confiscation, or merely by suggesting that the donor would be held in high esteem were he to honour the king with the gift of such a desirable property. By the end of his reign Henry VIII owned getting on for seventy houses or palaces, around half of which were in the Greater London area. These included the great royal palaces of Richmond, Nonsuch, the Bridewell, Baynard's, St James's, Oatlands and Greenwich, as well as those acquired from Cardinal Wolsey such as Hampton Court, the More, Whitehall and Tyttenhanger. Others included Beddington, forfeit to the Crown from Sir Nicholas Carew in 1539; Suffolk Place from the Brandons; and Elsyng, built in 1492 by Sir Thomas Lovell as a hunting lodge in Enfield Chase and acquired as a royal residence c.1540. These three and others like them were gratefully received from loyal, generous or indebted subjects, or in the case of Otford, from Archbishop Cranmer in 1537. Waltham Abbey, the last monastic house of all to be dissolved, came straight from the Church, but although his father had been a frequent visitor, and Henry VIII maintained apartments there, he forbore from annexing it to his estate. There were plans for a palace at Waltham-in-the-Forest, which would have given him the opportunity to build an ideal house on a green-field site, but he chose not to proceed with them, building only the hunting lodge at Rangers Road, Chingford, in 1543.

Royal Palaces

The new Baynard's Castle, on a site reclaimed from the Thames, was started by Duke Humphrey of Gloucester after 1428. After his death in 1447, it passed to the Crown and was used by both Edward IV and Richard III. Following refurbishment in 1501 it became Henry VII's major London residence. He removed its military aspect and turned it into a palace, much like Richmond and Greenwich in style. The dock was filled in and a walled garden was created. The frontage onto the river had an octagonal tower at the east end, and another at the west, with four half-hexagonal projections and a square watergate in-between. The octagonal south-east tower was some 26ft (8m) in diameter and may have been another of Henry VII's favoured donjons, furnished with the luxury of an attached garderobe tower. Alternatively, a view of c.1550 drawn prior to further western extensions shows that the south-west tower complex could equally have formed such a structure. The landward range, which may also have had corner towers, was accessed from Thames Street through a gatehouse. After her divorce, Katherine of Aragon retained Baynard's Castle and by 1550 had added extensions on the western side, terminating in a round tower in front of the site of the earlier dock. The palace was burnt down completely in the Great Fire, and was known only from drawings until excavations in the 1970s and 1980s.

From 1518, Henry VIII was building a new palace, the Bridewell, on the site of former Templar and Hospitaller properties on partially reclaimed land. This was necessary, mainly because his Westminster base had burned down in 1512. Originally there were two courts on the west bank of the Fleet, and a Thames-side entrance front with polygonal turrets at each end, separated from the inner court with its royal apartments by a walled garden. Access was by boat to a watergate and thence along a gallery. As at the More, brick arches springing from deep chalk piles gave the building some stability in this marshy corner outside the city walls, and more land was acquired during the construction, thus enabling a third courtyard to provide landward access as well. The riverfront had corner towers and other projections providing views over the river, while the main court had ranges of four-storey buildings and a great hall. The long gallery running up the western side of the palace, probably single-storey with viewing platforms, overlooked more gardens.

Henry VII carried out improvements at Greenwich Palace as did Henry VIII, who was born in the palace; he concentrated his collection of armour and weapons there, building a tiltyard and high towers from which the action could be observed by favoured spectators, to share his vision of chivalric display. The octagonal tiltyard towers at Greenwich were four storeys high, with turrets extending a further two storeys upwards, themselves topped by conical stair turrets. Two towers on Blackheath built in 1516–18 were joined by a third at Greenwich, which was still in use, having been refurbished, in 1525–26. Henry's armoury became the basis for the Royal Armouries, now based in the Tower of London and in Leeds (West Yorkshire). The palace in its final Tudor form consisted of three courtyards with a five-storey tower by the river and polygonal turrets on the lower ranges, a pair of which flanked a watergate.

Nonsuch Palace was built from scratch by Henry VIII on a green-field site offering none of the complications of the existing structures present at Greenwich or Whitehall. It was built of locally sourced chalk and freestone, as well as large quantities of worked stone from Merton Priory, which was suppressed in 1538, the year building started at Nonsuch. Designed around two courtyards, it was entered through two gatehouses with semi-octagonal turrets. The palace suggests the type of Tudor palace exemplified by St James's, but Nonsuch was quite different in two major respects. Firstly, it was neither intended for, nor capable of accommodating, the 1500 or so members of Henry's court, and was planned as a hunting lodge for Henry and his much smaller riding court. Thus there were fewer public spaces, no great hall, and lodgings for only a small establishment, covering a third of the area of Hampton Court, and barely a tenth of Whitehall's. Secondly, it was an architectural indulgence incorporating features that could only belong in a world of conspicuous consumption. The corner towers were jettied out as pavilions floating in the sky, connected by covered galleries along the tops of the connecting ranges, and the whole was either hung in slate or covered in ornamental plasterwork. It is difficult to find parallels (hardly surprising really, the clue being in its name – nonpareil) for this extravaganza other than the ostentatious structures that had provided temporary accommodation for the king and his entourage at the Field of the Cloth of Gold, an out-and-out exercise in public relations held outside Calais twenty years previously. Although virtually all traces have disappeared, excavations have revealed the ground plan and much of the architectural detail of this hybrid or transitional building, with its veneer of Renaissance motifs superimposed on a traditional late-mediaeval carcass. Although completed after Henry VIII's death and lived in by Elizabeth I, Nonsuch was demolished in the 1680s. It was surrounded by pleasure gardens and hunting grounds with a banqueting house built on a low mound 350yds from the house, which incorporated cellars, and it was surrounded by an irregular octagonal retaining wall of brick-faced chalk. At four of the corners were circular 'bastions', perhaps intended to have some symbolic meaning, or merely

to echo Henry's enthusiastic interest in his programme of coastal fortifications.

The site of Oatlands Palace, Weybridge, lies off Thames Street. The present Palace Gardens are bounded by a length of Tudor brick walling and an archway, which is all that remains of Oatlands Palace. The later house, now a hotel, is on the site of a hunting lodge 1 mile further east. The original house was moated and use was made of the brick revetments of this moat as foundations for a new range of buildings when Henry VIII expanded the accommodation. How much of the original house he demolished is uncertain, for views drawn in his daughter's reign clearly show that at least one range from the old house with, at each end, a large brick tower house, each with a higher octagonal stair-turret, was

21 St James's Palace, the Great Gatehouse of Henry VIII's palace of 1540, remodelled and heightened 200 years later.

retained in Henry's new building from 1537. The original wings were probably removed, allow-ing a new inner court to be built. The moat was backfilled and turned into a paved courtyard, leaving just enough of a ditch to act as a culvert for drainage of both rainwater and sewage. Brick vaults over other parts of the moat provided foundations for other buildings. The most noticeable introduction was the high Prospect Tower at the heart of the palace, which, like those at Nonsuch, was jettied out to make an enclosed viewing platform at the top.

St James's Palace was built by Henry VIII in 1531–40 on the site of a monastic hospital. It became his main London residence and consisted of four courtyards surrounded by ranges of apartments and services. There was a chapel but no great hall. The most significant survival is the four-storey brick gatehouse with half-octagonal corner turrets, which opens into the present Colour Court.

Palaces Taken Over from Cardinal Wolsey

The first stage of Hampton Court was what is now known as the Clock Court, a quadrangle of ranges entered through Anne Boleyn's Gate. It included a great hall to one side and lodgings on the others, and was built by Wolsey between 1514 and 1528, on the site, possibly moated, of a Hospitaller manorial complex. A new moat was dug for the Tudor palace but had been backfilled completely by Victorian times. A section was re-excavated in 1908 to expose the bridge. In 1994 trial trenches found that the moat had been 11ft 6in (3.5m) deep. In a short period, Wolsey had expanded his palace by adding the Base Court with the Great Gatehouse. This was originally two storeys higher than it is now and was the centrepiece of the widest and grandest entrance front of any of the Tudor palaces, royal or otherwise. Shortly after Wolsey had made a gift of the palace to Henry VIII in 1529 in a belated, but ultimately futile, attempt to save his career and reputation, extensive alterations were carried out. These enlargements and remodellings produced five major courtyards and projecting wings, which were added to the entrance front. The imposing presence of Wolsey's two original gatehouses was intended to emphasise his power and invulnerability, ironic in later circumstances. Henry VIII added new kitchens, a house of easement that occupied one of the front projecting wings straddling the old moat, an enlarged great hall, multiple royal lodgings and a covered gallery. He also finished the royal chapel that Wolsey had begun in 1520. The 'Bayne' donjon tower, adjoining the king's chambers and affording the only access to the new first-floor gallery, was one of Henry's very first additions to Wolsey's house. As its name suggests, it held a private bathroom and bedroom for the king's sole use, plus a study, library and jewel house, all spread across three floors. Such provision underlined the new twin domestic preoccupations with comfort and privacy. As at Greenwich, but much later in his reign, Henry VIII built a tiltyard, enclosed by high brick walls incorporating five viewing towers, one of which survives. He never saw it used. The gatehouse between the Clock (sometime inner, sometime fountain) Court and the (later) Fountain (some-time Inner) Court was rebuilt by William Kent for George II in 1732.

Whitehall Palace, formerly York Place, was enlarged from 1514 by Wolsey, who built a new great hall and a long gallery overlooking the Thames. Westminster Palace had burned down in 1512, but it was not until after Wolsey's fall from grace that Henry VIII actually seized this group of buildings, adding royal apartments. Henry's palace from 1529 joined up with the south-ernmost parts of Great Scotland Yard, as well as with his own new leisure complex of tiltyard, tennis courts etc., which spread across land between what is now St James's Park and Whitehall itself. This thoroughfare was enclosed between two new gatehouses, one becoming known as the Holbein Gate, and the other as the King Street or Whitehall Gate, and both were designed to restrict access on this scattered site, and to protect the king from public view. Owing to its piecemeal development, the palace lacked the integrity of its contemporaries, sprawling along the north bank of the Thames, and secured by walled-off areas guarded by gatehouses and porters' lodges, defining defensible space rather than a fortified complex as such.

In 1520, Wolsey, holding the abbacy of St Albans among other livings, acquired the Manor of the More, at Rickmansworth. Both he and Henry VIII, who took it over in 1530, enlarged the buildings, wrapping an outer quadrangle of ranges around the earlier one, building a base court outside the original entrance, throwing a new bridge across the moat on the east, and building a gallery to the north in order to provide views over the new gardens that nestled within the arms of the outer moats. By 1556, the manor had fallen into ruin and had become a squat. Within 100 years it had been demolished. At Tyttenhanger, the present house is of the seventeenth century but is on the site of a palace that Henry VIII acquired from Wolsey in 1529.

Tudor Episcopal Palaces

Fulham Palace was largely rebuilt by Bishop Fitzjames from 1506, replacing the mediaeval buildings of the palace of the bishops of London. The late-mediaeval hall, dated to c.1480, was unusual in that it had a storey over it containing a private chamber, and an adjoining solar block. These buildings formed one range of a quadrangular court entered through a simple brick archway. The kitchens and buttery at the other end of the hall were removed to allow the construction of a new chapel in the nineteenth century. Otford Palace was built around 1515 for the See of Canterbury by Archbishop Warham, taking Wolsey's Hampton Court as his model. There were two courtyards but only the octagonal three-storey north-west tower and part of the gatehouse of the outer court survive. Part of an adjoining range has been converted into cottages.

22 Otford Palace, the north-west tower of the palace of the archbishops of Canterbury, built in 1515, and extorted from Archbishop Cranmer by Henry VIII in 1537.

23 Lullingstone Castle, the sixteenth-century gatehouse of the fortified house of the Hart family, who still live there.

24 Drayton Manor, the gatehouse, along with some boundary walls, is all that remains of this former fifty-room house in use before 1547.

Other Tudor Great Houses

A large group of newly wealthy families and institutions showed their wealth by building smaller-scale palaces. Royal servants such as Sir John Cuttes, treasurer to Henry VIII, built Salisbury Hall within its moat, and Richard Breame built the so-called Boleyn Castle in Green Street, Newham. This sixteenth-century brick-built house had a detached octagonal four-storey brick tower with a higher stair-turret in its grounds. Much was still standing until the 1950s when partial demolition took place, the job only being completed in the 1970s. Lullingstone Castle came to the Hart family via a courtier of Henry VII. It originally had two imposing gate-houses and stood within a moat. The surviving brick outer gatehouse of c.1530 is three storeys high with four polygonal angle turrets. It has defensive features – battlements, arrow loops – but apparently only for effect. Bruce Castle, Tottenham, was begun by Sir William Compton in 1514 on the site of an earlier house; he had been knighted by Henry VIII on the field of battle two years previously. Next to his moated house was a detached, circular brick tower, 21ft (6.5m) in diameter with blank arcading on the outside, which was of military aspect but with no known purpose. Even the owner in around 1700 confessed to having no idea of its origin.

Other examples include Well Hall, Eltham, a house that stood within a rectangular outer moat of which only the western arm survives, but was linked to the complete inner moat, within which a two-storey L-shaped range of Tudor buildings stands, now used as an art gallery. In the fifteenth century the house was owned by the daughter of Sir Thomas More. After the Dissolution, Canonbury Tower, a manor of the priors of St Bartholomew's, was taken over by Sir John Spencer, Lord Mayor. He built a four-storey tower at the north-west corner of his new house, forming an open courtyard with three ranges, parts of which still survive hidden inside later terraces. In Church Road, West Drayton, the gatehouse with polygonal turrets and remains of the outer walls survive from the fifty-room Tudor manor house, which was acquired by the Pagets in 1547. At Hall Place, Bexley, an earlier, possibly moated house was rebuilt c.1547 by a Lord Mayor of London, and later work of the seventeenth century included a four-storey stair tower.

The Inns of Court

Inns of Court were built in the same tradition as Tudor manor houses and palaces, and Oxbridge colleges. Gray's Inn and Lincoln's Inn in Holborn take late-mediaeval houses as the basis of a courtyard layout entered through a gatehouse. At Lincoln's Inn the hall dates from 1492 and the gatehouse from 1518, being a smaller version of Bishop Morton's at Lambeth.

Tudor Naval and Military Development

Much of Henry VIII's effort to develop the navy was centred on the Thames. By 1500, ship-building yards had started up at Blackwall, Poplar and Wapping, and were developed under Henry VIII for launching, refitting and victualling warships. New naval shipyards were opened at Deptford and Woolwich launching the *Great Harry* in 1512, and *L'Henri Grâce à Dieu* a year later. A naval storehouse was built in West Street, Erith, in 1512, and the site of the Cistercian Abbey of St Mary Graces was developed as a victualling yard for the navy, incorporating a bakery for ship's biscuit, and as a naval storehouse for such essentials as cordage and sails. Another former monastic site, St Clare's near the tower, became an armoury.

Home Defence and the Spanish Armada of 1588

Some threats to security were domestic, if xenophobic. In 1517, London apprentices rioted against aliens, and were subdued by the Duke of Norfolk with 2000 troops. A few of the lads were hanged as an example and things settled down again until a familiar external threat was renewed. One of the best-known images of the time of Elizabeth I is of the queen reviewing her troops at Tilbury, but these troops are not part of the regular professional army that we are familiar with today. Many of them were militia, ordinary civilians who had practised their military skills at the local butts in their spare time. In 1498 a special area had been set aside for archery at Moorfields, accessed by a causeway from the gate, opened in the city wall in 1415, with archery practice being officially encouraged throughout the sixteenth century. In 1537, Henry VIII incorporated the Honourable Artillery Company as the 'Fraternity or Guild of Artillery of Longbows, Crossbows and Handguns'. Artillery practice grounds were laid out off Bishopsgate where Artillery Lane still marks its southern boundary; at Bunhill Fields in Finsbury, where the HAC still have their HQ and armoury; and in Tuthill Fields, Westminster. The militia, a force levied county by county by lords lieutenant, was periodically mustered. The militia returns for 1539, for instance, record eighty-five archers and 167 bill men equipped with rough pikes from the Hundred of Blackheath, just one element of London's total force of 15,000 militiamen between the ages of 16 and 60 who marched past their sovereign at Westminster that May. In 1554 Sir Thomas Wyatt and his rebels, in rebellion against Mary I's Spanish marriage, had been joined by a force of 500 London Militia sent to defeat them, and were welcomed into Southwark. The city establishment however, remained loyal to the Crown, and locked the city gates; Wyatt's men were repulsed by the defences of London Bridge, and were forced upriver to cross the Thames at Kingston, but the city gates remained locked and they were defeated at Temple Bar. The Inns of Court raised a volunteer force from among the lawyers and their clerks in 1584. In 1588 the Surrey Militia mustered at St George's Fields, Southwark, to repulse the Armada. The 1588 Militia Muster's target of 20,000 men for London, produced only 17,883, of whom 10,000 were armed, and 6000 were trained. From Middlesex came 1000 infantry, half of whom were trained, and a troop of eighty horse. No wonder Elizabeth needed her heart of a lion. The militia had not always been totally reliable, so it was as well that Elizabeth delivered some morale-stiffening rhetoric.

Warning of the approaching Armada was relayed by the age-old method of chains of beacons built on inter-visible high-points. The system had been refurbished in 1585 with one chain running from Beachy Head (Sussex) to London, and another chain running along the north Kent coast with its final links at Beacon Wood, Dartford, Shooters Hill and Greenwich. The chains then ran northwards, with a beacon on Monken Hadley church tower outside Barnet, for instance. The usual hilltops and natural features were used as well as other suitable sites such as Tumble Beacon, Banstead, a pre-historic barrow.

four

Stuart and Georgian London 1600–1815

These times saw enormous political, religious, social, economic and military change, with each dimension inextricably bound up in all the others. The political order underwent the most fundamental of changes when the monarchy was defeated by the forces of republicanism on the field of battle, only to be restored by the impetus of the military. The developments that underpinned the Industrial Revolution brought with them an escalation in the intensity of conflict as the French, or Napoleonic Wars demonstrated the industrialisation of warfare with concomitant casualty inflation. While mediaeval battles had seen roughly 10 per cent of combatants becoming casualties, the increase in the use of efficient gunpowder weapons meant that by the 1600s this figure had doubled, and extended to include those non-combatants unfortunate enough to be caught up in besieged towns, among armies living off the land, or in territory subject to scorched earth policies. What we now call collateral damage could be justified by reference to such divines as Thomas Aquinas who judged that in a 'just war, the gain of victory' outweighed the death of innocents. A fatalistic observation originating in the Thirty Years War was that war could not be 'carried around in a bag': bystanders could not be insulated from the violence, and would be hurt. Armies were becoming better trained, better armed, better led, less concerned about civilians getting caught in the crossfire, and altogether more disciplined in the business of killing, in a world moving ever closer to total war.

London in the Civil War

Many of the political events leading to the Civil War inevitably took place in London, the seat of government. Although Charles I was confident of the support of the city oligarchy, he was steadily losing that of the apprentices, which might have been expected, but he was also losing the middling ranks of craftsmen and artisans. Relying on the forces available to him under Colonel Lunsford, whose appointment as Lieutenant of the Tower of London had been unsuccessfully opposed by the citizenry, the king in December 1641 expected to subdue opposition in Parliament with a *coup de main*, in effect, imposing martial law. A mob of up to 10,000 armed Londoners surged to protect the MPs, denying Charles his chance to seize those he perceived as the ringleaders. The oligarchs were bypassed, and the Lord Mayor, having ordered the Trained Bands to fire on the mob, was assaulted and deposed. The city gates were barred against the king and those troops loyal to him, forcing him to leave, eventually to fetch up at Nottingham in August 1642 where, raising his standard, he effectively declared war on his own subjects. If the size of the mob sounds large, and some contemporary accounts claim it was even larger, it must be remembered that in London at the time there were at least 20,000 apprentices – young men who were energetic, fearless, excitable, adventurous and readily incited.

Among Europe's capital cities, London must have been unique in not being surrounded by great girdles of ramparts and bastions, or bristling with cannon and manned by standing bodies of troops. Circumstances of both history and, more particularly, geography, had combined to make such defensive provision unnecessary. Over the years the city had outgrown the old mediaeval city walls, retaining only the gates in any reasonable state of repair, and then only to serve as territorial markers or to house criminals or debtors. However, two events in November 1642 combined to emphasise the danger of leaving London unprotected in this novel state of war. The first was the sack of Brentford by the advancing Royalists, which brought the horrors of war uncomfortably close to London homes. The second was the Battle of Turnham Green, which highlighted the fact that London's security depended, for the most part, on the discipline and courage of citizen soldiers, the Trained Bands. By autumn 1642 plans had already been set in motion to establish a circuit of defence works around the extended city. Roads into London were obstructed with posts and chains, and cannon were mounted in earthen batteries. After Turnham Green, work accelerated, and the new defences were essentially complete by May 1643. The Venetian ambassador at the time made the observation that the defences would keep people in as well as out, and there existed some paranoia over a fifth column; the fortifications were expected to enforce loyalty and a commitment to Parliament in a population containing a significant proportion of Royalist sympathisers. The construction of this continuous circuit of forts and entrenchments around the wider city was an enormous undertaking. The circuit of 11 miles (18km) in all, included the square mile of the old city, the Palace of Westminster, marking the western extent of growth, the suburbs east of the tower, and Southwark, south of the river. The labour force, recruited or conscripted from London's population of 355,000, numbered tens of thousands, including women and children, who marched out to work with flags

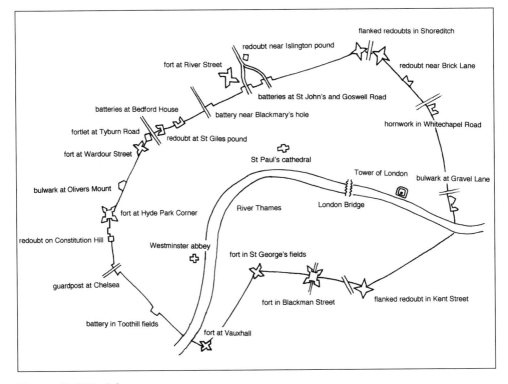

Figure 3 Civil War defences.

flying and drums beating. It was most likely organised both on a parish basis and by occupation or trade through the livery companies, with different categories of shops being ordered to close on specified days of the week in rotation. Phillip Skippon, commanding the London Trained Bands, had experienced warfare on the Continent, having been at the sieges of Maastricht (1629) and Breda (1624–25) and its recapture in 1637. He would have overseen the fortification project, with the detail worked out by imported Dutch engineers and their construction supervised by Colonel Mainwaring (*sic*). This latter was an alderman who led the eighteen companies of the Trained Bands, numbering 8000 militiamen. The work appears to have been completed by autumn 1643, when some 200 cannon had been emplaced. In Whitehall, at the very heart of government, cannon were mounted in 1643 in the ground floor of the Privy Gallery linking the Holbein Gate to the Banqueting House, covering the approach from Charing Cross. This battery was renewed in 1685 at the time of Monmouth's Rebellion, and only demolished in 1723.

Starting at Vauxhall, south of the Thames, the line ran anti-clockwise below Lambeth and Southwark to a point on the Thames a quarter of a mile east of the tower. On this stretch south of the Thames were four forts, that where the Newington road entered was particularly substantial with four bastions. Across the river the line ran north across the Whitechapel Road to Shoreditch, incorporating five works, horn-works, bulwarks and flanked redoubts. The line then turned west to run across the top of the city and on to Tyburn, this stretch containing seven works on the line itself, similar to those to the east. Additionally, there were two works in advance of the line either side of the road to Islington. One was a small redoubt, but the other was the substantial Fort Royal with four demi-bastions, connected to the main lines by a covered way and mounting some nineteen guns. Twelve of these were Cannon Royal, firing a 63lb (28kg) shot up to 1500yds, and gun positions were spaced at the appropriate intervals to allow intersecting fields of fire. A full range of the available guns was available, so, as well as the heavier Cannons Royal, there were also Culverins, which fired a smaller shot greater distances, and anti-personnel weapons such as Falcons and Robinets, which fired a 12oz (350g) shot. Another fort similar in design to Fort Royal but with fewer cannon stood at Wardour Street. The line then ran to Hyde Park Corner with another large fort, and then to Constitution Hill. At the point where the road went through the line at Chelsea Turnpike, there was a defended guardhouse, and Tothill fort, south-west of Westminster, was the final battery before the line re-joined the river opposite Vauxhall. According to Vertue's map of 1739, there were twenty-three strong-points altogether, while one contemporary observer, Lythgoe, reported twenty-eight works. A contemporary map known as the Stukeley Plan has been interpreted as showing the existence of an inner line of fortifications, and this could account for discrepancies. Where the old city walls and gates survived, they would, in extremis, have been brought back into use, but after Turnham Green, London was not really threatened again. While slight indications of earthworks survive, in Hyde Park for instance, most of the works were demolished very quickly, and were soon to be forgotten, although the fort at Whitechapel is reported to have been a prominent structure until 1807.

The nature of the works themselves is not always clear, but they were definitely not durable or impregnable. Contemporary description and representation both point to the construction of a number of different types of sconce, flanked redoubt, battery, and horn-work. This would appear wholly likely given the materials involved, the speed of construction, the theoretical models of military engineering that were current and accessible at the time, the experience of those who might have designed and built them, and the example of other contemporary fortified places. Although there are indications that some parts, specifically the gates of the bigger forts, may

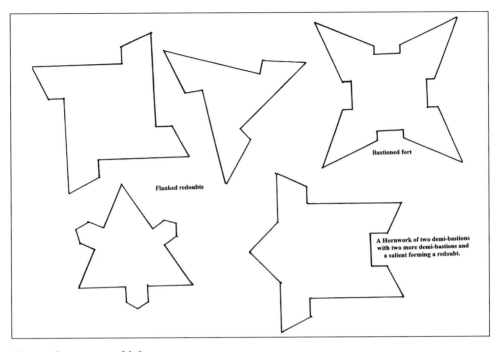

Figure 4 Components of defences.

have been revetted in stone or brick, the works were predominantly of earth with timber palisades, storm poles, stakes and iron spikes. Contemporary illustrations show inner works very like the log-built blockhouses of the Canadian or Russian backwoods, possibly derived from post mills. Roads would have crossed the ditch by drawbridge, and barricaded by logs and chains. Sentries had timber sheds, tiled with shingles, as guardhouses by the roadside. Some of the moats were kept full of water where possible, although opinion was divided: some argued that dry ditches could provide safe corridors for troops to deploy under fire, others that the additional hazard of water took the impetus out of an attacking force. The swampy land south of the river may have provided the possibility for deliberate flooding of the approaches, and the involvement of Dutch engineers would suggest such exploitation of water in the defences. Where the ditch has been excavated it was found to have been 4ft 6in (1.4m) deep and 16ft (5m) across. An outer bank would have helped to create a glacis to the field, and an inner one would have effectively doubled the depth. As sophisticated as the metropolis may have been, its defences were essentially fieldworks, a naivety that was the norm in Civil War fortifications, with the possible exception of those at Oxford. There were two outlying redoubts at Mile End defending the road into London from the east, and all roads into London had checkpoints where traffic could be controlled and those entering or leaving might be monitored. In order to secure the southern route into London, Parliament ordered that the Henrician blockhouses on Blackheath and at Greenwich, near the observatory, be garrisoned, along with those on the river at Gravesend and Tilbury. Surprisingly, although the tower continued to epitomise the military aspect of the city, very little work was carried out to bring its defences into the seventeenth century. It can only be surmised that Legge's Mount was given a bombproof vault over cellarage during the Civil War, since work in the 1680s removed this vault when the bastion was heightened.

Despite the presence of Royalist sympathisers, Parliament ensured that London's resources were mobilised against the cause of Charles I, financing the war effort through compulsory

25 The Tower of London, Legge's Mount was adapted in 1682, by removing a vault, probably inserted in the Civil War, and by raising it by 20ft (6m) to mount two tiers of cannon, in six casemates on one level, and *en barbette* on the roof.

weekly assessments. Despite the apprehensions of many of the rank and file, the London Trained Bands formed the first Parliamentarian field army. To safeguard its interests, in January 1642 London's Common Council elected a Committee of Safety dominated by Parliamentarian supporters. This body took over from the Commission of the Militia, thereby controlling the city's military resources. Although the London Trained Bands fought successfully at the two Battles of Newbury, and at the Relief of Gloucester, they were not always so dependable. Londoners fighting in Waller's army in Sussex and Hampshire had to be sent home in 1643 as they lacked discipline, and after the defeat at Cropredy Bridge in June 1644, the Tower Hamlets Trained Band deserted to a man, making straight for home. This may have been an indication of a willingness to enlist in order to protect home and family, but an understandable reluctance to operate away from home for too long. In 1647 there was a struggle for control of the London Trained Bands between the Presbyterian city fathers, the army, and Parliament, which was only resolved by the Parliamentarian General Fairfax marching on London with troops from Hounslow Heath following riots by apprentices and discharged soldiers from both sides, possibly orchestrated by the city. The Trained Bands refused to fight against the army and were then taken over by Parliament, encouraging the speedy resumption of normal mercantile business. The fortifications were then demolished to prevent London becoming a centre of reaction against the Commonwealth, as there was a genuine danger that the Royalist forces that launched the Second Civil War in 1648 might have expected support from London. Skippon, commanding the militia, managed to ensure that support went no further than lobbying Parliament to make peace with the imprisoned king. Apart from some unorchestrated rioting and looting, the king's execution in 1649 provoked little response. The city was under the thumb of the army, enforcing the payment of taxes, and it was not until 1660 that the largely pro-Royalist city would get its king back.

Although London was not attacked, there were widespread instances of destruction neverthe-less. Fortunately, the majority of the forts and the circuit of rampart and ditch were built on open land away from the most built-up parts of the city, but there were still demolitions. Houses in Whitechapel, Shoreditch and Bloomsbury were razed, isolated buildings that might impede fields of fire were flattened, as were other buildings that might have provided cover to an attacking force, and sheds and lean-tos that had encroached onto the old city walls were also torn down.

Civil War Sites Around London

After the fall of Brentford in November 1642, in which at least 500 Parliamentarian troops were killed, the victorious Royalists occupied Syon House, setting up gun batteries to control the river traffic, and taking advantage of the Parliamentarian evacuation of Kingston-upon-Thames at the same time. But within a week the Royalist forces had fallen back on Oxford and Reading, and the Parliamentarian garrisons resumed their duties. Few properties were newly fortified but the owners of Carew Manor, Beddington, a moated house of the fifteenth and sixteenth centu-ries, scoured their moat and repaired their drawbridge in order to sleep more soundly at night, and there must have been others. The palace of the archbishops of Canterbury at Croydon was garrisoned by Parliament. Kingston-upon-Thames figured once more in 1648 when it became the starting point for one final rising for King Charles, led by the earls of Peterborough and Holland and the Duke of Buckingham. This adventure ended with the Cavaliers being routed on Surbiton Common. Other buildings had more mundane uses, Greenwich Palace for exam-ple becoming a biscuit factory supplying troops in Scotland during Cromwell's campaigns, and afterwards being occupied by Dutch POWs. A century later, prisoners enjoyed less palatial sur-roundings. Prior to the alternative of transportation to Australia, which began in 1786, prison hulks were used after the American War. In 1782 there were over 1000 prisoners in hulks such as the *Retribution* moored off Woolwich, rising to a peak of 2500 by 1815.

London's Walls and Gates

The walls played little part in London's emergency fortifications of the Civil War period, and were approaching the end of their useful life. Aldgate had been rebuilt in 1607–9 at the request of James I who paid for it as a ceremonial entry to the city from Westminster, but was demolished in 1761. A part reconstruction was incorporated into the rebuilt Aldgate House, a sixteenth-century property of the Gresham family; the reconstruction was carried out by the antiquary Ebenezer Mussell in 1760, and stood until its demolition in 1911. Aldersgate was rebuilt in 1666, and Cripplegate was repaired in 1663, but both were to be demolished in 1760–61. Bishopsgate was repaired in 1648, and completely rebuilt in 1733 in the Baroque style, only to be demolished in 1761. Moorgate was rebuilt in 1672, in a similar style to Bishopsgate, and was also demol-ished in 1761. Wren may have been responsible for rebuilding the purely ceremonial Temple Bar in 1670, replacing a gate built by about 1350. The Bar was removed to Theobalds Park in Hertfordshire but has now been re-erected near St Paul's Cathedral. Newgate, excavated in 1875–1909, had been rebuilt in 1672, and in 1777 was the last gate to be demolished.

Headquarters for the New Army

Britons had long resisted the existence of a standing army, relying on ad hoc bodies of troops being raised for specific expeditions and for finite lengths of time. During the civil wars, the majority of combatants, both officers and other ranks, were essentially amateurs, but an influx of mercenaries experienced in warfare on the Continent, and the establishment of Cromwell's New Model Army consisting of cavalry, infantry, artillery and engineers, had contributed to a new professionalism. This involved leadership on merit rather than birth or social position, continual drilling, the practising of prescribed manoeuvres and the inculcation of discipline, both personal and corporate. The social, religious and political problems presented by the Commonwealth were ultimately to be stifled by the imposition of martial law, which necessitated keeping the army in existence. The Restoration of the monarchy in 1660 was to a great extent dependent on the army, now 40,000 strong and under the command of General Monck, later the Duke of Albemarle. Charles II deemed it politic to dissolve this force, but sensible to raise the nucleus of a new one, the body that would become the Coldstream Guards. Other regiments followed, but as a way of earning revenue they were often leased out to foreign powers. As a further safeguard, Charles ensured that the militia was placed under the command of those nominees who could demonstrate unquestionable loyalty to the Crown.

To maintain them, armies need a bureaucracy located physically close to the seat of government, and the rambling buildings of Whitehall Palace provided such premises. A *corps-de-garde* had been built in 1641 in the Horse Guards Tiltyard, and Cromwell's military administration had occupied the Cockpit, now the Downing Street complex. This provision was enlarged and developed under Charles II, with a new guardhouse in the Tiltyard, designed in 1660 by the deputy of Inigo Jones whose nearby Banqueting House had unhappy associations for the new king. From 1675 until 1683, Scotland Yard housed the War Office, which moved to Little Wallingford House in 1689, relinquishing quarters for the New Model Life Guard of Horse. The Old Horse Guards building, with its Foot Guards wing to the south, was open by summer 1664, having been established by Monck as HQ of the army commander-in-chief. The Navy Board had premises on Tower Hill from 1620–1788, but the Admiralty Board moved into a new building in 1693, both ending up in Somerset House in the next century but retaining premises in Whitehall. The army's civilian administrators worked from dedicated offices at 7 Whitehall Gardens from 1710.

The Tower of London

Work at the tower was to focus more on the internal buildings rather than the actual defences, although a line of cannon mounted on Tower Wharf is marked on maps from the early 1700s. The new developments were all intended to improve the tower's function as a magazine and armoury, and a number of accretions around the White Tower were cleared away on the grounds that they represented a fire hazard in too close a proximity to the large amounts of powder stored within. A new route from the wharf was also created by bridging the moat and breaching the inner and outer walls, in order to make the distribution of powder to the forces more efficient. The range running north from the Wakefield Tower to the Wardrobe Gate was converted into a temporary armoury and office for the Ordnance Board while the demolition of the structures around the White Tower was carried out, and two grand buildings were

26 The Tower of London, the New Armouries were built in 1664 as an ordnance store.

then constructed as replacements. The Great New Store House survives as the New Armouries along the east curtain, but the other, the Grand Store House, an imposing two-storey block of twenty-three bays, shallow projections at each end and central pediment, was later replaced by the Waterloo Barracks. It housed an armoury of weapons, artfully displayed in the traditions of earlier collections at Hampton Court and Windsor Castle. Accommodation for the garrison, the two-storey, timber-framed, weather-boarded Irish Barracks, had been completed by 1670. In 1666, Sir Bernard de Gomme was instructed to draw up plans to modernise the outer defences with artillery bastions. One proposal provided for a bulwark outside the Lion Gate, while the other, much more ambitious, scheme sketched an angular enceinte with three full bastions to the north and a demi-bastion at each corner of the river frontage, similar to another of his unrealised plans at Liverpool. A plan of 1682 shows, on the wharf outside St Thomas's Tower, a triangular bastion, which was also never built. In 1683 Legge's Mount was remodelled. The first half of the eighteenth century saw the White Tower radically altered with enlarged round-headed windows and Portland stone facings, and lodgings, now known as the Old Hospital Block, built. In 1755 the inadequate Irish Barracks was rebuilt in brick as a three-and-a-half-storey block of fifteen bays. A fire in 1774 destroyed the old mediaeval and Tudor apartments centred around the Lanthorn Tower, providing the opportunity to build a new Ordnance Office, opened in 1780 but itself badly damaged by fire eight years later.

Buildings Used by the Military

Although barracks would not commonly appear as discrete structures for a while yet, as billeting on civilian households, only formalised in 1689, remained the norm, there was still a need to house bodies of troops, particularly in the metropolis. Horse Guards itself was only properly rebuilt from 1750, incorporating barracks, but in the meantime the Royal Mews, now the National Gallery site, accommodated Horse Grenadiers from 1683 until 1788, and there

27 Hampton Court Cavalry Barracks built in three phases in 1662, 1689 and 1713.

28 Kensington Palace Barracks of c.1700, the only surviving wing.

was temporary stabling for a troop of Horse Guards in Buckingham Gate. The Savoy Hospital was taken over by the military in 1642, continuing in use as military hospital until 1679 when it became barracks for Foot Guards. In 1776 a fire destroyed much of the structure, which by

now contained a mustering centre for recruits, an infirmary and a prison for deserters awaiting execution at Tyburn. In 1761 a mutiny, in which some prisoners and at least one innocent
bystander were killed, was put down.

Hampton Court Barracks, a range projecting from the Tudor main front, was built in 1662 for
the Foot Guards, and was enlarged in 1689 to house Horse Guards as well. A further expansion
in 1713 allowed for horses to be stabled on the ground floor of the Horse Guards section, with
guardrooms under the barrack rooms of the Foot Guards. Kensington Palace Barracks, of which
a single block survives, was built around 1700 for cavalry. The Royal Hospital, Chelsea, for veter-
ans and pensioners, was begun in 1682 for Charles II by Wren. It was built in 1682–91 in direct
imitation of the 1670 Les Invalides in Paris and contemporary with Dublin's Kilmainham Royal
Hospital, and was refurbished in 1805. At Chelsea, an initial single courtyard was enlarged by
two additional ones in 1686 and by a chapel/hall connecting range of 1692, in order to accommodate nearly 500 NCOs and other ranks. A guardhouse and offices were added from 1809.
The neighbouring house of Sir Horace Walpole was converted into the infirmary in 1809, but
was destroyed by bombing in 1941.

The Thames Defences in the 1600s

The Navigation Acts of 1651 passed by the Commonwealth Parliament and aimed at challenging
the Dutch hegemony in trade, led to three Dutch Wars between 1652 and 1674, concluded by
the Treaty of Westminster. Despite a string of English successes at sea, in 1667 a Dutch fleet
sailed up the Medway sinking English ships and burning Sheerness, but fortunately chose to
do no more than threaten the Thames. This was just as well, as the Thames defences above
Tilbury Fort were far from impressive. Little had been done since the times of Henry VIII or the
Armada scare, with only a battery at Woolwich hastily thrown up by Prince Rupert and a boom
designed by an engineer from Deptford Dockyard. The tower remained as a last-ditch defence
but here only minor improvements had been carried out when the walls of Legge's Mount
were raised by 20ft (6m) in 1682–86 in order to allow six casemates for artillery to be built.
Once the immediate danger from the Dutch was past, Bernard de Gomme, the royal military
engineer from the Civil War days, was commissioned to build the state-of-the-art fort at Tilbury
that he had proposed some years previously. Ironically, it was just that absence of fortifications
around London that had enabled the rapid expansion that took the population to nearly
1 million by 1800, 10 per cent of the country's population, with its very defencelessness
increasing its attraction as a target.

Despite the innovation of a small standing army, the defence of the realm continued to rely
on the services of part-time, semi-trained amateur soldiers. The Honourable Artillery Company
had been chartered in 1537 as a volunteer unit, but the main force, at least for the time being,
was the militia. The muster of 1695 provides a snapshot showing the size of this force. London
had an establishment of six regiments, the Orange, White, Green, Yalow, Rad and Blew, each
consisting of eight companies, and totalling 6770 men. Tower Hamlets, famed for supplying
personnel to the London Trained Bands in Civil War times, could still raise 2000 able and effective men, duly qualified, in two regiments. The combined Middlesex parishes fielded twenty-six
companies totalling 3361 men in the County, Rad and Blew regiments, some 423 men below
establishment. However, they also raised 282 men in four troops of horse to fight alongside
Southwark's two troops of the Surrey Militia with a further 132 troopers. Fortunately, since the

Civil War, there had been little opportunity for the militiamen to be put through their paces. Monmouth's rebellion in 1685 was sufficiently remote from London to elicit no more than a passing interest and, despite some anti-popery rioting after King James II had fled the country, the Glorious Revolution of 1688 had little impact on Londoners in terms of active conflict.

Shipbuilding and the Royal Navy

Early in the seventeenth century the Dutchman Cornelius van Drebble is said to have demonstrated a submersible, based on William Bourne's 1578 designs, in the Thames, but the idea of using buoyancy tanks that could be filled and emptied was not to be properly developed for another 100 years. There was, however, an established shipbuilding industry on the Thames, and between 1615 and 1652 the East India Company built their Blackwall Yard for repairing and victualling their own ships. In 1661 they added a wet dock, and then the Brunswick Dock of 8 acres (3ha) in 1790. From 1591–1618 over 300 ships totalling 90,000 tons had been built in the East India Company's yards at Deptford and at Blackwall. Their ships were essentially well-armed merchantmen, capable of driving off all but the most powerful or determined of attackers, but from 1608, specialised warships were being built in Woolwich Dockyard. In 1637 the 102-gun First-Rate HMS *Royal Sovereign of the Seas* was launched, being rebuilt in 1660 as the *Royal Sovereign*. By the 1720s there were over fifty shipbuilding or ship-repair yards between London Bridge and Blackwall, and by the end of the century they were not only responsible for over 15 per cent of the tonnage built in Britain but also for generating a strong network of other suppliers producing everything from cordage to instruments and uniforms. London would later develop as an important centre of engineering with Henry Maudslay, the pioneer of machine tools, working at the Woolwich Arsenal in 1789 and opening his own engineering works in

29 Deptford Victualling Yard, the colonnade in front of the Guardhouse, with the gateway to the left, dating from 1783–88.

30 Deptford Victualling Yard, the two rum warehouses with the nearer bow windows marking the superintendent's house.

Westminster Bridge Road, Lambeth, in 1797. He worked with Samuel Bentham and Marc Brunel to revolutionise the mass production of parts, particularly wooden blocks, for the sailing ships of the Royal Navy, not only in the shipyards of Deptford and Woolwich, but in Chatham and Portsmouth as well.

There are a few survivals from these pioneering days. Of Deptford Dockyard the Master Shipbuilder's House, some officers' houses and a later shipbuilding shed can be found in Prince

Street. The nearby Czar Street commemorates the time Peter the Great of Russia spent learning the shipbuilding trade there. Deptford Victualling Yard, rebuilt in 1783–88, is represented by a gateway, a colonnade, two houses for officials, and seven three-storey houses for officers, along with two former rum warehouses and stables. At Woolwich the superintendent's house of 1778 stands at the centre of later structures from the steam era, in a yard entered between a pair of stone pillars carved with the fouled anchor of the Admiralty and past the colonnaded guardroom.

31 Woolwich Dockyard, the superintendent's house of 1778.

32 Greenwich Hospital, Queen Mary's wing, completed by 1740. This World Heritage Site is now occupied by the University of Greenwich.

After its ignominious role as a factory for army hard tack, the palace of Henry VIII and Elizabeth at Greenwich was demolished and a new palace begun in 1664, but only one range, the King Charles Block, was built. In fact, William and Mary had a preference for living at Hampton Court, where they employed Sir Christopher Wren to modernise the inadequate Tudor buildings, handing over Greenwich as a naval hospital. Naval pensioners moved in from 1705, and by 1815 there were over 2700 on site. The buildings were completed by about 1740, but the chapel had to be rebuilt in 1790 after a fire. A separate infirmary was built in 1763 later becoming the Dreadnought Seamen's Hospital, and the Manor House on Crooms Hill was built by 1700 for the Lieutenant Governor of the Royal Hospital. In 1807–16 new wings were added either side of the Queen's House to accommodate the naval asylum for the children of sailors in the Royal Navy that had started in Paddington in 1798. This, combined with an existing school for the children of pensioners, and a gymnasium and assembly hall were added later. The infirmary was the terrace of houses, now Nos 34–38 Maze Hill, built in 1807.

London Docks

Trade into the Port of London, measured by the combined tonnage of ships entering the docks as a percentage of the national total, hovered around half: 59 per cent in 1686, 54 per cent in 1718, and 49 per cent in 1772. This represented a larger share of total foreign trade: 77 per cent in 1700, 67 per cent in 1737 and 65 per cent in 1792. In the 1720s there were three wet docks, twenty-two dry docks, and thirty-three docks for laying up, repairing and building, all below London Bridge. In 1800 the West India Dock was begun, consisting of two parallel wet docks covering over 50 acres. For a nation whose growing imperial power was based on trade, these

33 The former armoury of the West India Docks guards.

installations could be very vulnerable to attack or sabotage. In 1805 two circular, domed guardrooms were built, flanking the entrance through the inner wall, which was demolished in 1932. One was an armoury for the military guard and the docks' own militia and the other, demolished in 1923, was a lock up. The Docks Police Force was formed in 1802, and two pairs of cottages for constables and a detached one for the sergeant were provided. A ditch and outer wall were built in 1802 to protect the docks from all comers, with a timber drawbridge over the ditch until 1809 when a permanent brick bridge was built. This wall was mainly dismantled in 1928–29 and the ditch had been backfilled in 1892. A restored length of wall forms the boundary of the garden of the Excise Office of 1809. In 1806 the East India Dock, covering 32 acres (13ha), was built at Blackwall.

Munitions Production

Gunpowder works were central to the successful operation of any army, and Parliament had benefited from the fortuitous location of important works in the London area. Tolworth, from 1560, Bedfont, established in 1609 on the banks of the River Crane, Stratford's Three Mills and St Thomas Mills from the early years of the seventeenth century, and Southwark, opened in 1630, had all fed the Parliamentarian war machine. In the years following the conflict, further mills were opened: Hackney and Clapton (1652), Enfield Mill at Enfield Lock (1653), Tottenham and Walthamstow (1656), Waltham Abbey (by 1665), North Feltham (1668) and Wandsworth (late 1600s). The Worshipful Company of Gunmakers' Proof House had moved to Aldgate in 1657 and then around 1757 into the less built-up environment of 46–50 Commercial Road, Stepney, being rebuilt in 1826. Artillery grounds were established at Victoria and at Spitalfields, with part of the St Mary's Spital site being leased to the Guild of Artillery, accessed by Artillery Lane, and sold for development in 1683.

 As early as 1565 there had been an ordnance store at Woolwich supplying the nearby Royal Dockyards. A hundred years later the site had been expanded to store mainly guns and ammunition. In 1696 the two Royal Laboratories opened to manufacture gunpowder and pyrotechnics alongside the Carriage Department, which mounted cannon for use by the king's army and navy. In 1717, following a serious accident at the main contractor's workshop in Moorfields, it was decided to set up a foundry at Woolwich where cannon could be cast to order, and Dial Square was built at this time. By 1620 Tower Place had been replaced by a new building, probably designed by Vanburgh, which in 1741 became the initial home of the RMA. In 1805, at the suggestion of George III, the complex became known as the Woolwich Arsenal.

34 Woolwich Arsenal, the surviving wing of Dial Court, named for the sundial that sits between the two piles of stone cannonballs. Built in 1717, the whole complex was known as the Great Pile. Arsenal FC began as the Dial Square Football Club.

35 Woolwich Arsenal, this was Vanburgh's replacement building for Tower Place *c.*1717. Variously known as the Board Room, the Model Room and, after the Second World War, as the Officers' Mess, it housed the Royal Military Academy until 1806.

Riots and Aid to the Civil Authority

While British troops were engaged in foreign wars for much of the century, the main dangers to eighteenth-century Londoners came from their fellow citizens. The general reluctance to establish a police force meant that when things got out of hand it was the soldiers, utterly untrained in crowd control and often panicked into precipitate and disproportionate action, who were sent in. Troops, readily available from the tower or the Whitehall Tiltyard, waded in with predictably lethal consequences. London had a long history of mob violence, and sometimes it took very little to set it in motion. In 1710, the sermons of Dr Sacheverel, a High Tory demagogue, were sufficient to incite a mob that threatened the Bank of England itself, at the time lodging in the Grocers' Company Hall. It was only saved by the prompt action of the Horse Guards from St James's. The bank had only recently been brought into being in order to handle the issue of government bonds to the public. These loans to fund the wars against France from 1689–97 and 1702–14, became the basis of the national debt, so the bank was soon associated, in the minds of the rioting classes, with oppressive taxation. The year 1715 was a particularly good one for the mob. Alehouse brawls between gangs of youths armed with firearms, political riots around anniversaries such as the Restoration of Charles II, and general fears of Jacobite conspiracies all brought the rioters onto the streets. The Calico Riots of 1719 and 1720 in Spitalfields, and the Anti-Irish Riots of 1736 in Shoreditch, Spitalfields and Whitechapel, were all suppressed by guards from the tower aided by the Tower Hamlets Militia. In 1738 the guards were called out to quell the Gin Act riots, during which several informers were stoned to death by the crowd. Security became such an issue that Lord Bute set up his own private force of 'butchers and bruisers' in 1761.

The famine years of 1725, 1740 and 1775 saw rioting prompted by very basic wants. London, it must be remembered, was a seaport with all the attendant problems of sailors and their pastimes. In 1748 sailors from HMS *Grafton* were robbed in the Star Tavern in the Strand, returning with their shipmates to wreck the place. The next night they attacked the 'Crown' and the brothel next door. Troops were summoned, arrests were made, and three of the sailors were hanged. Such small-scale events could be very much bigger. Just as the return of discharged soldiers from the Hundred Years War had filled honest tradespeople with dread, then the events of 1763 resurrected such fears, as the end of the Seven Years War saw a sailors' uprising when a reported 5000 sailors disabled every vessel in the Port of London and marched on Westminster. The so-called Battle of Temple Bar saw the HAC called out to deal with the mob from their new HQ at Armoury House, Finsbury, built in 1734–36. Much of the trouble was caused by purely economic rather than political pressures. People feared losing their livelihoods through unfair competition or technological advances, and the low-paid saw little scope for improvement. When they took action, authority's response was invariably harsh. In 1768 seven coal heavers were convicted of causing an affray, having attacked the house of one of the lord mayor's men seeking to end their industrial action over pay and conditions. An inevitable guilty verdict saw them hanged in Stepney, with 300 soldiers present to keep order. Luddism provoked riots, with attacks in 1765 on premises housing the engine looms that could do the work of six weavers. In 1769, a soldier was shot dead by weavers, those responsible were hanged and troops were quartered in Spitalfields itself. Politicians also joined in the fun if it suited their designs. Riots to support John Wilkes in 1768 at Lambeth's St George's Fields, suitably recorded in the annals of radical mythology as a 'Massacre', saw twenty killed or wounded when troops opened fire. The supposed ringleaders of either spontaneous or fomented disturbances, even if they escaped being shot by the guards, could still end up at Tyburn, or wherever an example needed to be made.

The culmination of all this unrest was the Gordon Riots. On 2 June 1780, Lord George Gordon, suspecting that Parliament was about to relax the restrictions on Catholics holding public office, presented an anti-Catholic petition at Westminster, supported by thousands of people 'of the middling sort'. The guards managed to clear a way for MPs to leave Parliament, but the mob then took over what had, up until then, been an orderly demonstration, embarking on the destruction of Catholic chapels and the homes of prominent Catholics. Prisons and other official buildings were attacked, including the Bank of England and the Royal Exchange, defended by the London Military Association alongside the regular troops. Rioting continued over the next week; the Horse Guards were called out to control the area around Westminster, and as many as 10,000 troops were mobilised to protect homes and businesses. Tented camps for the infantry were established in Hyde Park and St James's Park, as well as in Hampstead and Highgate. Detachments of the Horse Guards, the 3rd and 4th Dragoons, and the 3rd Dragoon Guards were stationed in Lincoln's Inn Fields, Knightsbridge, St George's Fields and in Islington, carrying out regular patrols around the city, Westminster and Southwark. The Surrey Militia, with a battalion based in Fulham from 1759, were well-placed to intervene, but militia regiments were brought from outside London, with, for example, the Cambridgeshires from Ely guarding Kenwood, the home of the Lord Chief Justice, who was widely suspected of being a secret Catholic. Two regiments of the Hampshire Militia were camped on Blackheath. By 7 June, the troops had restored order, and Gordon was escorted to the tower on 9 June. He was tried and found not guilty, but the lord mayor was fined £1000 for negligence in not reading the Riot Act promptly enough. This act had been promulgated in 1715, and it indemnified soldiers from prosecution for murder once it had been read aloud to gatherings of over a dozen people. The week of disorder left 285 dead, a further 173 being treated for gunshot wounds, 450 arrested, 160 brought to trial and 25 hanged. One of the effects of such riots was, amid acute public reluctance, the expansion of a police force. In 1792 seven new police offices were established, new magistrates' courts were opened, and the armed Bow Street Patrol Service was expanded. In 1800 the Thames Police Force was created, and in 1805 a horse patrol of sixty men was formed to combat highwaymen, expanded shortly after by a further 100 men on foot. All this would eventually lead to the Metropolitan Police Act in 1829. When the Bank of England was built by Sir John Soane from 1788, it incorporated musketry galleries and an on-site barracks for the use of a permanent guard. Lessons, as they always say, had been learned.

The Volunteers

As well as these bodies of official police, the 1780s saw the formation of voluntary armed associations to safeguard property against the 'rabble' seeking to advance radical policies through strikes, riots and demonstrations. However it was not until the impact of the French Revolution had been felt, and war with France had actually broken out in 1793, that serious attempts were made to establish a wholly military volunteer force properly recognised by the authorities. An Act of Parliament (Geo III, 34) of 1794 abolished the Trained Bands in London and provided for the establishment of six militia regiments. Lords lieutenant were permitted to raise volunteer forces alongside these, forming volunteer associations in each parish. Very little came of an April 1794 attempt to raise a regiment of volunteer infantry and a troop of cavalry under the name

'The Loyal London Volunteers'. However, the Nore mutiny in 1797 brought about a greater sense of urgency. The mutineers had reached Dartford in an attempt to suborn the London guardships and to cause a blockade of the Thames. The London merchants were already experiencing the economic impact of a 25 per cent fall in trade caused by the war, so the sailors' cause alienated many who might, in different circumstances, have supported them. Doubt over the reliability of the Royal Navy, Britain's traditional protection against foreign invasion, prompted a small increase in recruitment to the volunteer units. By 1798 the Cornhill Military Association had formed with fifty-three members, with others in Bishopsgate and Farringdon Within by 1799, and Marylebone forming a body of 800 volunteers by 1801. Disparagingly known as 'Bluebottles', they later became the more dignified Royal York St Marylebone Volunteers. Troops of cavalry were formed in Islington, Westminster and Uxbridge and in 1800 food riots caused the volunteers to be called out to relieve the militia. Kent's closer proximity to the enemy possibly influenced a higher level of recruitment there. From 1794 nearly twenty troops of yeomanry cavalry were raised in the county, with two in Chislehurst and Sevenoaks, each with three officers and fifty troopers. Most of these units were disbanded after the Peace of Amiens in 1802, but when war was renewed the next year many re-formed with much greater success. A force of 10,000 infantry was formed in eleven regiments in four divisions in the city, joined by large numbers of men from the East London parishes plus Westminster, Marylebone, Knightsbridge, Holborn and Clerkenwell, Southwark and the suburban parishes of Surrey and Middlesex. There were, in addition, the cavalry units, which had re-formed, and units made up of dockworkers and watermen. Nearly 30,000 men mustered for a grand review in Hyde Park in 1803 and on Blackheath the next year. The stated aim of these volunteers, the vast majority of whom came from the middling classes, was to 'protect Property, preserve the Peace of the Metropolis on occasions of Rebellion, Insurrection, Civil Commotion, and all other Cases of extraordinary emergency'. Only in fact incidentally to counter a French invasion, but more importantly to head off any attempt on the part of the lower orders to emulate the French Revolution. Nearly all these volunteer units had been disbanded by 1814 when Napoleon was thought to be safely out of circulation on Elba.

The Thames Defences in the 1700s

Throughout this period, the Tilbury-Gravesend axis remained the key military component in the defence of the river approach to London. To complement the long-established Tilbury Fort on the north bank, a new fort at Gravesend was built in 1780. Although there were permanent military camps at Warley on the Essex side, and Dartford on the Kent side, the vital ability to move troops around as a quick response to any enemy landing was sought. The solution was the construction of three jetties on each side of the river between which six barges could be winched backwards and forwards across the river between Gravesend and Tilbury on hawsers. A review of defences in 1794 decided that any additional works should be built downriver from Tilbury. Batteries were built on both sides of the river, some gunboats manned by volunteer Sea Fencibles were commissioned, and a line of warships was moored across the river at Lower Hope Point. The only activity at the Tower of London during this period appears to have been aimed at improving the facilities of the Ordnance Office and extending the barrack accommodation. As well as coast defences, there were proposals to block a potential invasion taking an inland route. A scheme of 1795 to protect London from invasion through Essex included an entrenched camp north of Chelmsford, never to be carried through. To the south of Chelmsford a line of entrenchments with bastions was actually built but never armed. It began at Widford, astride the old A12 road, running in a dogleg east and south for about 5 miles.

Military Establishments in the Napoleonic Wars

The expansion of the regular army during the wars necessitated the construction of barracks to house them. New cavalry barracks were built at Knightsbridge in 1792, consisting of a three-storied pedimented mess to house thirty-five officers in some degree of domestic comfort, and two long wings with stables on the ground floor with rooms for the troopers above benefiting from equine central heating. Also included were a riding school, stables for the officers' horses and a magazine. On the opposite side of the road was an infantry barracks for 500 men built around a courtyard. Hounslow Cavalry Barracks, built in 1793 on the site of an army encampment of long standing, contained similar elements to those at Knightsbridge but on a less constricted site. The two long ranges of stables and barrack rooms, one with a forage-barn on the end, faced each other across the parade ground. These were relatively substantial and permanent buildings, but the government's policy of distributing troops of cavalry around the country on internal security duties saw temporary timber barracks being built in 1795 at Romford and in Croydon. The Royal Artillery barracks at Woolwich had been started in 1775, becoming, as Douet points out, the longest residential building in Georgian Britain, over 1000ft (305m) long in ninety-four bays with space for 4000 men and, accessed through a triumphal arch, all the services behind this vast facade organised in a grid of buildings that included three riding schools. The Royal Military Academy, for training the army's intelligentsia, artillery and engineer officers, had opened in 1741 in a building in the Warren, or Woolwich Arsenal, moving to new premises on the common in 1806. The Royal Engineers

36 Woolwich Artillery Barracks was begun in 1775 and this shows just one of the six elements which make up the grand front stretching 1000ft (300m).

37 Whitehall, New Horse Guards built in 1750 to house the military High Command and to provide convenient barracks for the household troops. (Photograph: Pam Osborne)

Barracks on Woolwich New Road dates from 1803. Hyde Park Barracks was built around 1800, and parts may survive behind the later police station. On Gray's Inn Road, Holborn, there were new barracks for the London and Westminster Light Horse Volunteers, in use from 1812–28. The Duke of York's HQ off Sloane Square was built in 1803 as the Royal Military Asylum for the children of soldiers' widows. It subsequently became a military HQ, particularly for volunteer units. With a grand Doric portico facing onto playing fields, it is now the Saatchi Gallery, shops and apartments. The Whitehall complex had also developed throughout the eighteenth century. Horse Guards was rebuilt as a War Office in about 1760, with integral barrack accommodation for the Life Guards, Royal Horse Guards and three Guards regiments; the Old Admiralty (now Ripley Buildings) was built in 1723–26; and Admiralty House in 1786–88. No. 3 Grafton Street, Mayfair, was built in 1767 as an official residence for Admiral Earl Howe, the First Lord of the Admiralty at the time.

New powder works had opened throughout the 1700s at Balham, Hounslow and Wimbledon, and there was a need for secure storage to stockpile supplies for emergencies. Purfleet on the Thames, located in Long Reach, where warships traditionally took on gunpowder, was selected for new powder magazines that were begun in 1760 and completed nine years later. There were five gabled magazine buildings, each holding around 5000 barrels of powder, with walls 2ft (60cm) thick and sand-filled attics. A guard was provided as the complex was rapidly becoming Britain's prime powder magazine, eclipsing the Tower of London. A proofing house was built in 1781 to work in conjunction with the Woolwich Laboratories, and in 1787 Purfleet took its first delivery of gunpowder manufactured at Waltham Abbey. With the outbreak of the French wars, the magazines were provided with barracks for 100 men to safeguard the depot against the possibility of raids upriver, and in 1798 a local body of volunteer cavalry was raised as the Barstable and Chafford Troop. One of the five magazines and the clock-tower gatehouse of the barracks remain. Dating back to the Restoration, Waltham Abbey powder mills had become one of the largest producers in the country, and to ensure continuity of production it was taken into public

38 Whitehall, Old Admiralty (now Ripley) Building, built in 1723 to provide a board room and accommodation for the lords of the Admiralty.

39 Hyde Park powder magazine, designed by Wyatt 1805–6, to house munitions for the volunteers who would defend London against Napoleon. It only ceased functioning as a magazine in 1948.

ownership in 1787 on the eve of the French wars, during which it supplied 25,000 barrels of gunpowder a year to Purfleet and Woolwich Arsenal. Sited alongside the River Lea, further canals were dug to move volatile materials around the site. The barges used for this operation were lined in leather and were propelled by human muscle to avoid the problems of bolting horses or sparking horseshoes. Many of the early structures may still be made out at the Royal Gunpowder Mills site. The new Hyde Park powder magazine opened in 1805 storing guns and ammunition for the use of the volunteers. It was designed by James Wyatt, architect to the Board of Ordnance and was replicated around the country.

Communications

The development of London as the HQ of the armed forces required some system by which signals might be transmitted quickly and reliably. From 1794 a chain of naval signal stations was established along the entire South Coast. Using a system of flags and balls in prearranged code groups, every passing ship was challenged and identified. A weekly record was despatched by each post to the Admiralty, which was cross-checked with ships' logs. For night-time use, lanterns were displayed in set patterns. While a number of systems enabled local HQs to keep in touch with formations of troops stationed in camps spread along the South Coast, the Admiralty in London wanted to be kept in the loop. A shutter telegraph system, providing open and shut combinations for seventeen letters of the alphabet, was developed, initially linking London with Deal via Chatham, and then with Sheerness as well, its first two posts being at New Cross and on Shooters Hill. By 1796 the line to the HQ of the Channel Fleet at Portsmouth via Putney Heath had been completed. A continuation of this line to Plymouth and Falmouth, started in 1805, was never finished, and existing lines were shut down in 1816. By 1803 a network of beacons along the South Coast would have been used to give warning of a French landing and to alert anti-invasion forces. Dried furze was stored under thatch to be used in such an emergency. Along these chains of coastal beacons, Bexhill, Brighton and Chatham marked the start of other chains connecting directly to London. Different methods were used to improve the transmission of signals, including the lamps and white lights used by General Roy in his trigonometrical surveying of the previous decade, and a military telegraph was established from London to Norwich in 1803, employing relayed visual signals.

One of the ways in which Horse Guards was able to deploy troops in emergencies, avoiding the country's atrocious roads, was to make use of the canal system. In 1798 in response to the disturbances in Ireland where French troops had landed in support of a republican uprising, the Duke of York ordered reinforcements of eight regiments of militia, over 8000 men, to be transported to Ireland by canal. This method was found to be successful and became quite common in the years following, with numbers of both regular troops and militia being carried from Paddington canal basin up the Grand Junction and Trent and Mersey canals for embarkation at Liverpool.

Mapping

Major-General William Roy (1726–90) worked on mapping Scotland for military purposes from 1747 until 1752, in order to avoid any repeat of the Jacobite uprising of 1745 by securing the strategic routes. Having had his proposals for carrying out a similarly complete survey of England continually rejected, it was only when the French suggested that the Greenwich Meridian was not as accurately defined as the one passing through France, that he was commissioned to begin a survey. Finally, in 1783 he began a process of triangulation that would only end in the 1850s. His starting point for the initial baseline was the large flat area of Hounslow Heath, much of which is now covered by Heathrow Airport. Initially a steel chain, 100ft (30m) long, and wooden rods 20ft (6m) long, were used for the measuring, but these were found to fluctuate with the weather, so glass rods were substituted. The baseline of 5.19 miles (8.352km) extended from Heathrow to Hampton. In 1791, after Roy's death, the Duke of Richmond, Master of the Ordnance, who had recently instigated the Ordnance Survey, found on visiting the sites that the wooden posts marking the two ends of the baseline had begun to rot, so cannon barrels were planted vertically in the ground, and despite upheavals over the years, both may still be found. One is near the northern perimeter fence by Heathrow's main police station, while the other is in open ground in Hampton near Roy Grove and Cannon Close. From 1791 the Ordnance Survey was run from the Tower of London as a branch of the military under a serving officer, Major-General William Mudge, who in 1816 disabused civilian map sellers of the notion that these new maps were public property. After a fire in 1841, the OS moved to the vacant Royal Military Asylum in Southampton, but had to be evacuated to Chessington in the Second World War after successive bombing raids.

five

The Victorian Period *c*.1815–1914

Following the successful conclusion of the French wars in 1815 the perceived threat to the security of the nation's capital city switched from an external aggressor to the enemy within. The army was required not only to police the ever-expanding empire but also the streets of London. By the middle of the century, external threats once more dictated military policy, prompting far-reaching modernisation of the navy's warships and a radical reorganisation of the army, which included the recruitment of a volunteer force. By the century's end, London could be described as a garrison town, with a significant proportion of its inhabitants in uniform and a sizeable section of its workforce occupied in servicing the military machine. The build-up to the outbreak of war in 1914 saw an ever-accelerating expansion of this military dimension in London.

Civil Unrest

Those who expected that the end of the Napoleonic wars would herald a period of peace and stability were to be disappointed. In 1816 mass public meetings to protest against the Corn Laws resulted in troops being called out. Other violent events of these years saw an attack on the Tower of London; the Cato Street Conspiracy of 1820, which planned to assassinate the entire Cabinet while they dined in Grosvenor Square; and riots prompted by the official attempt to downplay Queen Caroline's funeral. Blocking the cortege's official, low-profile route, the mob forced a diversion of the procession under Temple Bar and through the city, headed by the lord mayor. Troops opened fire on the queen's supporters who objected to the unceremonious return of her body to Germany. Such military action was not confined to London. In May 1826, 700 men of 1st Bn Scots Guards, having marched from Windsor to stay overnight at Knightsbridge Barracks, were embarked on a flotilla of narrow boats at Paddington canal basin to travel the 260 miles to Manchester to aid the civil power during a period of unrest involving the weavers and their objections to the new machinery being introduced into cotton production.

In 1829 the Metropolitan Police was formed as a force of 3000 men in seventeen divisions to police London, and it was hoped that there would henceforth be less need for military intervention in civil matters. The River Police had been formed in 1798 to patrol the Thames, especially the rapidly expanding London Docks, and were aided in their task by Royal Navy vessels, the brig HMS *Port Mahon* up to 1837, then the brig HMS *Investigator* until 1857. HMS *Royalist* was moored as a hulk off Somerset House for the use of the River Police from 1841–56, and the sloop HMS *Scorpion* was loaned to the River Police at Blackwall, 1858–74. The city force was formed in 1839 to police the Square Mile, but in more rural areas it was still felt necessary to recruit volunteer units essentially for policing duties. The West Kent Yeomanry, along with many similar units, had been formed in 1794 as a response to the social and military upheavals of the French wars. Most similar voluntary bodies had been disbanded in 1814, but they survived until 1827. Within three short years, however, it was deemed prudent to re-form them with seven troops, three of which were based in Chislehurst, Dartford and Sevenoaks.

By the mid-1840s, the stability of most of Europe was threatened by revolutionary movements. In Britain, the Chartists were seen by the government and the propertied classes as a real threat to the established order. In 1848, a mass rally on Kennington Common prompted the enrolment in London of 85,000 special constables, backed up by large bodies of troops tucked away out of sight. The government's fear was that it would be impossible for the new police forces, even if greatly augmented by volunteers, to withstand the pressure of large mobs moving on arsenals. On 12 June 1848, the West Essex Yeomanry, also re-formed in 1830, was called out to defend Waltham Abbey powder mills and Enfield Lock small-arms factory against the expected Chartist revolution. Typical of these yeomanry corps was the Uxbridge unit, re-formed in 1830 as a response to rural disquiet characterised by rick burning. With an initial establishment of eighty troopers and three officers, paid training took place on eight days a year. Additionally, a racecourse was laid out at Harefield Place nearby, in order to improve both the men's riding skills and as motivation to acquire better mounts. After the excitement of the Chartist experience, when the corps had been put on standby but not actually deployed, numbers increased and a second troop was formed. Ultimately the unit was to become the Middlesex Yeomanry Cavalry, providing three companies of Imperial Yeomanry for the South African Wars, and then becoming the 1st (County of London) Yeomanry in 1908.

Anticipating the rise of a revolutionary movement, from 1845 a number of improvements to the defences of the Tower of London were put in hand. These included a general refurbishment of gun emplacements, the insertion of musketry loops, and, most obviously, the construction of the North Bastion in the middle of the outer wall between Legge's and Brass mounts. This was the drum-shaped gun tower with casemates on three floors that was destroyed by bombs in October 1940. Even as late as 1872, when a plan by Horace Jones, the City Architect, for the new Tower Bridge called for two high towers (much as was finally built but with two bascules that would be drawn up on chains like drawbridges), the army's Surveyor General of Fortifications, delighted by the way the Gothick design echoed that of the Tower of London, suggested that batteries of cannon might be mounted on the bridge to defend the Pool of London against threats from within or without.

The Army in the Nineteenth Century

Command and organisation

For much of the century the administrative departments of the army were scattered around the St James's area, particularly Pall Mall and Carlton House Terrace, but with outliers such as the Ordnance Office in Pimlico. A plan of 1883 for combined offices for the army and navy next to the Old Admiralty was not carried through. Instead, an Admiralty extension was added in 1888–1905, and a new War Office was built. This building on the site of Whitehall Gardens, now known as the Old War Office, was designed by William Young of Glasgow, and was completed by his son in 1906, re-using some internal fittings from Cumberland House (1763) and Buckingham House (1795); the previous War Department offices at 80–91 Pall Mall were demolished in 1908.

The second half of the nineteenth century saw the implementation of radical changes to both the governance and the organisation of the army. In 1855 its command structure had been centred on Horse Guards and such hitherto civilian elements as the Commissariat brought under military control. Over the next three decades the system by which commissions were obtained was rationalised, phasing out both the purchase of regular commissions and promotions and the grant of militia and volunteer commissions by lords lieutenant. The political control of all the various elements was centralised in the department of the Secretary of State for War, and the manufacture of weapons was taken over by the government. The majority of these reforms were carried out by Edward Cardwell, serving under Gladstone and best remembered for his localisation programme. Although regiments often enjoyed informal links to communities and benefited from traditional recruiting grounds, their home postings were generally serendipitous. Cardwell set up a system whereby each regiment of line infantry was allocated a fixed depot. This provided a permanent base for its two regular battalions, alternately deployed at home and overseas, a home for its militia battalion(s), and a focus for its volunteer battalions. Here recruits would arrive for initial training, drafts would assemble to be posted, supplies and munitions would be stored, and administrative functions would be performed by a permanent HQ staff. Cordial relations could be maintained with a local community no longer fearful of having alien and licentious soldiery billeted on them. Taking the East Surrey Regiment with its depot at Kingston-upon-Thames as a model in 1881, we find the regular 1st and 2nd Bns, formerly the 31st and 70th Foot; the 3rd and 4th Bns, formerly the 1st and 3rd Royal Surrey Militia; and four volunteer battalions, two of which became the 5th and 6th Bns in 1908 with HQs at Wimbledon and Kingston, while the other two joined the all-volunteer London Regiment as its 21st and 23rd Bns, with HQs at Camberwell and Battersea. The other local London regiments such as the Royal Fusiliers and the Middlesex Regiment all underwent a similar restructuring.

Barracks
Immediately after the end of the Napoleonic wars, the dispersed nature of the army's administrative departments was echoed by the chaotic nature of barrack provision. In central London, troops largely inhabited ancient buildings like the dilapidated Irish Barracks in the Tower of London, Hounslow Cavalry Barracks, or the rented Portman Street Barracks behind Oxford Street, with an assortment of orderly rooms scattered around Horse Guards and Whitehall. From soon after 1820, embedded within the centralised planning of Nash's Metropolitan Improvements scheme, were four new barracks: St George's, Wellington, St John's Wood and Regent's Park. St George's Barracks, on the north side of Trafalgar Square, was built in 1826 as the main recruiting depot for London, and was initially planned as three ranges to house an infantry battalion. In the event, only one range was built, demolished by the 1880s for the National Gallery whose new extensions were built in 1885–87. Wellington Barracks was built near Buckingham Palace on Birdcage Walk in 1833. It consists of a long three-storey range of twenty-seven bays with a linked pavilion at each end, the whole extending to nearly 500ft (150m) in length, with the parade ground in front, separated from the road by two Doric lodges. Its stucco finish makes it appear like a Nash terrace. The chapel was destroyed by a V1 rocket in 1944 with large loss of life, and many of the nineteenth-century buildings were demolished and replaced by modern accommodation blocks from 1979. The Royal Artillery had kept horses at St John's Wood Farm from 1804 for the brigade of artillery stationed near the Master Gunner's House in St James's Park. In 1812 new artillery barracks were built next to the farm

40 Wellington Barracks, opened in 1834 to house the Foot Guards, and still in use.

on Ordnance Hill, and in 1824–25, a riding school, measuring 185ft by 65ft (55m by 20m) had been built for the Cavalry Riding Establishment, which moved to Maidstone in 1830. Horses were stabled at Ordnance Mews, St John's Wood High Street, and the barracks were used by the Foot Guards Recruit Depot for a year, and then until 1876 by a succession of infantry battalions. The Household Cavalry moved in as lodgers while their Knightsbridge Barracks was rebuilt, erecting temporary wooden stables only demolished in 1969. The RHA saluting battery was stationed at St John's Wood from 1880 in order to carry out their ceremonial duties in central London. A succession of rebuildings leaves the riding school as the only remaining original structure. Barracks had been planned for the north part of Regent's Park in the original development plan but the earmarked site was let to the Zoological Society of London in 1826. The barracks, designed by Nash in 1820–21 for 450 cavalrymen and 400 horses, was ultimately shifted eastwards to a site on Albany Street, its buildings being grouped around a courtyard. Since the officers preferred to dine out at their clubs there was no mess initially, but subsequent additions and replacements provided for the Chapel School in 1857, an officers' mess in 1866 and a hospital in 1877. A major rebuilding in 1891 included the riding school with a 60ft (18m) span with steel trusses, which remains in use as garages, and new barrack blocks. While these four sites provided much-needed accommodation for Household troops and the guards, there was still a pressing need for more. William IV hated Buckingham Palace so much that he offered it up as a potential barracks for the Foot Guards in 1834. Sadly for him, it was deemed unsuitable. The foundation stone of the new Waterloo Barracks in the Tower of London was laid by the Duke of Wellington in 1845, and completion came shortly after his death in 1852. Chelsea Barracks in Pimlico, built in 1855, was the first barracks design chosen by competition, and its chapel of 1861 survives. Knightsbridge Cavalry Barracks followed in 1878–80, a replacement for its Georgian predecessor and, like Chelsea, rebuilt in the 1960s. Only the pediment from the officers' mess survives, over the new gateway.

41 The Tower of London, Waterloo Barracks, together with the adjacent officers' quarters, now the HQ of the Royal Regiment of Fusiliers, was begun in 1845 when the Duke of Wellington laid the foundation stone.

42 Hounslow Barracks, the keep/armoury added to the earlier barracks in 1871 as part of the localisation depot of the Royal Fusiliers. It is an example of the larger double version with three towers.

The architectural style selected for the majority of the new localised regimental depots was mediaeval and castellated, generally including a large keep with corner turrets and battlements, and an arched gateway. None of this was functional in a military sense but the keeps were immensely strong with a fireproof iron frame supporting grids of rolled, wrought-iron I-beams carried on cylindrical cast-iron columns, and mass-concrete slabs for floors. This emphasis on strength and solidity was so that they could fulfil their prime purpose of providing secure storage for large quantities of arms, munitions, uniforms and equipment, which could be issued to volunteers and reservists on mobilisation. Hounslow was already in use as a cavalry barracks when its keep was added in 1876. This is one of the few double keeps, for barracks serving two regiments. It is a three-storey block with a higher tower at each end of the front face, and another in the middle of the rear face. The original accommodation for the cavalry troopers at Hounslow had been the usual arrangement of stables with rooms above for the men who would welcome the horse-fired central heating in cold weather. The new standard accommodation for the troops was the two-storey barrack block with eight twenty-eight-man dormitories, washrooms and sergeants' rooms in the centre by the stairs. Food was still collected from the kitchen and eaten in the dormitories. A twenty-eight-bed hospital, officers' mess, institute for the troops' recreation and a drill shed completed the complex. By 1884, Hounslow Barracks had its own underground railway station, since renamed. At Kingston-upon-Thames, the armoury of the East Surrey Regiment was designed by the same hand as the keeps but is in the form of a two-storey block with a central three-storey gatehouse and a castellated tower at each of the forward-facing angles. Few other buildings survive on this site but all are in yellow brick with red-brick facings.

By the early years of the twentieth century the need for modern accommodation for the infantry had been recognised. The War Office commissioned designs that would better meet

43 Kingston-upon-Thames, the gatehouse/armoury of the localisation depot of the East Surrey Regiment, built in 1875. While designed by Major Seddon, the same architect as the other depots such as Hounslow, it is quite different.

44 Caterham, one of the radically new barrack blocks of the Guards Depot built between 1901 and the cuts of the incoming Liberal government in 1906. The soldiers' rooms were connected by airy balconies and the NCOs had rooms in the tower annexe connected by walkways to the main block.

new standards for hygiene, health and social relations. The Guards Depot at Caterham was one of the first exemplars of this new thinking. From 1905, it housed the troops in airy, two-storey barrack blocks with balconies, proper sanitation and with rooms for NCOs in attached annexes. There were canteens and mess rooms, an institute for recreation, and sports facilities. A new depot for the Middlesex Regiment at Mill Hill, later known as Inglis Barracks, was built in 1905 with three large barrack blocks and an officers' mess. Alongside the traditional fighting arms, the support services were gaining importance and an Army Service Corps depot was established in 1905 in the old Woolwich Dockyard, with Connaught Barracks, formerly the Royal Ordnance Hospital, nearby on Woolwich New Road. Woolwich Artillery Barracks continued to develop throughout the Victorian period, gaining a new Commandant's House in Rush Grove, and the Garrison church of St George, built in 1863 and retained in the ruined state to which it was reduced by bombs in the Second World War. On Frances Street, Cambridge Barracks, the New Royal Marine barracks, was built in 1847, with the Royal Marine infirmary, Red Barracks, added alongside in 1858. Both were demolished in the 1970s but their gate lodges were retained. The Royal Artillery's Greenhill schools of 1856 in Hillreach have now been converted into dwellings.

The Militia

On 28 July 1833 by command of King William IV all lords lieutenant and colonels of militia were commanded to attend at St James's Palace to confirm the order of precedence for militia regiments determined by their date of formation. In 1850 there were eight regiments of militia in the Greater London area with two more being raised by 1853. Many militia units volunteered for foreign service and the Royal Westminsters were stationed at the Citadel in Corfu in 1855–56 in order that regular units might be released for service in the Crimea. As we have

45 Uxbridge, The Shrubbery, 222 High Street, house for the adjutant of the 58th Royal West Middlesex Militia.

46 Uxbridge, the Load of Hay Public House, formerly the forage barn of the Royal Elthorne Regiment of Militia Light Infantry, formed in 1853 with its depot in The Greenway.

seen, as part of the army reforms the militia regiments were integrated into the numbering and territorial systems of the regular army in 1873 and were allocated barrack space and training regimes. The Middlesex Regiment had four regular battalions so its militia battalions were numbered 5th–7th. Many of the militia battalions volunteered to serve in South Africa, most being employed as garrison troops manning the lines of blockhouses erected to restrict the movement of the Boer commandos.

Uxbridge was already the HQ of the 58th Royal West Middlesex Militia whose adjutant lived at The Shrubbery, 222 High Street, now a pizza restaurant, with other permanent staff quartered at Hillingdon End. However, the Royal Elthorne Regiment of Militia Light Infantry was formed in 1853 as a wholly new unit with its depot in The Greenway. Remarkably, although the barracks itself in Enfield Place has gone, there are tangible reminders in some surviving buildings. The former dry canteen is now the Militia Canteen PH and the forage barn is the Load of Hay PH. Three officers' houses, 64, 66 and 68 The Greenway, also remain.

The Volunteer Force

The Rifle Volunteers 1859–1908

At least two major factors were instrumental in the setting up of the force of civilian volunteers that became the Rifle Volunteers in 1859. The first was a general feeling, arising from the recent experience of the Crimean War and the Indian Mutiny, that British troops were deficient in their shooting skills. The second was the fear that the France of Napoleon III was poised to invade Britain. The Royal Commission set up by Palmerston had initiated an expensive and comprehensive building programme to fortify Britain's naval bases and sea approaches. As well as seaward-facing batteries of heavy guns to oppose a direct assault, the ports' landward approaches were also provided with lines of mutually supportive forts. It was obvious that the regular troops, half of whom were away defending far-flung outposts of empire at any one time, would be incapable of manning these enormous fortifications, and that it would need large numbers of part-time soldiers to do the job. There would be an advantage in these troops having permanent affiliations to the military and receiving training. A number of essentially private armies were being established around the country so it was seen as desirable to bring them into a national fold. On 23 June 1860, a grand volunteer review was held in Hyde Park, and the National Rifle Association held its inaugural competitive shoot on a 1000yd range at Queen's Butts on Wimbledon Common on 2 July 1860, when Queen Victoria fired the first round, duly scoring a bull's-eye that had been prepared earlier.

Rifle Volunteer units sprang up everywhere that there were mainly middle-class men to organise them. This was the urban man's opportunity to emulate the rural yeomanry, to be seen to be patriotic and willing to defend his nation and all it stood for. The City of London quickly raised three corps, each of at least battalion strength. The county of Middlesex raised twenty-seven corps, most of which survived to become full battalions in 1881, affiliated to the Middlesex Regiment, the Rifle Brigade, the Royal Fusiliers or the King's Royal Rifle Corps. Some Rifle Volunteer corps were recruited en masse from such discrete organisations as the staff of Harrow School, the employees of the Royal Small Arms Factory at Enfield Lock, the Post Office, the Internal Revenue or the Bank of England. Others were drawn from a particular occupational group such as printers or dock workers. Wider groups such as expatriate Scots working in London formed corps, while many others were simply drawn from the inhabitants of a defined neighbourhood. Those parts of Essex, Hertfordshire, Kent and Surrey, that now comprise London boroughs, also raised corps, subsequently affiliated to their own county regiments. In the beginning, officers were elected, uniforms were designed and paid for by the membership, weapons were kept in the wardrobe and drilling was carried out in the open air. Such was the response in terms of numbers and enthusiasm that the whole movement was in danger of getting out of hand and, somewhat reluctantly, the War Office decided to take over. Local corps were amalgamated into administrative battalions, standards were set for training and units received payment on the basis of the number of 'effectives', that is men trained to those set standards. In return for this financial support from the taxpayer, units were required to provide a secure store or armoury for their arms and ammunition, minimal accommodation for a unit orderly room and instructor, somewhere under cover to drill, and some sort of range for live-firing of their rifles. Although units might be able to travel to Bisley periodically to use the NRA ranges, it was more realistic to find local provision, and even public houses were persuaded to set up miniature indoor 25yd ranges. The invention of the Morris Tube, a sleeve inserted into the barrel of the rifle thus reducing its bore, enabled full-size rifles to fire smaller-bore ammunition over these shorter ranges.

As well as the many corps of rifle volunteers there were artillery and engineer volunteers and a few, albeit short-lived, units of light horse. The artillery units were primarily formed to man coast artillery batteries in time of war and were based close to their guns in order to practise on them *in situ*. Despite attempts to raise volunteer units of field artillery, the regulars maintained that the gunnery and team-handling skills involved could never be mastered by part-timers. Although a significant proportion of volunteer artillery officers had previous military experience (over a third in the Middlesex unit for instance), the regulars' intransigence and the War Office's refusal to finance horses to pull the guns combined to force these units to disband. The London and Middlesex units chose to amalgamate in 1871. Not until 1900 would this problem of the lack of trained gunners for the Home Defence Force be addressed, and even then the Army Council continued to oppose the very principle of volunteer field artillery until 1908. The first Volunteer Engineer unit was formed in January 1860 from the staff of the South Kensington Museum as the 1st Middlesex Corps, with companies dotted around the wider city. An associated 1st London EVC formed in 1862 in Old Jewry and then 27 Barbican, along with the 1st Tower Hamlets EVC in Victoria Park. Members tended to be drawn from the construction industry or the railways, but Royal Engineers were also responsible for the army's signalling and other electro-mechanical functions such as searchlights and submarine minefields. An all-officer Engineer and Railway Volunteer Staff Corps was formed in Westminster by 1865. Members, either qualified civil engineers or senior managers of railway companies, were responsible for integrating the railways into the military infrastructure in time of war.

The short life of the Volunteer Light Horse units can be put down to two main factors. Counties without a yeomanry unit might be able to support a corps of light horse, but there were successful yeomanry units based in the semi-rural areas of Middlesex, West Essex, Hertfordshire and West Kent, ringing the metropolis. The other factor was cost. The 1st and 2nd Middlesex Light Horse Volunteers had annual subscriptions of 2 and 5 guineas respectively, initial joining fees, and both required an outlay of around £15 for the hussar-type uniform. Most expensive was the cost of keeping a suitable mount for drills and ceremonials, reckoned to be at least £1 per week. Setting up a troop of horse cost £300 and maintaining it cost £100 per annum. No wonder that these units, attempting to recruit from the

urban artisan or professional classes, could not survive. The Surrey LHV based in Clapham
lasted from 1861–68, and the 1st Middlesex LHV, formed in 1861 with HQ at Tattersall's,
Hyde Park Corner, despite amalgamation in 1866 with the 2nd Middlesex LHV, with HQ at
111 Regent Street, had disbanded by 1871. Even the Light Cavalry troop of the long-
established and socially superior Honourable Artillery Company (HAC), though regularly
performing ceremonial duties, was forced, under the terms of a new charter, to re-form as a
horse artillery battery in 1891.

The Territorial Force 1908–20

The South African wars had shown that the regular army quickly became stretched when
confronted with significant overseas commitments, highlighting the vulnerability of a country denuded of regular troops, so the Secretary of State for War, Haldane, began the process of
turning an amorphous collection of volunteer units into a centrally organised state-funded
Home Defence Force. Territorial Associations were established on a county basis to provide
the administrative support, and most units simply transferred *en masse* into the new Territorial
Force (TF). The new force was organised into fourteen freestanding divisions, each with three
infantry brigades of four battalions apiece; a cavalry brigade of three yeomanry regiments
with a horse-artillery battery; three brigades of field artillery and one of howitzers; two engineer field companies and one of signallers; ammunition columns to support each artillery
unit; three Service Corps supply and transport companies; and field ambulances attached to
each cavalry and infantry brigade. The twenty-four infantry battalions of London's two divisions were provided by the newly formed, all-volunteer London Regiment, which absorbed
mostly existing units. Thus the 1st to 4th Bns came from the Royal Fusiliers, for instance, and
the 22nd and 24th Bns from the Queen's Royal West Surrey Regiment. These new battalions
were encouraged to retain their traditional titles, so, for example, the 28th Bn continued as
the 'Artists' Rifles', the 12th Bn as the 'Rangers', and the 8th Bn as the 'Post Office Rifles'.
The 25th Bn was a cyclist unit used for reconnaissance and message carrying. The numbers
26 and 27 were unallocated as the two infantry battalions of the HAC refused to accept such
a lowly status and remained outside the system, being notionally in the 1st London Division
as attached Army Troops. The Inns of Court Regiment based in Lincoln's Inn operated as
an officer-training corps. Many of London's schools maintained junior OTCs, the successors to Cadet Corps going back to 1860. London's outer suburbs provided units for others
of the TF's divisions, from Essex and Hertfordshire to the East Anglian Division, and from
Kent, Surrey and Middlesex to the Home Counties Division. London's four yeomanry regiments provided the London Division's cavalry, and those of Kent and Surrey formed part of
the South Eastern Mounted Brigade with HQ at 43 Russell Square, providing the cavalry
element of the Home Counties Division. The West Kent Yeomanry, which had provided
the 36th Coy Imperial Yeomanry in the South African War, based one of its squadrons in
Bromley, with a riding school on Bromley Common; a squadron of the West Essex Yeomanry
was at Waltham Cross; and elements of the Hertfordshire Yeomanry were in Barnet, Islington
and Harringay.

  One very specialised unit was the London Balloon Company, composed of enthusiasts for
military flight. Parading in central London where the opportunities to practise their skills were
limited, they held annual camps at the Farnborough (Hampshire) Army Balloon School. Never
very well equipped, it saw out the balloon era, some members becoming proficient fixed-wing
pilots and subsequently joining the RFC.

Volunteer drill halls

While many officers, often members of the professions, allowed use of their own homes or business spaces for corps purposes, it soon became apparent that dedicated premises were needed, and the drill hall was born. At first, any available public hall, chapel or trade hall was used, usually on a shared basis. Gradually halls were acquired or purpose built. This process may be seen in Lambeth, for instance, where 167 Lower Kennington Lane (formerly 51 Newington Place), a four-storey terrace house, was in use from 1860 until 1865 as the HQ of 19th Corps Surrey Rifle Volunteers. The nearby Redcross Hall, built in 1887 with decoration by Walter Crane, was used by the Cadet Bn of the Queen's Royal West Surrey Regiment, and by about the same time there was a purpose-built drill shed in New Street (now Braganza Street) for the Queen's 4th Volunteer Bn, on the land behind a pair of houses that served as orderly room and armoury. Nearer the centre of London it would appear that a large number of volunteer corps continued to use either private houses or public buildings for longer than was common in the suburbs or elsewhere in the country. Houses in the Adelphi, Park Village East in Regent's Park, Fitzroy Square and Russell Square, and offices in Lincoln's Inn and Gray's Inn were still in use in the early 1900s, as were Somerset House, the Guildhall and the Custom House. The HAC's barracks in Finsbury, Armoury House, had been built in embattled Tudor style in 1857.

Drill halls, while serving a common function, were all very different in style and in layout. The essential elements of the drill hall were the orderly room where the unit's administrative functions were carried out; a secure armoury for storing arms and ammunition; a large space where drilling could take place on winter evenings or in inclement weather; a residential space for the permanent staff instructor, usually a retired regular NCO and/or a caretaker; an indoor miniature range; a canteen or mess for other ranks; and separate messes for officers and sergeants. Beyond these basic requirements, anything else such as a billiards room, library or gymnasium constituted a bonus provided by the largesse of a wealthy CO, or as an inducement to recruits in a competitive market. Many drill halls shared the ambience of the gentleman's club but had to cater for a range of demands. The busy professional might want to sit in a comfortable club room reading the papers over a glass or two of port in the evening, whereas the young energetic chap in his sedentary occupation in a government office preferred to work out or fence, especially if coached by a professor from the Life Guards. The Volunteer Annual (Metropolitan Corps) for 1903 lists over seventy volunteer units in the London area, each attempting to recruit suitable members by offering, at their respective

47 Finsbury, Armoury House, the imposing HQ of the Honourable Artillery Company, built in 1857 in a martial Tudor style.

drill halls, opportunities for training in military and physical skills, recreational and leisure pursuits, implicit social advancement and networking, and the use of facilities not always available to the working man. One of the earliest purpose-built drill halls, that of the 19th Middlesex Rifle Volunteers, known as the Bloomsbury Rifles, in Chenies Street, Bedford Square, is now an exhibition space. It was built in 1883 with a four-storey front block and a hall measuring 50ft by 70ft (15m by 21m) behind, with a stage at one end. The ground floor contained the orderly room, the sergeants' room, and a mess room with a bar for other ranks. On the first floor were the officers' mess and the colonel's room. One floor up was a billiard room, a kitchen with dumb waiter, and a room for the caretaker. On the third floor, arranged on a mezzanine floor around the double-height billiard room, were the caretaker's living accommodation and spare bedrooms. Another grand, central London drill hall in Duke's Road, Euston, is that of the 20th Middlesex Rifle Volunteers, known as the Artists' Rifles, and now the Place Theatre. It was designed by its colonel, the architect Robert Edis, its front adorned with terracotta plaques of Mars and Minerva, reflecting the unit's dual concerns. Despite once being commanded by the artist Lord Leighton, president of the Royal Academy, and attracting such famously martial figures as Dante Gabriel Rossetti, William Morris, Burne-Jones and Millais, and advertising such warlike pursuits as lawn tennis, regattas, riverside picnics and smoking concerts, members recruited mainly from local craftsmen nevertheless won the bayonet v. lance, and the bayonet v. bayonet prizes at the 1902 Royal Tournament. Another drill hall of this period was that of the 2nd City of London Rifles at 57a Farringdon Street, which still displays the city arms over the door.

Some volunteer premises had short lives. One example is 256 Gray's Inn Road, the barracks of the London & Westminster Light Horse Volunteers, which was abandoned by 1828 when the unit disbanded. The buildings, including the stables, were taken up by the Royal Free

48 Euston, Dukes Place, the terracotta panel of Mars and Minerva, signifying the twin preoccupations of the 20th Middlesex Artists' Rifle Volunteers.

49 Westminster, 56 Regency Street, the drill hall of the volunteer electrical engineers, later to become the Royal Signals HQ, and now apartments.

Hospital in 1842 and improved and replaced, starting with Sussex Wing in 1856. It has been the Eastman Dental Hospital since 1931. The establishment of the Territorial Force in 1908, on a more official basis, brought about the building of more functional drill halls, emphasising the military nature of the activities taking place within. It was also necessary to provide premises for the new, more specialist units of the TF. An example of such provision is the drill hall of the RE Electrical Engineers, at 56 Regency Street, Westminster, opened in 1900. Other premises used by TF units in the centre of Westminster included the offices of the Engineer and Railway Volunteer Staff Corps at 8 The Sanctuary by the west front of Westminster Abbey, and the drill hall of the 23rd Middlesex RV, built in 1899 at 9 Tufton Street. Six years later Lutyens built Faith House, the church hall of St John, Smith Square, next door at No. 8. Some units were fortunate enough to find a home in which they stayed for decades, or in a few cases over a century. The 4th Volunteer Bn East Surrey Regiment, later 23rd Bn London Regiment, was given land by Lord Wandsworth on which to build a drill hall on St John's Hill, Battersea, the building that is still in use in 2011 by their successor unit. Others such as the 3rd County of London Yeomanry (Sharpshooters) moved around. From their former RHQ in the old Army Recruiting Office at 13a Cockspur Street, Trafalgar Square, they went to 4 Park Village East, a villa of 1824 in Regent's Park. In 1902, the regiment fell in at the old St George's Barracks, Trafalgar Square, later moving to Horse Guards, but by 1912 their RHQ was at 90 Henry Street (now Allitsen Road) in St John's Wood, a building whose final military use was by US marines guarding the embassy in Grosvenor Square. The Inns of Court Regiment has stayed in the same area through all its changes from infantry, to officer training, to cavalry, to armour, to amalgamation with the Roughriders, to signals and yeomanry, still in 10 Stone Buildings, Lincoln's Inn. Horsed cavalry needed regular drill time in riding schools in order to improve their members' riding skills.

In 1903, Messrs Tillings Riding School in Peckham was used for drill by the 2nd County of London Yeomanry (Westminster Dragoons), the HAC carried out horse drills with the Royal Horse Artillery at St John's Wood, and the Loats Road riding school, Clapham, was used by the 4th County of London Yeomanry (Sharpshooters) and the Surrey Yeomanry.

Training the army
The middle of the century saw the development of the professional training of officers. The Royal Military Academy (RMA) at Woolwich had been built in 1808 to train the army's gunners and engineers. By 1864 there were opportunities for officers to progress at different stages in their careers through the academy, the artillery college, and the advanced class. By 1890, around the time that flying was being explored in Aldershot (Hampshire), there was a balloon section. While the officers studied the theory, the cadets drilled on the guns, with live firing, initially on Woolwich Common, but transferred to Plumstead Marshes on humanitarian grounds.

The Woolwich Repository had been set up by Congreve to implement his methods of handling heavy artillery, and he defined it as a School of Mounting and Dismounting Ordnance, using his own well-tried training programme. In 1820 the Rotunda, a permanent tent-like structure designed by Nash for the Prince Regent's use in Hyde Park, was dismantled and re-erected at Woolwich, housing an historical teaching collection of military artefacts, particularly artillery. Behind the Rotunda, Repository Wood became a training area incorporating realistic landscape features such as ponds where the cadets could practise erecting pontoon bridges, and moving artillery using basic mechanics with sheer-legs, ropes and pulleys. Additionally, a front of fortification was constructed to include all the elements of modern defence-works with moats and counter-scarps, casemates and gun-mountings behind parapets. Cadets then learned how to mount and dismount heavy guns. To keep the cost down these works were constructed in rammed earth rather than brick, but it was found that if turves were laid with bonds, similar to those employed in brickwork, they were perfectly strong enough for the exercises. Some of these ramparts and ditches can still be seen around the Rotunda and Napier lines. A series of photographs, taken in 1858, show the range of activities undertaken by the cadets. It was around this time that the engineers left for Chatham (Kent). In 1859 the School of Artillery was set up at Shoeburyness (Essex) and some of the work with the heavier guns was transferred there. In 1900, the Woolwich Repository closed, its staff moving to the ranges on the coast at Lydd (Kent). Onslow Hall on Richmond's Little Green was a cavalry college from 1857.

Around the same time that the RMA opened in Woolwich, the Honourable East India Company started its own training school for the military cadets who would officer the armies of the Indian presidencies. This was at Addiscombe, and offered a two-year course. Only the gymnasium in Havelock Road, currently converted into apartments, survives of this college. After the Indian Mutiny, the company began to hand over its military functions to the government and their college closed in 1869. Most other military training was undertaken on the job, or bought in. Army Service Corps officers were offered courses in procurement at the London School of Economics.

With the sudden increase in the numbers of both regulars and volunteers requiring practice in outdoor rifle shooting, new ranges were desperately needed, but it was not until after the TF's formation that the extensive ranges at Purfleet, on land purchased by the War Office in 1906, and completely separate from the magazine's existing 200yd proofing range on the east bank of the Mardyke, were completed. In the new complex there were three blocks of 1000yd ranges, graduated in increments of 100yds from firing positions to stop butts, the most commonly used distance being 400yds. Between them, the five ranges contained seventy numbered targets but more riflemen than this could be accommodated if necessary. The main feature distinguishing Purfleet from all contemporary ranges is the construction method used for the butts. Owing to the marshy nature of the ground, the butts, rather than consisting of the normal massive earth banks, are built of open brick boxes supporting a stepped concrete platform carrying the conventional sand layer, the whole reinforced by brick buttresses. Troops were brought to the Musketry Camp, opened in 1914, by railway, and a tramway served the cordite store inside its earth embankment, continuing on to the powder magazine. Another tramway served the butts, introducing the possibility of moving targets. The range remained in use until 1961.

The Defences of London in the Years before the First World War

The seaward defences of London

During the Napoleonic Wars, the defensive strategy for the Thames had been to push the fixed fortifications as far forward as possible in order to destroy hostile forces before they could get anywhere near the capital. This policy was followed throughout the nineteenth century but on a larger scale. Fears of a French invasion resurfaced periodically during the second half of the century and the government, particularly conscious of potential dangers to the powder magazine at Purfleet and the arsenal at Woolwich, decided to build new works to guard the Thames: a fort at Shornemead, and a battery at Coalhouse. However, these measures failed to solve the continuing vulnerability issue as the development of, particularly French, armoured warships and the perceived bellicosity of Napoleon III once more underlined London's lack of protection against such threats. As part of a national review, the Royal Commission on the Defence of the United Kingdom of 1860 recommended that forts be built at Shornemead, Coalhouse and Cliffe, all mounting heavy guns, both in casemates with iron shields and in open batteries facing

50 Woolwich Dockyard, one of two Victorian emplacements mounting replica 32- or 68-pounder smooth-bore muzzle-loaders.

upriver. At the same time, improvements were made to Tilbury and New Tavern forts. These forts were part of an integrated system involving boom obstacles, submarine minefields and, from 1887, wire-guided Brennan torpedoes. By 1900, the fear of raids by fast-moving torpedo boats had prompted the building of new low-profile batteries of quick-firing (QF) guns, supported by searchlights (DELs) for night firing. Closer to the centre, there is little evidence that any permanent defences were constructed. At Woolwich Dockyard, there are two gun positions, probably mounting 32- or 68-pounder smooth-bore guns, and dating from the middle years of the century. The guns currently emplaced are on replica slide mounts that traverse on a front-racer and pivot. While thought to be a practice battery, these guns may nevertheless represent the only fixed defence between Tilbury and the tower at this time. With Purfleet and Woolwich, London Docks provided just as tempting a target for raids. In the early 1900s Millwall Docks could accommodate 24,000 tons of grain, the Royal Albert Dock's cold stores had a capacity of 250,000 carcasses of mutton, and the Surrey Commercial Docks held 1 million tons of timber. The Royal Docks covered 230 acres (90ha) of enclosed water. In 1914, a new PLA police office was built at West India Docks near the earlier guardhouse but little attention appears to have been paid to everyday security, let alone serious defence.

The landward defences of London

These fixed defences were complemented by army units based at strategic points to intercept enemy landings, or else behind lines of fieldworks, blocking potential lines of enemy advance. In 1888, a defence scheme, similar to that of 100 years previously, was planned. North of the Thames it consisted of a strongpoint at North Weald from which a line of fieldworks stretched to the Thames near Canvey Island. South of the Thames a further dozen similar strongpoints were spaced at intervals down the Darenth Valley from the Thames near Dartford, then along

51 Farningham Redoubt, the tool shed, one of the standard buildings in these London Mobilisation Centres. The tools were stored for use by the navvies who would dig the trench systems connecting the centres in the event of an invasion.

52 North Weald Redoubt, the caponier under the entrance bridge, defending the ditch of one of the more overtly fortified London Mobilisation Centres.

the crest of the North Downs from Westerham to Guildford. These strongpoints, along with storehouses and forward depots, served as tool stores, armouries and magazines, and were known as the London Mobilisation Centres. They were all defensible, with some being provided with gun emplacements built into their ramparts. The whole scheme, only to be implemented in the event of war, was called the London Defence Position, and by 1903, when the War Office issued a handbook to the volunteer force, the infrastructure was apparently largely in place. The two lines totalling around 72 miles (115km) would be manned at the level of 2000 troops to the mile (1250/km), and the majority of these troops would come from volunteer artillery and infantry units, with a stiffening of regulars. Once war had broken out, a great deal of instant digging was required, using civilian labour and estimated as achievable, given seven days' notice, by 35–40,000 labourers in just four days. Mobilisation centres can be seen at North Weald, Farningham and Fosterdown, among others. Proposals to link up with the extensive complex of defences ringing the Medway towns were, surprisingly, never realised.

The Royal Navy

The Royal Naval College moved from Portsmouth to Greenwich in 1873, occupying the naval hospital that had closed four years previously. During the final years of occupation by naval pensioners, the west wing of the King Charles Block had finally been completed, and Trafalgar Quarters, now almshouses, had been added for administrative staff. In 1879, soon after the college started, the Engineering Laboratory, now an interpretive and information centre, was added, reflecting the increasingly technical demands being placed on naval officers. In 1873, the Royal School of Naval Architects, now the Henry Cole Wing of the Victoria and Albert Museum in South Kensington, had opened. HMS *Buzzard*, the RNR drill ship renamed *President* in 1911, was moored in the Thames. There was a RNR drill hall in Commercial Road, Lambeth, in use until 1909. HMS *Frolic*

(1872) formerly *Rainbow*, the RN Artillery drill ship, was moored off Somerset House, and HMS *Sharpshooter*, renamed *Northampton*, operated as a sea-going training ship from 1895–1921.

Munitions Production in Victorian London

All of London's other activities tended to overshadow those of an industrial character. However, if one looks closely it is evident that from the early days, there had been a strong tradition of military production, with the bulk of the country's gunpowder manufacture located around the capital, with over thirty powder works in the greater London area. An integrated and well-coordinated system had developed, with small arms and cannon being manufactured at Enfield and Woolwich, secure arms stores at the Tower, powder stores downriver at Purfleet, and more ammunition works across the river at Crayford. There was a well-established shipbuilding industry on both banks of the Thames producing warships whose guns would be made at Woolwich. Along with the wholly new and fast-developing aircraft factories, all these facilities would be greatly expanded in the run-up to the First World War.

Shipbuilding

There had been a shipbuilding industry at Deptford and Woolwich since Tudor times, with the East India Company's yard at Blackwall producing ships for the Far East trade, and Woolwich and Deptford dockyards building ships for the Royal Navy, the latter yard launching HMS *Beagle* in 1820. Thames-based shipyards played their part in the new revolution in naval architecture when the Royal Navy's first steam-driven warships, HMS *Lightning* and HMS *Comet*, were built at Deptford in 1822–23, equipped with engines built by Maudslay's of Lambeth. The Thames yards,

53 Woolwich Dockyard, the Mould Loft of 1815, one of the earliest industrial buildings at what would become the Admiralty's first experimental steam factory.

both public and private, formed the major focus for the development of steam power. The Royal Navy, attempting to manage its changeover to steam power, found itself handicapped by the inability of private suppliers to meet its needs with sufficient speed, so the Admiralty decided to develop its own state-of-the-art facilities. Thus Woolwich Dockyard was provided with its steam factory, opened in 1844, bringing the benefits of automated mass production to the process of ship construction. The Thames Ironworks, starting out in 1837 at Leamouth Wharf in Bow Creek as Ditchburn and Mare, launched the twelve-gun brig HMS *Recruit c.*1840, but in 1855 Mare was bankrupted through underestimating the cost of building warships to tight Admiralty contracts. Following a takeover by Peter Rolt, the yard won the contract for the first ironclad, HMS *Warrior*, in 1860, and a cast-iron commemorative plaque cut from the hull of HMS *Warrior* may be seen at Canning Town Station. However, the size of these new ships along with foreign competition would be the undoing of the industry. The Thames Ironworks had launched HMS *Minotaur*, the first iron-hulled, 400ft (120m) long, armoured frigate from the Canning Town side of the Lea, but Millwall Ironworks was to experience problems with another vessel of that same class in 1866. Despite the kudos of being chosen to build the SS *Great Eastern*, Scott Russell had been forced into bankruptcy after her difficult and protracted sideways launch from the Napier Yard in 1859.

Nevertheless, by 1865 the Thames shipbuilders were experiencing a boom, with nearly 30,000 jobs in the yards. The Thames Ironworks had the capacity in 1863 to construct warships and mail steamers, totalling 25,000 tons and 10,000 tons respectively, at the same time. The Millwall yard had been taken over by C.J. Mare & Co. but HMS *Northumberland's* protracted launch was to prove difficult, with the long hull running aground, and they too went out of business while the ship was high and dry. In 1869 the Admiralty closed down both their Deptford and Woolwich yards, signalling the final collapse of the industry on the Thames. The roofs from the slips at Woolwich were dismantled and re-erected at Chatham Dockyard.

54 Whitehall, the Admiralty extension of 1888–1905, built along the northern edge of Horse Guards Parade, to accommodate the increased bureaucracy needed to drive the naval arms race with Germany. (Photograph: Pam Osborne)

55 Deptford Dockyard, two Victorian boat sheds, apart from the recently refurbished Master Builder's House, the only remnants of this once-thriving shipyard.

When there was a revival in the industry in the next decade, it was to take place elsewhere, mainly on the Clyde and the Tyne. Smaller warships continued to be built by Thorneycroft's of Chiswick and Yarrow's of Poplar for a while, but they too had moved away from the Thames by 1906. Only the Thames Ironworks struggled on, building 144 warships between 1837 and 1912, including ships for the Greek, Spanish and Russian navies, and Prussia's first iron-hulled warship, the SMS *König Wilhelm*. In 1895, they built one of the first of a new category of warship for the Royal Navy. HMS *Zebra* was a torpedo boat destroyer, which, by the time they launched HMS *Grampus* in 1910, had evolved nearer to the destroyer proper. The last ship to be built by Thames Ironworks was the Orion-class dreadnought HMS *Thunderer*, displacing 22,000 tons, 580ft (175m) long, crammed with the new technology and costing £1.9 million. Mounting 10 x 13½in guns in five twin turrets, and with a secondary armament of 16 x 4in guns, she had a crew of 1100 men, and was completed in 1911, being fitted out downriver at Dagenham. In a squadron along with three of her sisters, she fought at Jutland in 1916. Some of the buildings involved in these operations still survive at Deptford, Woolwich and at Burrells Wharf on the Isle of Dogs, where the only surviving examples of many Victorian shipbuilding processes on the Thames can be seen, as can the slipways used to launch these enormous ships. Excavations by Thames Discovery have uncovered the slips laid down for the fraught launch of Brunel's *Great Eastern*, giving clues as to what went wrong. Thames Ironworks is remembered now mainly as being the origin of West Ham Football Club.

Munitions production

Woolwich Arsenal employed between 6,000 and 10,000 men in the three major departments: the laboratory, the Royal Gun Factory and the Royal Carriage Department, the latter two merging in 1907 as the Royal Gun and Carriage Factory. In 1860, William Armstrong had presented the rights to his new breech-loading rifled guns to the nation and along with a knighthood, he was appointed superintendent of the Royal Gun Factory at Woolwich in gratitude. The

56 Woolwich Arsenal's main gatehouse in characteristic machicolated red brick. The lower part dates from 1829 and the upper parts and the bell tower from 1859 and 1897. Note the mortars, cast in the Royal Brass Foundry, on the wings.

57 Woolwich Arsenal, buildings in the Royal Carriage Works where gun carriages were designed and built.

58 Woolwich Arsenal, the entrance portico to the Shell Foundry of 1856. This shows the inner face, the outer having three sets of wrought-iron gates, re-sited at ROF Patricroft but repatriated and now preserved *in situ*.

Crimean War prompted the establishment of the Armstrong Gun Factory to manufacture guns out of wrought iron, and to be their sole supplier to the government. Woolwich proceeded to manufacture guns of all types and sizes for the army and the Royal Navy, who were both stimulating and exploiting developments in the private sector. By 1875 Woolwich was building 80-ton RML guns for the navy. In 1855 the Shell Foundry, with its 233ft (70m) high chimney, opened to produce shells for rifled and smoothbore cannon, test firing on Plumstead Marshes. Artillery also needed paper and cloth products for cartridge bags, percussion caps, felt pads and protective clothing, and these were all manufactured at Woolwich. There were research facilities at the Royal Laboratories and Metallurgical Department, later to be the Royal Armament Research and Development Establishment at Fort Halstead. Rockets, mines, torpedoes and bombs were all developed and manufactured, and the complex was served by barges using the Ordnance Canal, and by a narrow-gauge railway. In 1856 loading was speeded up with heavy cranes on the Ordnance Pier. By 1876 it was no longer possible to test fire heavy guns on site, so the customised barges *Gog* and *Magog*, equipped with railway lines, were brought into service to carry the guns downriver to Shoeburyness. In 1880 the new Lee-Metford rifle was given trials at Woolwich prior to entering manufacture at Enfield. This rifle would go on to become the MLE Mark I in 1895, and then the SMLE, adopted by the army in 1902, and still in production as the Mark IV in 1950. Another nascent development at Woolwich was the Balloon Equipment Store whose purpose was to make experimental hydrogen-filled balloons suitable for military operation. Set up in 1878, it moved to the RE depot in Chatham four years later. The Grand Store had been built at the end of the Napoleonic Wars and now it was expanded by in-filling. Security depended on the high walls, the controlled access through the main gate, and armed guards based in the Arsenal.

59 Woolwich Arsenal. The Grand Store was begun around 1814 but the wide spaces in-between the blocks were in-filled in Victorian times with less grand structures.

60 Woolwich Arsenal's riverside access was protected by these two guard houses, one of which housed the body of the Prince Imperial the night before his funeral, his body having been brought back from Africa where he had been attached to a British force fighting a colonial war.

The Enfield Small Arms Factory opened in 1816 and expanded in the 1850s with a steam-powered factory built for mass production in operation, turning out over 1700 rifles per week by 1860. In 1886, the last water-powered machines were replaced, leaving the factory powered by sixteen steam engines and employing 2400 men. During the 1880s and 1890s new rifles were being developed, and Enfield, along with BSA at Sparkbrook (Birmingham), and the London Small Arms Connaught Works at Old Ford Road, Bow, in operation from 1867 and accessed through Gunmakers Lane and linked by canal to the Enfield factory, together produced 2000 rifles a week. Among the buildings from these times still standing at Enfield, are the factory of 1854–56 with its clock tower, stores and workshops, the water tower, the police station and the workers' housing. The whole site is now a new residential village.

Like the Woolwich Arsenal and the Enfield Factory, the Royal Gunpowder Mills at Waltham Abbey were pushed into large-scale change by the military's demands during the Crimean War. Steam-powered gunpowder mills were brought into use and new buildings were developed to exploit the new processes incorporating tramways, cranes and auxiliary engines. Five of these T-shaped structures, with central beam-engine, underfloor drive shafts and a boiler house with coal yard, had been built by the end of the century, these steam mills being 50 per cent more efficient than the water-driven ones. Improvements in the core task of milling gunpowder

61 Enfield Lock, the steam factory, Britain's major producer of military rifles.

62 Enfield Lock, the police station/guard room.

63 Waltham Abbey, The Lodge, Powdermill Lane. Built *c.*1825 as the Clerk of the Cheques' house, it was later used as senior officers' quarters, and then as offices.

by exploring the potential of hydraulic power for instance, were accompanied by efforts to produce powders for use in specific weapons. Heavy artillery needed powder presented in particular ways to avoid being blown apart by the sheer volume required to propel a large projectile. Brick-vaulted magazines were built to hold the powder produced on-site prior to its move by barge to Purfleet for storage and issue. As alternatives to gunpowder appeared, some of the facilities could be converted to the processes involved in the production of cordite and guncotton, and other specialist buildings were constructed. While the armed services' peacetime need for gunpowder was quite modest, the outbreak of the First World War created a new and heightened demand for gunpowder, particularly for fuses in cordite shells. A number of industrial buildings from this period, on what is now a public site, can be seen along with some domestic buildings for staff and infrastructure. Hounslow Powder Mills operated from 1828 until 1920, on a site long-used for the purpose, and under a parent company that had bought up much of the private sector of the industry. Its so-called 'Shot-Tower', however, is more likely to have been a water tower.

The powder magazines at Purfleet continued in use throughout the period, receiving an additional proof house and proofing range. Every particle of powder made for government use at Waltham Abbey or at private works such as Hounslow or Dartford, was delivered here to be examined, tested, approved and taken into store with, at any one time, 52,000 barrels weighing 2300 tons being stored. A permanent guard of two officers and eighty men, a detachment of artillerymen who tested powder in cannon and mortars, and a workforce of 100 lived in the 'Garrison', as it was called. Only twenty of these civilian workers actually worked in the magazines, with others tending the storage hulks in the river, or working as craftsmen, making the special shoes worn in the magazines, for instance. Along with their families, a community of around 1100 was resident at the magazine complex by 1871. The fire risk and security issues were constants. In 1878 the garrison was increased and civilian police were drafted into the area after news of a proposed raid by the Fenians had been received. Nothing came of it but the security at the site was greatly tightened. These measures included a permanent police guard of three sergeants and nineteen constables of the Ordnance Store Corps.

Health and safety issues prompted the move of the Proof House of the Worshipful Company of Gunmakers from Aldgate, in the heart of the city, out to Stepney, at 46–50 Commercial Road. It was rebuilt in 1826 with the Proof Master's house, receiving offices and copper-lined powder magazine and proving chamber. Next door was the Gunmakers' Hall, which was built in 1872 but sold off in 1927.

Military aviation

The early history of flying is associated with a number of sites in the London area, particularly Woolwich, where the Royal Engineers Balloon Section had been set up in 1890 to explore military applications. Short Brothers established a Balloon Factory under some railway arches in Battersea in 1903. By 1909, flights by fixed-wing aircraft were taking place, but it would be a further three years before the implications for warfare were taken on by the military. The Parliamentary Aerial Defence Committee had been persuaded to sponsor a display of military flying at Hendon by Grahame-White in May 1911, involving, among other spectacles, the bombing of ground targets, and it was this fortuitous event that went some way to persuading the sceptics at the War Office. By the middle of 1914, there were three aircraft factories producing machines for the services: Grahame-White at Hendon, Handley Page at Cricklewood, and Airco, later to become de Havilland, at Colindale.

Medical care and welfare

Although the nineteenth century was a period of near-continuous military activity, the number of casualties caused by direct enemy action was dwarfed by those caused by disease. The development of barrack facilities involved attempts to include adequate medical provision. After the horrors of the Crimean War, a Royal Commission was set up to look into the planning and layout of military hospitals. It approved the pavilion plan, in which two-storey ward blocks ran at right angles to a central spine, affording maximum light and ventilation. The Royal Herbert Military Hospital at Woolwich, named for the late secretary of state who had encouraged the work of the Royal Commission, was the first of this new style of hospital, and opened in 1865. This became the standard for subsequent military hospitals, including the Queen Alexandra Military Hospital on Millbank, which opened in 1905. One of the Commission's major criticisms had been levelled at the regimental hospitals present at many depots, and the first of a new style of sixty-bed barracks infirmary was built at Hounslow Barracks in 1861. It consists of a two-storey central block containing the administrative and surgical elements, flanked by single-storey ward blocks benefiting from all-round light and air. A similar arrangement was achieved at the Caterham Guards Depot in 1875. In 1902, the Army Medical College moved out of the Royal Victoria Hospital at Netley (Hampshire), first into temporary premises at St Ermin's Hotel in Caxton Street, and then, in 1905, into new buildings on Millbank, including RAMC barracks, buildings that now house the successor institution to Chelsea College of Art, alongside the Tate Gallery.

While medical discoveries and treatments were reducing the impact of many diseases, the military were particularly badly affected by venereal disease (VD), often regarded by authority as self-inflicted. The rate of infection in Britain ran at 181–206 per 1000 servicemen in 1830–47, a rate six times higher than that in France or Belgium. By 1862 this had risen even higher,

64 Woolwich, Shooters Hill Road, Royal Herbert Hospital, the pavilion-style military hospital that opened in 1865, improving on the earlier example of the Royal Marine Infirmary in Frances Street.

65 Westminster, Millbank, one of two barrack blocks built 1898–1901 for the newly founded Royal Army Medical Corps. A third side of the parade ground is filled by the RAMC medical college of 1905. The adjacent Queen Alexandra Royal Military Hospital closed in 1977 but much of it survives in use as storage and offices for the Tate Gallery. The RAMC buildings now form part of London's University of the Arts.

to 442 per 1000, while it stood at only 70 per 1000 in France. On HMS *Warrior* for instance, 220 out of the 771 crewmembers were treated for VD. Attempts were made to use legislation to solve the problem, but the three Contagious Diseases Acts of the 1860s provoked outrage, and were vigorously opposed by Josephine Butler and other campaigners for women's rights, leading to their repeal in 1886. One way of keeping bored young unattached males on the straight and narrow was to provide them with more wholesome alternatives to their traditional leisure-time pursuits. The Institute, later to become the NAAFI, was introduced into new barracks, providing reading and games rooms. In Westminster, Manning House in Francis Street was set up as a Guardsmen's Institute in 1867. Off base, temperance coffee houses and evangelistic organisations tried in their various ways to save our soldiers. The growth of the officers' club was a feature of this time, with the general area of St James's becoming the home of the Cavalry Club (1890), United Services Club (1816), Junior Naval and Military Club (1874–75), and Army and Navy Club (1848–51). One aspect of Victorian philanthropy was the endowment of homes or schools for orphans and almshouses for pensioners, often with very specific target groups. In Wandsworth the Royal Victoria Patriotic Asylum, was built in 1857 for the orphaned daughters of servicemen, as was The Friary in Francis Street, Westminster, set up for the orphans of guardsmen in 1865. The King William Naval Asylum, in St Johns Road, Penge, opened in 1847 as almshouses.

Military influence on the civil landscape

The majority of military architects had usually been trained at Woolwich as Royal Engineers, going on to design both military and public buildings. Notable examples include Colonel Joshua Jebb, who designed Pentonville Prison in 1840, providing the model for successive prisons until 1870 when Wormwood Scrubs replaced it as the standard design, and Captain Francis Fowke, architect of the Royal Albert Hall. This work was completed by another military man, Major (later Major-General) Henry Scott, who also completed Fowke's work on the Victoria and Albert Museum. Fowke's design for the Natural History Museum was selected but his untimely death in 1865 prevented its implementation and Waterhouse took over.

One obvious feature of the Gothick style was the application of pseudo-mediaeval motifs such as machicolation and castellation to buildings. This was particularly true of prisons such as Brixton, Pentonville, Wandsworth and Holloway, which was consciously, if erroneously, modelled on Warwick Castle. Barracks also followed this path, and examples include Armoury House, Finsbury, built in 1857 in a rusticated Tudor style, and Hounslow and Kingston-upon-Thames with their pseudo-keeps. Civil engineering proposals, such as for Tower Bridge, often incorporated overtly military motifs.

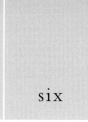

six

London in the First World War

For the first time in several hundred years, Londoners were to find themselves on the front line of a war whose conduct they could do little to influence. While young men flocked to the colours in their thousands, their loved ones remained behind to face the terrifying ordeal of bombing, which drew no distinction between military and civilian targets. As the world moved ever closer to total war, women worked and died in munitions factories, hardly a family avoided the dreaded telegram from the War Office reporting a loved one's death in action, and all but the wealthy and privileged few suffered from shortages and disrupted services.

The Defence of London

The Thames defences

By 1914, advances in the science of ballistics meant that the new breech-loading (BL) guns, mounted further downriver from the narrows, could dominate the estuaries of the Thames and Medway with their longer ranges of up to 7 miles (11km). Many old rifled muzzle-loading

66 Purfleet (TQ793538), defensible submarine-spotting tower mounting an AA gun which contributed to the shooting-down of a Zeppelin in 1916.

guns (RML) were removed and QF guns were substituted. An indication of how far forward the defences had been shifted was the position of the fire-control post for the Thames, which was now at Grain, between the mouths of the Thames and Medway, about level with Southend, and many miles from Tower Bridge. These technological advances necessitated modifications to the old forts, and such structures as Electric Light Director Stations, range-finder observation or position-finding (PF) cells, and the DEL positions themselves can be seen superimposed on their roofs. Coalhouse Fort was designated the Examination Battery, and suspect merchant ships were required to anchor under its guns until cleared to proceed upriver. The actual check was carried out by tugs from HMS *Champion*, a wooden warship moored in the river. Along the riverbank were more observation posts, one of which, a circular tower with loopholes protected by iron plates behind the present flood bank at Purfleet, was built early in the First World War specifically for submarine spotting, but was useful for generally monitoring the river traffic. The country's traditional reliance on the protection afforded by the Royal Navy is indicated by the presence of a flotilla of destroyers based at Sheerness in an anti-invasion role.

Defence against land attack

During the run-up to the outbreak of war quite an extensive invasion literature had sprung up. The *entente cordiale* of 1904 had removed France from her customary position at the top of the most likely potential aggressor charts, and substituted Germany, ruled by a grandson of the late queen. Although it seems highly unlikely in retrospect that there was ever a German plan to invade Britain, the possibility was not one that could be dismissed by the War Office. Given that a German occupation of the Channel Ports was unthinkable, the route an invasion might take was across the North Sea (or German Ocean) to hit the coast between north Norfolk and Harwich. Consequently, a large field army was based on the Norfolk-Suffolk border, with its HQ at Lynford Hall near Thetford, and smaller forces were stationed along the coast to act as an early warning system and to delay the advance of enemy troops once ashore. If the worst came to the worst, then the field works of the London Defence Position, its permanent skeleton complete in 1905, would come into play. Enough warning, it was optimistically assumed, would have been received for the trench lines and redoubts linking the mobilisation centres to have been dug, in just four days. Fortunately, it would appear that this never became more than a paper exercise, although Peter Kent reports that parts were dug in Essex in February 1915, along with another line to Maldon and Danbury Hill from Chelmsford. Pillboxes appeared on the east coast in the last year of the war as the military planners were unable to remove from their minds the fear of a German invasion designed to break the deadlock on the Western Front, but there appear to have been no new initiatives involving fixed defences anywhere near the centre of London.

Defence against air attack

When the attack on London came it was not the seaborne invasion foreshadowed in *The Riddle of the Sands*, but a wholly unexpected assault from the skies. The first Zeppelin raid was in May 1915, but it was not until September 1916 that AA defences were either organised or equipped to disrupt the airships' bombing operations. Given the pre-occupation of the army on the Western Front and elsewhere, the responsibility for AA defence was handed to the Royal Navy. With their established RNAS Armoured Car Squadrons as a basis, the Admiralty set up a mobile brigade armed initially with Hotchkiss QF guns and 1.5 pounder pom-poms, crewed by RNVR personnel aided by special constables on a part-time basis. There were also fixed 3in naval guns

67 A 3in 20cwt AA gun on a Peerless lorry, photographed at IWM, Duxford.

at Tower Bridge and Regent's Park manned by Royal Marine crews, as well as limited provision at Waltham Abbey, Thameshaven, Purfleet, and Woolwich Arsenal. As the Zeppelin raids continued, and civilian casualties and damage to both morale and property escalated, then attempts were made to increase the effectiveness of the AA response. The mobile brigade was equipped with French 75mm auto-cannons, specially mounted on Panhard or de Dion Bouton touring cars. There were also a number of 3in 20cwt Vickers guns on high-angle mountings on Daimler and Lancia trucks, later on Peerless lorries or towed on trailers, along with searchlights drawing their power from their towing vehicles' dynamos. This flying column was based at the Talbot Motor Company's works in Ladbroke Grove.

On receiving the alarm, the convoy would race along Oxford Street at high speed, heading for the Artillery Ground at Moorgate, which provided a suitable open space for their deployment. Late in 1915, Grand Duke Michael of Russia made the stables of Kenwood House, his eighteenth-century mansion in Hampstead, available to the brigade and here the whole force could be accommodated. The mobile guns would respond to air-raid warnings by taking up appropriate, predetermined positions, to supplement the permanently emplaced static guns. If the warning was very short, then an emergency position on Hampstead Heath was occupied. These deployments and redeployments often involved significant distances, with guns being moved from Finchley to Wandsworth, and Wanstead to Beckenham, for instance, depending on the direction of attack. Records show units travelling an average of 80 miles on some nights. By February 1916, there were nearly 150 assorted weapons available for the AA defence of London. In May 1916, a new trailer mounting for the 3in 20cwt AA gun was built at Ashford Railway Workshops, proving superior to the Woolwich Arsenal product and capable of being towed at up to 40mph. By this time, the control of London's AA defences had passed from the RNAS to the army, so HQ moved from the Admiralty to Horse Guards. The liaison with France, which had produced the 75mm guns, thirty-five of which were now emplaced around London, continued to bear fruit in terms of fire-control systems. The French camouflage techniques, developed by the set designer at the Paris Opera, also excited interest, and the London gunners were able to produce their own expert who rendered the vehicles of the mobile column nigh-on invisible using dazzle painting. On 1 April 1916, pom-pom guns at Purfleet powder works, including one mounted on the submarine-spotting tower, along with guns at Tilbury Fort, shot down Zeppelin *L15*, the first such success of the war. In August 1916, the mobile column was despatched to the Norfolk coast as it was decided, rightly as it turned out, that the Zeppelins could be defeated long before they got anywhere near the capital.

Compared to what the next generation of Londoners would be forced to undergo, the aerial onslaught was mild, but it nevertheless caused loss of life, fear and anger, and it was the indiscriminate nature of the bombing that most appalled people. A Zeppelin attack on Blackheath hit the ASC Reserve Horse Transport Depot, wounding nineteen men and some animals and destroying the YMCA hut, but such successes on military targets were fortuitous rather than intentional. The victims were usually civilian and the intended targets irrelevant. In one raid on the West End in October 1916, seventy-one people were killed, and other Zeppelin raids of the total of fifty-three claimed lives in double figures. However, worse was to come when a completely unexpected and disastrously effective daylight raid on London by twenty Gotha bombers in June 1917, heralded an escalation of the bombing offensive. On 13 June bombs killed 160 people, including eighteen 5-year-old children, when a bomb fell on Upper North Street LCC School in Poplar. Even the Royal Hospital Chelsea was bombed. Deaths approached 800, with 2000 injured in bombing attacks on London.

May 1917 saw another reorganisation of London's AA defences, when a network of sub-commands was created. The western sub-command, with HQ atop the reservoirs of the Metropolitan Waterworks on Putney Heath, controlled nineteen gun stations, thirty-six searchlights, and thirty-eight observation posts, covering the London area from Watford in the north, to Croydon and Bromley in the south, and from Windsor in the west, to Grove Park in the south-east. Similarly, the north sub-command's guns were spread between Ware and Chingford, and the east sub-command stretched from Rainham and Romford, north of the Thames, to Dartford and Sidcup in the south. This system, covering approaches from all directions, gave added support to the RNVR-manned batteries in the central sub-command at Hyde Park, Parliament Hill Fields, Deptford and Paddington Recreation Ground. By January 1918, these four sub-commands had fifty-five of the 3in AA guns. General Ashmore at the War Office developed the OPs into the Metropolitan Observation Service, the forerunner of the ROC, as part of the London Air Defence Area, establishing a gun belt 20 miles (32km) east of London, and a balloon barrage or 'apron', all integrated with the Home Defence fighter squadrons of the RFC and RNAS. The London Gun Barrier, initially in 1916 comprising only fourteen AA guns at Purfleet, Erith, Dartford and Plumstead, by early 1918, extended right around London, from St Albans through Epping, to Redhill, round to Staines, and ultimately equipped with sixty-one of the 3in guns and thirty-three adapted 18 pounders. The balloon apron began north of Tottenham, and ran to the east of Wanstead, Ilford, Barking, Plumstead and Lewisham. Fighter aircraft had to keep above 10,000ft (3050m) to avoid being caught by this barrier of taut steel cables. Forest Farm, Fairlop, was a balloon station, and a balloon training depot was set up in Richmond Park, with test sites on Kingston Hill and at Beverley Brook. Early in the war, an OP had been set up on the roof of the Imperial Institute in South Kensington, and a captive observation balloon was tethered at Crystal Palace, with OPs forming such an integral part of the system that by the end of 1917 each of the dozens of AA gun sites was allocated one or two

dedicated OPs. Searchlights were provided in the ratio of two per gun. Every possible van-
tage point was exploited for maximum effectiveness, searchlights being mounted, for instance,
on Old Lambeth Bridge, and on a timber platform, precariously straddling the Apsley House
Gate to Hyde Park, in order to illuminate targets for the battery of two AA guns, permanently
emplaced in the adjacent park.

This organisation, the response to the daylight raids on London by Gotha and Giant bombers, would form, in essence, the basis of British aerial defence into the Second World War, the
Battle of Britain and the Blitz. Ashmore's overriding principle was that of centralised coordination, with all the system's components communicating information through dedicated phone
lines, connected to significant locations such as Buckingham Palace and New Scotland Yard,
but, most importantly, to a central clearing house and control centre at Horse Guards. The
police and fire services were also included, and a public warning system was developed. A final
Zeppelin raid in October 1917 resulted in the loss of the entire force, possibly nine airships, but
raids by aircraft, Gothas and Staaken IVs, continued until May 1918. In the last raid, three aircraft
out of the thirty-three taking part were shot down by AA fire, and a further three by fighters.
Throughout the war however, of the 654 airships and aircraft that crossed the English coast on
raids, only fifteen were destroyed by the guns, and another seventeen by fighters. It is easy to see
the origin of the notion, so prevalent throughout the interwar period, that the bomber would
always get through.

Given the often temporary nature of the construction, and ninety years of subsequent redevelopment, it is not surprising that very little remains to be seen on the ground. Monkhams
Hill (TL386024), north of Waltham Abbey, was the location for an AA gun in February 1916.
The gun is listed as a 6-pounder Hotchkiss QF, but the surviving remains, a brick and concrete
platform with brick-built shelter/magazine, and circular, steel holdfast, would suggest that a

68 Monkhams Hill, the First World War AA position; the hold-fast was actually part of its refurbishment
for use during the Second World War.

69 Honor Oak Park, this First World War AA gun emplacement on One Tree Hill, was later converted for use as a bandstand.

3in 20cwt gun had subsequently been substituted. Indeed, excavation has shown the holdfast to be dated '1939' confirming that the position was re-used in the Second World War. One Tree Hill (TQ354743) at Honor Oak Park had been equipped with a 3in gun from its first reference in April 1915. The emplacement survives: an octagonal, concrete platform, the outline of its circular holdfast still visible, later adapted as a bandstand and standing alongside a 1977 Jubilee beacon. Archaeological investigations here have also suggested that traces of associated structures may survive below ground. The submarine-spotting tower at Purfleet (TQ793538), on which was mounted a pom-pom, still stands behind the flood bank. Some of the guns were mounted on timber towers or convenient existing buildings, while others had purpose-built concrete emplacements. At most gun sites, any accommodation provided was in temporary huts, as the preferred method in built-up areas was to billet crews in private houses, or else to locate them, as we have seen, in central points like HMS *Kenwood*, later Kenwood Barracks. Post-First World War sale catalogues, showing incidentally how quickly these defences were dismantled, list the only structures provided as Boarden huts, which were constructed out of corrugated iron and timber, with the only brick-built structures on site being the magazines.

Airfields for the fighter aircraft
The outbreak of hostilities saw Hendon requisitioned for the RNAS but, a year into the war, only four fighters, stationed at Hendon and Chingford, were available to defend London against attack. By 1916 this provision had increased, and Hainault Farm, Sutton's Farm and North Weald Bassett had been established as fighter bases for the defence of London, first against Zeppelins and later, Gotha bombers. By the end of the war Biggin Hill was fulfilling a basic coordinating role, with a centralised fighter operations room. These airfields were initially provided with canvas Bessoneau hangars, which afforded the fragile aircraft a degree of all-weather

70 Hainault Farm, the twin aircraft shed (51/17) at this First World War fighter station.

71 Hendon's Aerodrome Hotel of 1917, requisitioned for use as an extra officers' mess for the rapidly expanding RFC.

protection. Tents also housed the unfortunate personnel. In time, timber hutting was built for offices, workshops and living accommodation, and along with this came permanent hanga-rage. Hainault Farm, for instance, eventually received a pair of twin aircraft sheds. So that the fighters might stay in the sky for the longest possible time, a network of landing grounds was provided. Northolt, with some rudimentary lighting, was designated a night-landing ground, while Biggin Hill, Croydon, Grove Park, London Colney and Joyce Green all fulfilled the day role. Aircraft Acceptance Parks for the receipt of new aircraft from the factories were established at Brooklands, Hendon, Feltham, and Kenley, and these were usually provided with storage sheds, which were often paired GS hangars, as at Hendon and Kenley. Croydon, in its dual role as National Aircraft Factory and training airfield, was also provided with GS hangars.

Starting from such a tiny base in 1914, there was always a desperate need for trained person-nel to fly the thousands of new aircraft emerging from the burgeoning aircraft factories. New training airfields, to maintain and build on the momentum built up at Chingford and Hendon in the first year of the war, were set up at Croydon, Denham and Hounslow. A number of these new airfields had acquired quite large complexes of specialist buildings by the end of the war, particularly North Weald, Biggin Hill, Kenley and Sutton's Farm, where there was the complete range of airfield buildings: two large hangars with workshops, power house and vehicle sheds forming the technical site, while squadron offices, officers' and NCOs' messes, lines of barrack huts, regimental institute, and, beyond the farm itself, a women's hostel, all providing necessary permanent or semi-permanent accommodation. Civilian buildings were requisitioned where appropriate. Since 1935 the Chingford field has lain under one of the Lea Valley reservoirs, but recent investigations have uncovered possible traces under a strip of grass separating two reservoirs. It must not be forgotten that airships had a part to play in Britain's military avia-tion tradition, and the Wormwood Scrubs airship station, with its enormous windbreak, was only one in a nationwide network of such bases. Accommodation was, as ever in wartime, at a premium, and the Hillingdon House estate in Uxbridge was acquired in 1917 for the use of the RFC, with the house still serving as an officers' mess for the RAF.

London-Based Units in the First World War

London was very much a garrison town in 1914, providing a base for, at a rough but fairly conservative estimate, 25,000 regulars and 60,000 volunteers, representing about 1.5 per cent of the total population of 6 million. At the very least, a similar number must have been working in London's defence-related industries. The vast majority of these men would serve abroad, mainly on the Western Front, over the next four years, joined by hundreds of thousands more, both volunteers and conscripts.

Cavalry units
Even as early as 1914, when mechanisation was still some time into the future, cavalry was becoming an anachronism. The Household Cavalry was in the 3rd Cavalry Division on the Western Front, ready to sweep through the enemy lines and exploit the great breakthrough that never came. Infantry formations were still allocated cavalry to provide a forward screen, to carry out reconnaissance tasks, and to provide couriers, so the 19th Hussars from Hounslow began the war in separate squadrons, attached to infantry divisions as divisional cavalry. Once it became clear that many of these tasks were inappropriate they went to the 1st Cavalry Division.

King Edward's Horse (The King's Overseas Dominions Regiment) with their HQ at Chelsea, were sent to France as corps cavalry, to be deployed by the corps commander. As we have seen there were yeomanry cavalry units drawing their members from London's hinterland. The Essex Yeomanry went to France as divisional cavalry; the Hertfordshire Yeomanry went to Egypt, and then served as divisional cavalry in France; the East and West Kent Yeomanry regiments lost their horses, serving as infantry at Gallipoli, and were then amalgamated as the 10th Yeomanry Battalion of the Buffs, serving with Allenby in Palestine; the London Mounted Brigade served in the Middle East, Gallipoli and Salonika, in both mounted and dismounted roles; some of the London yeomanry reorganised as 103 Bn the Machine-Gun Corps during the last year of the war, serving on the Western Front; the 1st/1st Surrey Yeomanry were corps cavalry on the Western Front. Most of the second-line yeomanry units, such as the 2nd/1st Surrey Yeomanry, converted to cyclist units, which were based in East Anglia on anti-invasion duties right up until 1918, recognising a threat of invasion that lasted throughout the war.

Regular infantry units

The Guards Division, comprising the 1st and 2nd Bns of each of the four guards regiments, plus an extra battalion of grenadiers, along with GHQ troops, were sent to the Western Front immediately, serving there throughout the war. They were quickly joined by the Welsh Guards, newly raised in February 1915, and by another newly formed unit, the Guards Machine-Gun Regiment. A total of twenty-two battalions of the Royal Fusiliers (City of London Regiment) served on the Western Front, while four more served in Egypt, Gallipoli and East Africa, and a further twenty-one labour corps, training or reserve battalions were raised. In August 1914 the 1st Bn Middlesex Regiment, stationed at Woolwich, was sent straight to France, and the 2nd Bn followed them there from Malta. Of the forty-nine battalions eventually raised by the regiment, the majority served in France, with others at Salonika and in India. Other regular units from around Britain recruited in the London area, the 13th (Reserve) Bn Argyll & Sutherland Highlanders for example, formed at Blackheath in 1914, trained at the White City during 1915, then went to Dunfermline as a training battalion, and the 16th (Service) Bn the Rifle Brigade formed at St Pancras in 1915, before leaving for their depot in Winchester and thence to France.

Territorial Force infantry

The two London divisions of the TF each comprised three infantry brigades of four battalions, formed from the twenty-four battalions of the London Regiment (Royal Fusiliers). All the TF divisions were renumbered to fit into Kitchener's overall organisation, designed to show the order in which they were despatched overseas. The 1st London thus became the 56th Division, and the 2nd London became the 47th Division. Apart from the 1/10th and 1/11th Bns, which served in Gallipoli, Egypt and Palestine, the rest of the twenty-four original battalions were on the Western Front for the entire war. Of the second-line battalions, six served at Gallipoli, while the rest went to France; most of the cyclist companies manned the East Coast defences. The London Regiment raised a total of eighty-eight battalions in the course of the war. The other London volunteer regiment, the HAC, sent two batteries of horse artillery to France with the mounted brigades attached to the 47th and 56th Divisions. Two HAC infantry battalions served in France, and a third formed part of the garrison of the Tower of London. The 5th and 6th Bns of the East Surrey Regiment, the 4th Bn the Queen's Royal West Surrey Regiment, and many of the Queen's Own Royal West Kent Regiment's battalions formed the greater part of the TF 44th (Home Counties) Division, serving in France, but the 1/5th Bn, raised in Bromley, was to serve in Iraq, while its second- and third-line units stayed in Kent for the duration. The 4th, 6th and 7th Bns of the Essex Regiment served with the 54th (East Anglian) Division in India, on the Western Front, and in Italy. While all these formations were rapidly being moved out of the country, it remained necessary to protect the capital, and the 26th Reserve Brigade, including three battalions of the KRRC, formed part of the garrison at Wimbledon.

Recruiting and training the new armies

Right from the start of the First World War, the army was faced with an enormous recruitment and training task, as it was immediately obvious after the retreat from Mons, that the Old Contemptibles of the BEF would need replacement drafts in large numbers, coming either from the part-trained territorials or the wholly untrained volunteers required by Kitchener for his 'New Armies'. The established TF regiments signed up new recruits at their drill halls such as that of the Civil Service Rifles at Somerset House. Other recruits could sign on in police stations, at town halls or at local depots, but many passed through the Central Recruiting Office, a splendid neo-Georgian building with GR cipher, at 3–5 Great Scotland Yard, just round the corner from the Old War Office. Extra space was needed to administer the new armies, and Finsbury Court, Finsbury Pavement, was taken over as a War Office annexe, with 4 London Wall Buildings as the Infantry Record Office. Battersea Town Hall (Lower Hall) served as the recruiting office and HQ for the 10th Service Bn Royal West Surreys in 1915. Once recruits were secured, it was important to hang on to them, so training commenced immediately, even if no weapons, uniforms or equipment were available. In Battersea, Latchmere Road Baths was used for drill, and there was a board room for medical examinations at Nine Elms Baths. Wandsworth Town Hall in the High Street served as the recruiting office for the 13th Service Bn of the East

72 Victoria Embankment, Somerset House, the drill hall of the 15th (County of London) Bn The London Regiment (Prince of Wales's Own Civil Service Rifles) apparently currently (2011) scheduled for demolition.

73 Whitehall, 3–5 Great Scotland Yard, the Central Army Recruiting Office.

Surrey Regiment in 1915, with the orderly room at 380 Streatham High Road and the Buckhold Road yard of Young's Brewery being used for parades, while the men could be drilled in an adjacent camping field donated by a Mr Rawlings. Recruits were then sent to a more conventional training camp, or to the regimental depot. Ranges like Purfleet or Bisley were available for outdoor shooting. Recruiting centres were springing up everywhere. The 23rd Bn Royal Fusiliers, for instance, was enlisted at the Cecil Hotel in the Strand, while the former public schoolboys of the 16th Bn of the Middlesex Regiment gathered to sign on at 24 St James's Street at the very heart of club land. Units aimed at recruiting men from particular backgrounds seem to have selected racecourses as their assembly points: the University & Public Schools Brigade on Epsom Downs, and the 16th (Public Schools) Bn Middlesex Regiment at Hurst Park and Kempton, but the 11th (Public Schools) Bn Middlesex Regiment gathered at Woldingham Camp.

Such was the pressure to raise new units that local worthies were forced to resort to all sorts of gimmickry. Spared the disaster of the Pals Battalions, where entire generations of a locality were wiped out in an afternoon, London was nevertheless subjected to the lure of themed units. The MP Joynson-Hicks set about raising sportsmen's battalions the 17 and 23 Middlesex Bns

74 Purfleet Ranges, the reverse of one of the butts showing the hollow box construction.

(1st & 2nd Footballers). The 18 Bn KRRC (Arts & Crafts) was raised at Gidea Park, the house demolished in 1930. More controversial was the formation, early in 1918, of the 38th Bn Royal Fusiliers in the East End as an all-Jewish unit, specifically for service in Palestine, its march through London on the way to embarkation providing newspapers with plenty of opportunity for sneers and anti-Semitic comment. Two further such units were also formed, serving in the Middle East.

The enormous numbers of men suddenly under arms necessitated the instant production of a new officer corps. The 28th Bn of the London Regiment (Artists' Rifles) was converted into an Officer Cadet Training Unit (OCTU), operating in France, with its 2/1st Bn fulfilling the same role as 15 Officer Cadet Bn at Hare Hall, Romford, a grand house of 1768 now the Royal Liberty School. The Inns of Court Regiment, with three infantry companies and a cavalry squadron, moved to Berkhamstead (Hertfordshire) as 14 Officer Cadet Bn, training nearly 12,000 officers throughout the war. When the regiment was moved to Catterick (North Yorkshire) the Berkhamstead establishment became a training centre for officer-cadet instructors. At the start of the war, cadet corps based on regiments, in schools as Junior OTCs, or in Church Lads' Brigade contingents, provided copious numbers of recruits, many of them potential officers. Some were soon forced to suspend activities for the duration, since their instructors had disappeared into the ranks of the armed services. Overall however, the numbers of youngsters in cadet units more than doubled between 1914 and 1918. The sheer variety of experience available to youngsters included such widely differing units as the cadet battalion of the Household Brigade at Bushey, two newly raised sea-cadet units in Wimbledon and Richmond, and the exotic horsed Imperial Cadet Yeomanry, raised by the HAC in Finsbury. Many of these cadet units provided guards for the same sort of vulnerable points that were covered by the VTC. Some of the school OTC units such as that at Harrow, combined with other units for field days, later on in the war actually managing an exercise involving aircraft.

The Volunteer Training Corps

As early as 4 September 1914, the War Office allowed London County Council to raise a London Defence Force of volunteers who would be trained in the rudiments of military practice: drilling and shooting. Permission was given on the basis that no uniforms would be issued, only GR armbands. There was a concern that forces such as the VTC would divert men who would otherwise have been available for Kitchener's New Armies, so the War Office was less than enthusiastic about the development, but could not afford not to be involved. Once the ground rules had been laid down, there was an evident role for the corps, and a defined membership, which the Army Council could accept. Across the country local authorities usually took the initiative in recruiting these units. Stepney Borough VTC, for example, formed in March 1915 affiliated to 17th Bn London Regiment, and had their drill hall in Tredegar Road, Bow. Membership was aimed at those who were too old to serve in the regular forces, or who were in reserved occupations, particularly aiming at shopkeepers who were invited to drill and use the miniature range on Thursday afternoons, possibly their local early-closing day. They also attracted schoolboys too young to enlist but anxious to take part in some military activities prior to going for their initial training. VTC units guarded vulnerable points such as railway bridges or munitions factories, releasing regular troops for other duties. Local companies, such as that in Stepney, usually had around only 50–100 active members at any one time, but across the country a quarter of a million men had served by the end of the war. Other such units were the City of London Volunteer Corps with its own cap badge, showing how long the no-uniform rule lasted, and the County of London Motor Volunteer Corps, which provided privately owned vehicles with their drivers to operate as staff cars or ambulances. Some VTC units were raised for the express purpose of joining the army. Price's Candles Company in Battersea, for example, raised a company that then volunteered en masse for the 3rd (City of London) Bn, Royal Fusiliers.

Training camps

London's green lungs such as Wimbledon Common, Epping Forest or Blackheath might be adequate for the very basic initial training of new units raised from within the crowded metropolis, but anything more advanced generally took place in those areas that had become vast training camps. At least four battalions of the Royal Fusiliers went to Clipstone Camp (Notts), others were sent to Pirbright (Surrey), Tidworth (Wiltshire) or Aldershot (Hampshire). Several battalions of the Middlesex Regiment went to Colchester (Essex) and thence to Shoreham (Sussex). Many of the new battalions of the London Regiment trained in the enormous complex of Wiltshire camps at Sutton Veny, Fovant or Chiseldon. In 1915 the RHA moved into St John's Wood Barracks, requisitioning Lord's Cricket Ground for training.

The expansion of the army in the First World War was almost universally accommodated in vast tented, or later, hutted camps, either freestanding on green-field sites or open areas like racecourses, or as temporary extensions of existing barracks as at Hounslow. Smaller camps might be found attached to AA batteries. A number of portable huts had been used from early on in the war, but it was the invention of the Nissen hut in 1917 that was to revolutionise the field. The Nissen could be carried in easy loads, assembled with minimal tools, heated, ventilated, and then, when it had served its purpose, it could quickly be moved somewhere else. It could be adapted as living or hospital accommodation, as workshops, offices or storage. It is no wonder that tens of thousands were in use by 1918. Woldingham Camp, first used by infantry, then artillery units, and finally as an enteric hospital, had slightly more substantial wooden huts, some of which still stand as the cores of dwellings in Woldingham Garden Village.

The RFC, RNAS and RAF

Apart from the operations of the Home Defence squadrons based in their various airfields, most other flight-related activity was limited to training. The RNAS carried out basic pilot training at Crystal Palace, moving to Greenwich from 1917. Pilots of other than of fixed-wing aircraft, trained at No. 1 Balloon Training Depot at Roehampton on kite balloons, and at Wormwood Scrubs on airships. Hendon was home to the RFC School of Instruction for 18 Wing in 1916, with the RFC Armament School moving from Perivale to the grounds of Hillingdon House, Uxbridge, in 1917, staying there until autumn 1919. Towards the end of the war, Training Depot Stations, primarily designed to train British and US pilots on the new Handley-Page 0/400 bombers, were established at Chingford (No. 207), Northolt (No. 30) and Hounslow (Nos 42 and 62). The RAF Stores Depot was established at Kidbrooke in 1917 to distribute everything from aircraft spares to clothing.

Munitions and Logistics in the First World War

War on this unprecedented industrial scale required an almost unimaginable level of production. The army's apparently insatiable, and unsatisfied, appetite for shells, bullets and explosives generally, led to a political controversy triggering more government control over the means of production. Technological advances such as those in aviation created demands for products hitherto unknown. London took on a new role as one giant production line, churning out materials for the war machine. The new warfare also created a need for new techniques. The British Army School of Camouflage was set up near the powder magazine off the (West Carriage Drive) Ring in Hyde Park, its Dazzle Section being accommodated in Burlington House.

Aircraft production

Several aircraft factories had attached flying fields, some of which became operational military airfields. The RFC, a tiny organisation in 1914, quickly grew to over 100 squadrons by the end of 1916, and more than doubled in size the next year, requiring the application of mass-production methods to what had hitherto been little more than a cottage industry. While Hendon, Cricklewood and Colindale had managed to supply aircraft from the Grahame-White, Handley Page and Airco factories, there was only limited capacity on these restricted sites. In Kingston-upon-Thames, Sopwith was forced to expand its works on Canbury Park Road to build a new factory at Ham, and to contract out work under licence. Only by such measures might maximum levels of production be maintained. During the war years, Sopwith produced nearly 16,000 aircraft to forty different designs, Camels and Pups probably being the best remembered. Handley Page built a new factory near their Cricklewood works in 1916, but the solution to the universal capacity problem of limited capacity was seen to lie in the two National Aircraft Factories that were to be built in London with a third in Liverpool. The Croydon factory, originally planned for Watford, was actually built, but that intended for Richmond-upon-Thames was shifted to Manchester. The three sites would produce 30,000

75 Kingston-upon-Thames, Canbury Park Road, the offices of the Sopwith aircraft factory, built 1913–18

aircraft in a single year. The Croydon factory only functioned for a year before the Armistice, after which it became the National Aircraft Depot, responsible for destroying the thousands of surplus aircraft that the new RAF no longer needed. In 1920, under Handley Page's ownership, it began a new life as London's major civil aerodrome. Hanworth Park at Feltham had been built as an Aircraft Acceptance Park, with large storage sheds and a flying field. It also provided a home for Whitehead Aviation, who had moved their operation from a drill hall and skating rink in Townshend Road, Richmond in 1915, building BE2bs, Sopwith Pups, SE5as and DH9s. Fairey had a factory in Hayes making float planes, despatching them to Hamble (Hampshire) for testing, while nearby was a government-owned aero-engine factory from 1917. Waring & Gillow, the well-known furniture manufacturers, opened the Alliance Aeroplane Company at Acton airfield. In 1918, the Bohemia Cinema in Ballards Lane, Finchley, formerly the Alcazar, became the National Balloon Factory. At the end of the First World War many aircraft constructors faced bankruptcy and though some diversified into automobile manufacture for example, others went to the wall.

Some evidence of all this can still be found. At Hendon, the main building of the Grahame-White factory has been transferred onto the RAF Museum campus, and the Airco factory stands opposite the end of Colindale Avenue on the Edgware Road. Here, the three-storey neo-Georgian offices of 1915 are occupied by a school, while the A-frame sheds behind are in light industrial use. In Kingston-upon-Thames, the Canbury Park Road offices of the Sopwith factory, begun in around 1913, have now been converted into flats as 'Sopwith House'. At Feltham there are a few traces of the RFC base incorporated into the later RASC depot and barracks, while the currently (2011) derelict Hanworth House stands forlornly behind wire fences.

Explosives production

The combination of a war of attrition and frequent pushes taking place on the Western Front made vast demands on the munitions industry, the perceived mismanagement of which brought David Lloyd George into the key role of Minister Of Munitions. By the early years of the century, cordite had become established as the military explosive of choice, and a new plant within the established Royal gunpowder works at Waltham Abbey was in operation, along with the Dartford guncotton works of Curtis and Harvey. Obsolete buildings at Waltham Abbey were mainly converted to new uses, but a new nitro-glycerine plant was built. Surprisingly, a large number of explosives factories, keeping the army supplied with shells and ammunition, were in the London area. In 1903, the first Lyddite filling plant had been built in a remote spot on Plumstead Marshes, next to the Woolwich Arsenal, as the open marshy areas of the Thames Estuary were clearly unsuited to accommodating such works. Some were too near to built-up areas, as was demonstrated in January 1917 when the TNT factory in Silvertown, near the modern City Airport, exploded, killing sixteen workers and fifty-three local residents. At Blake's munitions factory in Wood Lane, Hammersmith, a hut where incendiary bombs were being produced caught fire and thirteen workers lost their lives. When finding a location for a factory there was a balance to be struck between the availability of a workforce and the dangerous proximity of surrounding dwellings, but it inevitably became necessary to site these works in populous areas. There were National Filling factories in Hayes, Abbey Wood, Greenford, Perivale, Stratford, Horley, Fulham and Southwark. That at Perivale covered 138 acres (55ha) and consisted of row upon row of gabled timber sheds in which the mainly female workforce filled shells by the thousand. A separate Trench Warfare Department ran factories at Erith and Walthamstow, and two in Watford. The Admiralty had its own filling factory in Stratford, and there were TNT plants in Southall, Hackney Wick and Rainham as well as Silvertown. Other specialist factories handled acetone, ammonium nitrate, picric acid, mineral jelly and cotton waste, while HM Guncotton Factory was at Colnbrook. From December 1914, Chislehurst Caves were used to store 1000 tons of TNT from Woolwich Arsenal, brought there by train and lorry. Local residents cannot have slept too soundly. J & W Nicholson's Three Mills gin distillery at Bromley-by-Bow used fermentation tanks to pilot acetone production using horse-chestnuts and acorns, often collected by schoolchildren. Some of the original powder works were granted an extended lease of life, with the Hounslow Powder Works, with origins in the sixteenth century at the latest, lasting until 1920. Much of the experimental work leading to the production of gas shells was carried out at Woolwich, with shell filling taking place at Greenford. However, one consignment that failed to make it to Woolwich was the load of highly volatile aluminium powder that formed part of the *Lusitania*'s cargo when she was torpedoed off the Irish coast in May 1915. Accusations that it could have caused the unexplained second explosion have been largely discredited due to the lack of eyewitness testimony to any lightning-like fire that would have resulted, and the absence of damage to the relevant parts of the ship's hull.

Weapons production

This was centred on Woolwich Arsenal for artillery, where a workforce of 65,000, 45 per cent of it women, was eventually employed by the end of the war, and on Enfield Lock, the main factory for small arms. The major new weapon of the First World War however, was the machine gun, and one of the key men in its development was Hiram Maxim. He first worked out of premises in the city, the 1880 Hatton House, off the Clerkenwell Road, but some matchmaking by Sir Ernest Cassel and the Rothschilds brought him together with Vickers, whose Crayford factory

became the primary source of his output. Vickers then brought his own designs into play, and the 0.303in Mk 1 gun came into use in 1912, remaining in use for over fifty years. A 37mm, 1-pounder gun for naval use, air-cooled models, and guns using AFV's integral cooling systems were all developed in their works in Fraser Road, Crayford. The enormous steel-framed erecting shop, dated 1907, survives from the complex of buildings that housed Vickers and their neighbours Fraser & Chalmers. The machine gun may have been seen as the star killing machine of the First World War, but the workhorse, responsible for the overwhelming majority of death and destruction, was the artillery piece. Woolwich Arsenal was a combination of laboratory, test bed, store

76 Clerkenwell Road, Hatton House, the original workshop of Hiram Maxim, the machine-gun manufacturer, from 1880.

77 Erith, Fraser Road, the Vickers-Maxim works of 1907 producing machine-guns which combined elements from both producers' models.

and manufactory, stockpiling weapons such as old naval 6-pounder Hotchkiss QF guns removed from such ships as the *Thunderer*, and fitting them to the new male Mark 1 tanks that appeared in 1916. The female Mark 1 tank was equipped with five Vickers machine guns from Crayford, and may have been thought more deadly. In 1918 a new three-storey range was added to the London Small Arms Company's Connaught works at Bow, expanding works that had produced rifles since 1867.

The Vickers works at Crayford survives, but most of Enfield Lock and Woolwich Arsenal have been redeveloped as housing, with only particularly significant buildings retained for conversion. Waltham Abbey is now open to the public, as is a part of the Arsenal. The ammunition storage sites at Crayford continued in use in the Second World War along with others, including that at Barking Reach. Enfield Lock's 'Rifles' public house of 1916, like those in the great munitions-producing areas of Carlisle and Gretna, was government owned. Controlling licensing hours and limiting actual opening kept munitions workers out of the pub and at their benches, resolving a problem only exacerbated by the comparatively generous rates of pay in the munitions industry.

Transport

At the beginning of the war virtually all transport was horse-drawn, and vast numbers of horses and carts were requisitioned for use by the army. The Army Service Corps set up a network of depots where transport and animals were assembled and the men to work with them were trained. In 1914, No. 1 Reserve Horse Transport (HT) Depot had been moved from Deptford to Park Royal, but Deptford remained the Reserve Supply Depot, served by a light railway and crane unit. On Blackheath, No. 2 Reserve HT Depot was set up in 1915, with its HQ in the Rangers House with the use of Macartney House. A fenced area north of the Dover Road (A2)

78 Grove Park, the former Greenwich Workhouse, which became an Army Service Corps transport depot assembling buses for service on the Western Front, and carrying out driver training.

contained huts and stables with a veterinary hospital to the south of the main road. The HQ of the Forage Department and the Women's Forage Corps was at 64 Whitehall Court, Westminster. As motor transport (MT) came into use, wholly new units needed to be developed. A driving school was set up at Plumstead and a complex of Reserve Depot, Recruit Reception and Training centres was established in the Lee area with satellites in Camberwell, Catford, Eltham, Kelsey Manor, Norwood and Sydenham. The old Greenwich Workhouse in Marvels Lane, Grove Park (SE12) became the depot for 3rd and 4th (Auxiliary) Omnibus MT Coys in 1914–19, and to whom 300 buses were supplied by the London General Omnibus Company based in Grosvenor Road, Pimlico. Here, drivers were trained prior to taking these buses to the Western Front as troop transports for the BEF and the RN division. Another reserve MT depot was Osterley Park, using further sites in Hounslow, Isleworth and Twickenham. The Home MT Depot in Short's Gardens, Drury Lane, was the centre of another web of sub-depots in central London. As the army's administration kept on growing, using premises dotted over the whole of the London area, so a concomitant need for personal transport mushroomed. By 1915, the formerly voluntary Local Auxiliary MT companies, No. 23 at Shepherd's Bush, and No. 28 at Regent's Park and Kensington Barracks, appear to have been taken under the wing of the military. The garage, stores and workshops for vehicles serving the GOC London was at Goldhawk Road, Shepherd's Bush, with the unit on ferrying duties for personnel from the Ministy of Munitions and the Ministry of Aviation, which were close by in Holland Park Avenue, while the War Cabinet drew from a car pool at Kensington Barracks. ASC personnel were accommodated as conveniently as possible, with one hostel for 250 members of the Queen Mary's Auxiliary Army Corps being in Holland Park. Another responsibility of the ASC was the army's mail, and 620 MT Coy was based in Regent's Park to serve the main sorting offices, such as Mount Pleasant. As MT became ever more important, the government sought more control.

The Talbot works in Ladbroke Grove, already under the technical direction of Rolls-Royce, was acquired by the Ministry of Munitions in 1918, and the Motor Radiator Manufacturing Co. Ltd of Sudbury, Wembley, was nationalised in 1918. Wolseley manufactured ambulances for the War Office and gathered fifty volunteer drivers to run those they had donated to the war effort.

Military hospitals

There were trained medical personnel in the TF whose function, in the event of war, was to establish military hospitals using the existing infrastructure. Five of these hospitals were in London: in Camberwell, Chelsea, Wandsworth Common, Denmark Hill and St Thomas' at Lambeth. Along with RAMC clearing hospitals at Chelsea and Surbiton, these would supplement the regular army hospitals at Millbank, Woolwich and Rochester Row. This network was run from offices in the Duke of York's HQ at Chelsea, and others in Harley Street, Holborn. Within a short space of time it became apparent that these would not suffice, and a number of solutions were found. A range of specialist hospitals took in appropriate cases: cardiac, orthopaedic or neurological for example. Others would specialise in specific treatments for typhoid or VD. A great deal of provision was needed for convalescence, of those returning to duty and those, particularly the limbless, who would have to learn to make their way in the world. It was an opportunity for fashionable society to demonstrate humanity and patriotism by making their town or country residences over to recovering soldiers. Londonderry House in Park Lane, and the Duke of Rutland's house in Arlington Street are examples. Both the Red Cross and Voluntary Aid Detachment set up mainly convalescent homes in borrowed houses. One in

79 Chelsea, the Duke of York's Headquarters was built in 1803 as a school for soldiers' orphans. In 1912 it became a drill hall for Territorial Force units including the 1st County of London Yeomanry, the London Irish Rifles, ASC, RE, and London's volunteer RAMC General Hospital and Field Ambulance units. Since then it has been home to AA regiments in the 1920s, bomb disposal units during the Second World War, and the SAS post-war. It now houses the Saatchi Gallery and private apartments.

Hampstead was staffed by female relatives and associates of the Artists' Rifles. The Queen Mary Hospital in Sidcup was specifically set up in 1917 to treat burns cases, pioneering plastic surgery, and Hampstead Military Hospital was restricted to RFC cases after 1917. London's enormous mental hospitals at Epsom, Ewell and Napsbury, for instance, were brought into service. The most delicate affliction was that dubbed shell shock. A number of private hospitals such as Latchmere were set up for officers, but other ranks very often had to take their chance in the mainstream system, often laying themselves open to accusations of cowardice or desertion.

Housing

One feature of the landscape, whose military origin is often forgotten, is housing built specifically either for military personnel, or for workers in the munitions industry. The Well Hall Estate in Eltham was built in 1915 as a low-density garden suburb of 1000 houses and 200 flats for workers at the Woolwich Arsenal. It was designed for the Office of Works by a pupil of Ashbee, hence its arts and crafts style. Its village appearance with timber and tile hanging, though picturesque, was deemed expensive and sadly, simpler, less traditional projects elsewhere became the model for municipal housing in the years after the war. A quite different approach to housing key workers can be seen at Aeroville, where 300 employees of Hendon Aerodrome were housed in a square of terraced neo-Georgian houses. Designed in 1917 by Matthews, the details include mansard roofs, dormers with pediments, and colonnades either side of the entrance. A third example can be seen at Barnes Cray, where, from 1914, some 600 houses were built to house workers at the Vickers-Maxim factories. Some are of concrete blocks, roughcast and colour washed. Roe Green in Stag Lane, Kingsbury, was built in 1917–19 by Frank Baines for workers at the Aircraft Manufacturing Company's factory at The Hyde. A mixture of houses and flats in blocks of four, these were laid out around a traditional village green at the garden suburb density of eleven dwellings to the acre (twenty-seven to the hectare).

80 Eltham, Well Hall, housing built for workers at the Woolwich Arsenal.

81 Hendon, Aeroville, housing built around a quadrangle for workers at the Graham-White aircraft factory on Hendon aerodrome.

Camps for Prisoners of War (POWs) and internees

Although POW camps in the form in which we tend to imagine them, with rows of huts and wire fences around them, existed in the First World War, the majority were simply large houses or even hotels acting as bases for work details, hospitals, or convenient open spaces. On 6 August 1914, enemy aliens were required to register at Police Courts such as Bow Street, Old Street and Albany Street in central London. If an alien was seen as any sort of security risk, then detention followed, for some, initially at Olympia. Many of these unfortunates were, in fact, naturalised British, and included, for instance, a sergeant with twenty years service in the TF, who was arrested at the RE drill hall in Bethnal Green. The two exhibition halls at Olympia had been built in 1885 as the National Agricultural Hall, and, with the conversion of a lodge into a guard-room, was considered suitable for holding internees, many of whom would be moved on to camps on the Isle of Man or elsewhere. The government had plans for White City, the derelict, 200-acre site of the Franco-British Exhibition, and the 1908 Olympic Games, but public opinion was against the idea, owing to the proximity of the site to central London. However, despite such objections, a large internment camp was set up at Alexandra Palace, built in 1875 with a hall to seat 12,000. Some 600 male enemy aliens of military age were delivered here in September 1915, and by April 1916, the camp's population had increased to 1600 Germans and 700 Austrians. Another north London camp was St Mary's Institution for the Poor, also referred to as Islington Workhouse, now part of the Whittington Hospital complex on Dartmouth Park Hill near Archway. This held mainly German businessmen who had lived in London for many years. While they were not seen as a security risk and enjoyed a high degree of unsupervised recreational activity, they were nevertheless behind barbed wire fences.

seven

The Interwar Years 1919–39

At the end of the First World War, Britain was exhausted and bankrupt, and had little choice but to cut defence spending to the bare minimum. Were Britain's security ever again to be seriously threatened, it was reckoned that any potential aggressor, particularly if it were Germany under the restrictions imposed by Versailles, would take at the very least, ten years to re-arm. Therefore, the government, with a certain amount of understandable justification, found it expedient to impose the Ten Year Rule. This allowed successive chancellors of the exchequer to pare defence estimates to the bone while arguing that there was no evidence of a need to re-arm. This policy was only abandoned in 1932, the year that the Defence Budget hit its lowest level. By the early 1930s, it had become apparent that Germany was rising from the ashes and was likely to threaten the peace of Europe, so rearmament slowly gathered pace. In the meantime the military had returned to peacetime routines as the Household troops changed the guard, trooped the colour, and provided guard detachments for the Bank of England and the Hyde Park magazine.

The RAF and its Airfields

Retrenchment and consolidation

Having finished the war with nearly 400 sites, the RAF was compelled to close over 90 per cent of them. Sutton's Farm and North Weald Bassett were all but razed to the ground, and Hainault Farm's flying field was returned to agriculture. Croydon, its National Aircraft factory busy destroying the thousands of surplus aircraft, by 1920 was establishing itself as London's main civil aerodrome, a status confirmed in 1928 after a complete rebuild. A year later it had become the busiest in Europe. By 1922 the RAF was down to just twenty-five sites, only four of which were in London. Of these, Kenley was HQ of 1 Group, Biggin Hill was mainly engaged in research and development, Northolt was concerned with the induction of new recruits, and Uxbridge was an administrative site. Additional elements of the RAF infrastructure were the stores depots at Ruislip and Kidbrooke, Finchley Hospital, and the research establishment at Hampstead. West Drayton Reception Depot, as HQ 21 Group, disbanded in 1930–34, its functions being taken over by Uxbridge. In 1935–36 a new RAF sub-depot was established at Orpington. Trenchard had to fight hard to keep an air force at all, as its role was widely seen very much as one of policing the empire rather than the role he envisaged for it as central to home defence, a function that the establishment continued to regard as the preserve of the Royal Navy.

It was in a climate of zero growth and minimal funding that a vulnerability, possibly to French belligerence, initiated the formulation of a number of air defence plans. The Steel-Bartholomew Plan of 1923, and the 52 Squadron, or Romer Plan of 1925, were both developments of the 1918 London Air Defence Area, but with extensions to north and west. They were predicated on the

82 Hendon, the parachute store (2355/25) at the rebuilt fighter station.

notion of a bomber force located in the so-called Wessex Bombing Area, and a fighter force deployed in an arc giving cover to both London and the bomber bases. The size of the scheme was governed by the usual balancing act between the desirable and the affordable, so the simple yardstick of parity with France's air force was adopted. Once the plan had been accepted, it was necessary to select the airfields through which it might best be implemented. For the fighter force protecting London from air attack, North Weald, Hornchurch, Biggin Hill and Kenley were chosen as Sector Stations, with Hendon and Northolt as backup. In 1927, to ensure that new installations retained some semblance of secrecy, Stanley Baldwin ordered that no military establishments should be shown on OS maps.

The Home Defence Scheme

Gradually, over the next few years, these fighter stations, and some of the new bomber stations, gained new improved buildings drawn from a centrally designed suite of plans. These are often referred to as Home Defence Scheme buildings, reflecting the phase of development in which they were designed and built. Five 'A'-type hangars (19a/24) were distributed between North Weald, Hornchurch and Northolt. The watch office was still basically a bungalow for the duty pilot (1072 & 2072/26) but that used for fighter stations had an upper storey containing a pilots' rest room. These were built at Hornchurch and Northolt, with the single storey version at Hendon. Two-storey barrack blocks, Type 'C' (104/23 and 230/27 among other variations), were built at Biggin Hill, Kenley, Northolt, North Weald and Hornchurch, the last two having Type 191/24 and 1524/25. The officers' mess at Biggin Hill came into service in 1931 to a neo-Baroque design by the Air Ministry architect, featuring a three-storey centre and two-storey wings. Often, existing buildings on site were requisitioned, as at North Weald where Ad Astra House had become the Station HQ, and at Kenley, where Flintfield House, demolished in 1980, initially served as the officers' mess, but was superseded by a grander, more conventional structure by 1931. The First World War airfield at Sutton's Farm had been demolished by 1921, and

83 Northolt, the guard room (166/23), almost identical to that built at the, by-then civilian, Croydon Aerodrome.

84 Biggin Hill, the particularly grand officers' mess built by 1932.

85 Hornchurch, the officers' mess (1524/25) identical to that at North Weald.

the new airfield was built some distance to the west of its predecessor and renamed Hornchurch in 1928, sharing the same officers' mess design as North Weald.

Re-orientation and expansion

As these airfields were being upgraded, and the size and efficiency of the RAF increased, so the world was changing. By the early 1930s, two things had become very apparent. Firstly, any aerial threat that might be facing Britain would be coming across the North Sea from Germany, and secondly, the RAF was in need of even greater enlargement than had previously been envisaged. These realities brought about the 'Expansion Period' involving the creation of many new airfields, a growth in the provision of flying training, the establishment of secure storage facilities for new aircraft coming off the assembly lines, and a realignment of forces, characterised by the Reorientation Plan of 1935 which located new bomber airfields in the eastern counties, poised to carry out raids on Germany.

By 1931, Biggin Hill had undergone a major programme of refurbishment not only for its role as a Sector Station in the fighter setup, but also as a school of AA warfare, helping to integrate the separate arms of aerial defence. To the two GS hangars surviving from the First World War was added an F-shed. Significantly, all three had been destroyed by enemy bombing by the end of 1940, ultimately to be replaced by T2 utility hangars. The Expansion Period airfields are characterised by elegant buildings, as their designs were influenced by Lutyens and given their seals of approval by the Royal Fine Art Commission and the Council for the Preservation of Rural England. Their style was neo-Georgian for the most part and they tended to be grouped in coherent and easily recognisable clusters according to their function. However, a number of concessions to their essentially warlike purpose were made. Many of them had bombproof roofs, some use was made of camouflage, and hangars were usually grouped in arcs to lessen the chance of their destruction by a single stick of bombs. While new airfields on green-field sites were given complete layouts of these buildings, most of our London airfields had been continuously developed in a piecemeal fashion from 1919 and received only elements of the

86 Biggin Hill, the Station HQ (352-3/31).

87 Croydon, the hangar built in 1927 as part of London's new aerodrome, and pressed into RAF service again in the Second World War.

new. Thus, although much of the vital work on fighter stations protecting the capital was already well underway, a 'C'-type hangar was provided at Hornchurch in 1935, and another at Northolt in 1938. Hornchurch also received a 'Fort'-type watch office (2062/34) but without the usual distinctive tower. When war came the RAF would need to requisition civilian aerodromes such as Croydon and Heston.

88 Heston, the experimental all-concrete hangar built by Jackamann of Slough for Airwork. It anticipates the Lamella hangars built in Germany.

Command

Uxbridge soon became an important centre in the command and control of the RAF, when HQ RAF South East Area in Kensington amalgamated with the South West Area as the new Southern Area in 1919, and moved to Hillingdon House, Uxbridge. Successive HQs were located here: Air Defence of Great Britain from 1926, Inland Fighting Area in 1926–36, Bomber Command until 1936, and 11 Group, RAF Fighter Command, until it moved to Bentley Priory in 1936. The Air Ministry occupied Gwydyr House, Whitehall.

Bentley Priory had been acquired by the RAF in March 1926 for use as a command centre. When Fighter Command was created in 1936, it set up its support branches (engineering, armament, signals and equipment) at Bentley Priory, and a Command HQ Operations Room with a table in the ballroom, a room measuring 50ft by 30ft (15m by 9m), and a switchboard and teleprinters in the adjacent Rotunda or picture gallery. With the construction of a gallery around its north and west sides, the Ops Room was nearing completion in December 1936 and GPO 'phone lines were installed. In August 1938 a Home Defence exercise showed that the new RDF (or RADAR) system was working, and the decision was taken to transfer the Filter Room from Bawdsey (Suffolk) to Bentley Priory. It was installed in a basement room hitherto used as an office-cum-lumber room, up and running by 10 November. January 1939 saw work start on an underground Ops Block capable of withstanding hits by 500lb (230kg) or 250lb (115kg) semi-armour-piercing bombs. Excavations to an average depth of 42ft (13m) necessitated the removal of 58,270 tons of earth, and the basic structure took 23,500 tons of concrete, much reinforced with steel, and required 4000 joints in the wiring for the air-raid warning system alone. There was discussion over the location of a standby alternative ops room in early 1939, and the GPO advised that it be located in the Leighton Buzzard area where the new Air Ministry central telephone/teleprinter exchange had been built as the

RAF Communications Centre. Liscombe Park, 2 miles to the west of Leighton Buzzard, was selected, and used mainly as a training centre for Ops Room and Filter Room personnel. In May 1939, the Filter Room at Bentley Priory was transferred upstairs to a room next to the Ops Room, possibly the former library where a wooden gallery was installed overlooking the operations table, and a hole was knocked in the wall at gallery level to interconnect these two rooms. Uxbridge meanwhile became HQ No. 11 Group Fighter Command with its own underground Ops Room.

Aviation training

Ironically in a period of austerity, from the early 1930s there had been a move to romanticise flying, ostensibly for its commercial and recreational applications, but always with a feeling that the country was going to be in need of a lot of trained pilots in the near future. A private airfield had been opened by Whiteheads at Hanworth towards the end of the First World War, and this was resurrected as the London Air Park in 1929 with a clubhouse in Hanworth Park House. Commercial companies such as de Havilland at Hatfield and British Air Transport at Redhill, set up flying schools, and flying clubs like Feltham joined the government-sponsored Civil Air Guard scheme. Stapleford Tawney, Redhill and Fairlop operated as training airfields early in the Second World War, subsequently becoming operational fighter stations when the bombers began attacking London.

Throughout the years leading up to war, Uxbridge continued to develop as the major RAF depot for recruits and personnel deployment, with schools of PT and drill, administration and anti-gas procedures, and the Short Service Officers' course. Alfred House in Cromwell Street, Kensington, housed the Air Ministry School of Control and the School of Meteorology.

The defence of London against air attack

Successive air defence plans, particularly the Reorientation Plan, re-introduced the notion of separating out airspace, creating a system that would include searchlight, barrage balloon, gun and fighter belts, but little, beyond the skeleton network of fighter stations, was actually provided. From 1922, the Territorial Army (TA) had taken on the responsibility for the AA defences, and the School of AA Artillery was established at Biggin Hill to train this new force, comprising just four AA brigades. Not until 1935, however, was there to be a real expansion programme, implemented by the conversion of eight battalions of TA infantry into AA gunners and searchlight operators, forming new units of RA or RE (TA). Unfortunately, little of the necessary equipment was forthcoming, partly because of economic depression, and partly because the thought of another war was too terrible to countenance. At the end of 1937, while the notional establishment of the new AA Command provided for 224 heavy AA guns in the London Inner Artillery Zone (IAZ) and the same amount again in the Thames and Medway defences, there were, in fact, fewer than 200 guns available for the defence of the entire UK. Although new guns had been designed, they had not been put into production, so many of the new TA units were manning old 3in guns that had seen service in the previous war. Only in late 1938 were the new 3.7in HAA guns appearing in numbers, and it was not until early in 1939 that the first 4.5in guns were actually emplaced. Because of all the delays, more of the static 3.7ins were produced, since the mobile version was more versatile, more complex to manufacture, and more expensive.

The other key piece in the air defence jigsaw was the Observer Corps ('Royal', from 1941). The success of the spotting service in the First World War had ensured that it remained an integral part of each successive interwar air defence plan. Cynics might argue that it was only because it was cheap to run and manned by volunteers that it was kept in the frame, but the value of a network of eyes and ears, consistently present on the ground, had been proven. The observers would complement the evolving radar cover, filling in the gaps caused by weather conditions or enemy action, and solving problems not yet overcome by the still-developing technology. The observer system was initially based in coastal areas, manned by special constables and coastguards, but quickly came to cover the whole country, with trained and enrolled observers serving in a quasi-military organisation from 1929, under the auspices of the Air Ministry, with its HQ in Hillingdon House, at RAF Uxbridge. The country was divided up into areas that reported to the fighter controls, or filter rooms. From 1937, the London area was covered by posts belonging to Observer Corps groups based in Watford (17 Group), Bromley (19 Group) and Colchester (18 Group), and Corps HQ moved to Bentley Priory in 1938. Each group consisted of triangles of posts connected to their centre by telephone. A post, at its most basic, consisted of a garden-shed sized hut and a telephone. The hut gave some shelter, and a place to mount the rudimentary plotting instruments that enabled observers roughly to report direction and altitude to Control. Posts were located in the open on high ground with good visibility or in built-up areas, on the roofs of high buildings.

The Army

Like the RAF, the army was swiftly demobilised at the end of the war, but some units were surprised to find themselves in Russia supporting the White Russian forces against the Bolsheviks. Indeed, two battalions (the 45th & 46th Garrison Bns) of the Royal Fusiliers were raised early in 1919 specifically for service in north Russia, and were disbanded in December 1919 when the campaign collapsed. At home, once the enormous numbers of troops had been dispersed, the army went back to its peacetime role of providing garrisons and the occasional punitive expeditionary force around the empire. A programme of mechanisation, particularly the conversion of horsed cavalry to armour, was undertaken and proceeded slowly until the urgency of rearmament speeded the process up by the mid-1930s.

London's TA units

The Territorial Army was re-formed in 1920 and was immediately given the central role in air defence. In 1922 the 51st (London) AA Brigade formed at the Duke of York's HQ in Chelsea, the 52nd at Acton, and the 53rd and 54th at Putney, all four becoming HAA regiments in 1939, and the Electrical Engineers were converted to searchlight troops. The biggest change of role in the 1920s, however, was imposed on the yeomanry regiments. The four London regiments all faced total transformation. The 'Rough Riders' converted to artillery, the Middlesex Hussars to signals, the Westminster Dragoons and Sharpshooters to armoured car companies in the Tank Corps, with the Dragoons becoming the corps' main source of officer material. King Edward's Horse was disbanded, and the Inns of Court Regiment continued as an officer training corps. The East and West Kent Yeomanries' earlier amalgamation was made permanent and the new regiment was converted to artillery, becoming the 97th Kent Yeomanry Field Regiment with four batteries, one of which, 388 Howitzer Battery, was based at Bromley. Still reliant on horsepower, riding practice took place at Woolwich and Sevenoaks on Wednesdays, and other drills on Thursdays. In 1920 the HAC was reconstituted as 11th (HAC & City of London Yeomanry) Brigade RHA.

The Essex Yeomanry and Royal Horse Artillery combined to become a regiment of field artillery in 1921, and the next year the Surrey and Sussex Yeomanry combined to the same end.

For the time being the existing artillery and infantry units were little affected, beyond receiving new equipment, but all this was to change in 1935. At last, something was to be done about the five notional, but hitherto largely non-existent AA divisions. The first step was to take eight infantry battalions from the TA's London Division and to convert them into AA units, forming the 1st AA Division with HQ at Uxbridge. The units involved were the successors of some of the best-known volunteer battalions: the Post Office Rifles, the Finsbury Rifles and the 1st Surrey Rifles for instance. Over the next three years more such units were absorbed into the expanding AA forces, with the 9th Bn Middlesex Regiment, based in Willesden, converting to a searchlight unit in 1938. As well as the conversion of old units, completely new ones were raised. The 36th (Middlesex) AA S/L Bn RE, TA was raised as a new unit in 1935 with HQ in a brand-new drill hall in Edgware opened by Secretary of State for War Leslie Hore-Belisha. There is a carved art deco panel of searchlight beams over the front porch. The 88th Middlesex AA Regiment RA, TA, was raised entirely from employees of London Transport in 1938. The 72nd (Middlesex) Searchlight Regiment RA, TA was raised as a new unit in 1938 with a brand-new drill hall on Vicarage Farm Road, Heston. Often units underwent a number of changes in this process. The 74th (Essex Fortress) AA Bn RE, TA for example, changed cap badges once again on becoming the 74th (Essex Fortress) Searchlight Regiment RA in 1940, based at another new drill hall in Tottenham High Road. The Post Office Rifles, by now the 32nd Searchlight Regiment RE, TA, also transferred to the RA in 1940.

More changes came in 1938 when the Militia Act made six months' military training compulsory for all young males. They were initially accommodated in dedicated hutted camps such as those at Lippitts Hill and in Richmond Park. New units were needed in which all these new recruits might subsequently serve after their period of training. All TA regiments were therefore required to clone themselves by finding a cadre of officers and NCOs to form the basis of a new duplicate unit. This gave the Surrey and Sussex Yeomanry Field Artillery the opportunity to resume their separate identities, with the Surrey regiment remaining in Clapham Park, and the Sussex unit returning to Brighton. The Sharpshooters formed a duplicate armoured regiment and the Middlesex Hussars split into two armoured signals regiments. Artillery units

89 Edgware, Deansbrook Road, the drill hall opened in August 1938 by Leslie Hore-Belisha, the Secretary of State for War, for 317 Coy 36th (Middlesex) Searchlight Regiment, RE, TA. The panel over the door depicts crossed searchlight beams.

90 Heston, Vicarage Farm Road, the drill hall opened in 1938 for the 72nd (Middlesex) Searchlight Regiment, RE, TA. In 1955 it was HQ of the 82nd AA Brigade.

did the same, the 1st London Brigade RFA becoming the 90th Field Regiment RA, TA, and its duplicate, the 138th Field Regiment RA, TA. Bromley's howitzer battery was hived off to form the basis of 143 Field Regiment RA, TA. The 6th London Brigade RFA was reorganised as the 52nd AT Regiment RA, TA at Brixton, with its duplicate becoming the 62nd AT Regiment at Stockwell. By the eve of the outbreak of war a further tranche of new AA units was being raised, including the 60th (City of London) AA Regiment at Bromley Road, Catford, the 88th at White City, and the 99th recruited from among expatriate Welshmen, and based at Iverna Gardens, once home to the 13th Bn London Regiment (Kensington Rifles).

Drill halls

Few new builds for the army appeared during the austerity years between the wars, as the available resources were channelled to the RAF Expansion Schemes. The major exception was the TA. Both its new AA formations and its yeomanry regiments reorganised as field artillery or armour, requiring premises with specialist training facilities and equipment storage, and some of these units got new drill halls. Many were built to the same standard as the neo-Georgian buildings of the RAF, with maple-block floors, oak panelling and marble fireplaces in the messes. The drill hall of the 98th (Surrey Yeomanry) Field Regiment RA (TA) at Clapham Park opened in 1939 in brand-new premises incorporating drill hall, interconnecting gun park, canteen and messes for other ranks, NCOs and officers, garages for the trucks that would tow the guns into battle, fuel compound, training rooms, offices, armoury and a flat for the resident caretaker.

Searchlight units needed even more space as their eight lights and attendant generators, all on wheeled chassis, needed to be kept under cover. For indoor use, in the hall, there had to be a minimum of 15ft (4.6m) up to the top of the side wall. Outside, there had to be enough unrestricted space to operate several lights at a time, circling through 360° from 15° upwards. At Ewell, opened in 1938, there were specialist training rooms for spotters, listeners, driving and maintenance and searchlights, as well as a large, double-height dark room painted to replicate

91 Ewell, Welbeck Close, Mercator House, drill hall, opened in 1938 for the 30th (Surrey) Searchlight
Regiment, RE, TA. It was a Home Guard base in the Second World War.

the night sky, all grouped around the spacious central hall itself. Ewell was built for 318 Coy
30th (Surrey) Searchlight Bn RE, TA, whose unit HQ was at nearby Kingston-upon-Thames.
Here were replicated all those facilities seen at Ewell, but with the addition of a sound locators'
training room and a wide rear-entrance passage with folding shutters to facilitate access for
the cumbersome equipment. Others had to make do with partial refurbishment. The Braganza
Street drill hall of 7th (Southwark) Bn Queen's Royal Regiment (West Surrey) had been built
in 1833 as a pair of semi-detached houses with a later drill-shed behind and had been home
to the battalion and its predecessors since 1865. In 1936 a partial rebuilding was started, and
the new HQ was finished in June 1938, opened by Major-General the Duke of Gloucester.
This provided a great improvement for the battalion but, when required to accommodate a
duplicate unit, the 2/7th Bn, in August 1939, only a former dance hall and gymnasium at St
George's Market near the Elephant and Castle could be found. Even the control centre of 1st
AA Division had to be improvised from redundant property. Brompton Road underground
station closed in July 1934, and was bought by the War Office as the London AA defences'
protected HQ and operations room. The street level lift-shafts and some of the underground
passageways remained in use into the 1970s.

Barracks, camps and depots for the regular army 1919–39

Little new provision was made for the regulars. Red Barracks, in Frances Street, Woolwich,
built as an infirmary for the Royal Marine Light Infantry, had served as the first depot for the
RAOC, but in 1921 they left for more spacious premises in Hilsea (Hampshire). At St John's
Wood, the RHA got new officers' and sergeants' messes in 1922, and Jubilee Buildings, five
storeys of married quarters for RHA other ranks, opened in 1935. Another expanding corps
with accommodation needs was the RASC. An HQ, driving school, Vehicle Reserve Depot,
MT stores depot, and heavy repair shop opened in Feltham around 1936, with an additional site
at Ashford earmarked for further expansion of the repair shop facilities.

92 Feltham, the RASC barracks and depot opened by 1938 as a Vehicle Reserve Depot, driving school and vehicle repair workshops.

Housing and welfare

'Homes Fit For Heroes' was an expression derived from Lloyd George's actual aspiration to create a land 'fit for heroes to live in'. The Sunray Estate in Herne Hill was built in 1920–21 by the Office of Works under Sir Frank Baines who opted for a simpler style than that employed at the wartime Well Hall, with steeply pitched tiled roofs and plain rendered walls. There were more such homes at the Long Drive and The Bye in Acton, where they were built out of experimental materials, mainly concrete blocks of various types, but also some interlocking hollow terracotta blocks. On Castlebar Road in Ealing are St David's Homes for Ex-Servicemen, incorporating eighteenth-century survivals but with a chapel of 1919. The Chapel House Estate, on the Isle of Dogs, was built in 1919–21 by Sir Frank Baines and consists of terraces of four cottages plus three-storey blocks of flats set around squares.

A feature of the interwar airfields was the provision of houses for married officers and other ranks. At Biggin Hill, dating from the 1920s, the detail is picturesque with gables, bay windows and tiled roofs on cottages in terraces of threes and fours. At Kenley, the other ranks' married quarters of 1929–31 are more formal with very little detail. They are either in terraces of four houses, or in pairs of semi-detached, probably reflecting a hierarchy of rank rather than the needs of individual families.

Welfare and medical care

Apart from the Star and Garter Home for invalid and incurable servicemen, which was built in 1921–24 on Richmond Hill, and Queen Mary's House, a military maternity home of 1922 on Heath Street, Hampstead, the majority of new building was for the RAF as the new service developed and consolidated its infrastructure from scratch. New buildings ranged from the RAF Club at No. 128 Piccadilly remodelled by Aston Webb in 1919–22, to the RAF officers' hospitals at Finchley (1918) and Uxbridge (1925), and the RAF Hospital at Finchley, which was staffed by permanent members of Princess Mary's RAF Nursing Service set up in 1927, to the Southern Area RAF Medical HQ at Uxbridge (1919).

93 Biggin Hill, married quarters built in the 1920s.

London Prepares for War

Civil Defence

The bombing of civilian targets, particularly in London, had made a deep impression on the authorities, who realised that efforts would have to be made to provide greater protection if such events were to be repeated. The Home Office-run Committee on the Co-ordination of Departmental Action on the Outbreak of War (CCDAOW) of 1923 was made the responsible body for the ARP organisation. Ten years later a report by the Air Raids Commandant set the agenda for the role of services in London, plans that were rolled out to other cities. Passive defence, the provision of shelters, fire and rescue services and suchlike, were seen as civil concerns. In 1934–35 efforts to prepare for bombing included wide-scale ARP exercises, further research into the destructive capabilities of 500lb bombs in order to gauge the required robustness of shelters, and work to expand and centralise the fire-fighting force on a wartime scale.

In anticipation of being subjected to a bombing campaign immediately on the outbreak of war, work started on the requisite infrastructure for the fire-fighting services in 1938. Emergency water supplies were organised, tapping into bodies of water such as the lakes and ponds in London's parks, and establishing underground tanks and improved pipelines and hydrants. Auxiliary fire fighters were recruited and trained, and equipment was sourced and stockpiled. Gas masks for civilian use were manufactured from 1936. From late 1938 the construction of air-raid shelters began, but despite pressure on the government to utilise the stations and tunnels of London's Underground railway, these were confined to the surface. Also in late 1938, plans were laid to evacuate large numbers of London's population to places deemed to be of greater safety. After Munich, all Civil Service departments were instructed to prepare for war by recruiting and training First Aid and ARP personnel drawn from within their own organisations. On 8–9 July 1939 practice alerts were carried out in fifteen counties, of which Surrey was one. This involved testing the blackout and sirens, and ensuring that volunteers and professionals turned out and understood their tasks. Civil Defence Control centres such as that under Caterham's Soper Hall were responsible both for running the exercises and testing their own efficiency under the eyes of Home Office observers.

In the expectation that enemy bombers would see London Docks as an enticing target, an Emergency Committee, consisting of representatives of the Admiralty, the Ministry of Transport and the Port of London Authority, was set up, co-ordinated by the Royal Navy's Flag Officer in Charge from an office in the PLA building on Tower Hill. Anticipating the later Home Guard-sponsored small-boat patrol, a civilian River Emergency Service was set up in 1938 using a fleet of privately owned motorboats, which included the writer A.P. Herbert's *Water Gypsy*. Attached to regular and territorial infantry units were Home Defence companies, composed of generally over-age ex-soldiers, and formed to provide guards for vulnerable points, duties that were performed by the VTC in the previous war, and by the Home Guard in the next.

eight

London in the Second World War

In order to understand the context within which both the anti-invasion and air defences of London operated, we must take a brief look at the three main elements of the bigger picture: the coast defences of the Thames Estuary, the capital's land defences, and the updated version of the London Air Defence Area (LADA), in the broader context of Air Defence Great Britain (ADGB).

The Thames Defences

By the beginning of the Second World War, the process of shifting coast defence batteries as far out as possible, which had been begun in 1905, had continued, so that Shoeburyness, and Fletcher Battery on the Isle of Sheppey, formed the outer limits of the fixed defences. While large targets could be engaged long before they were able to approach close enough to cause damage in the Thames Estuary, small, fast craft were always going to pose a threat, especially at night, as they could do a great deal of damage among massed shipping in confined spaces with mines, torpedoes or gunfire. As in the previous conflict, QF guns with CASLs, booms, minefields, and patrol vessels were all employed to counter this threat. A new 6in gun battery was built at Canvey to cover the boom, from which anti-submarine nets were suspended, with searchlights mounted on the boom itself. OPs on the roof of Coalhouse Fort reported to a defensible blockhouse on the riverbank from which the minefields were controlled. An emergency battery of two 5.5in guns was built on the fort's roof, above the Victorian casemates. Cliffe Fort was one of several bases for the Thames Auxiliary Naval Force, which patrolled the river in launches, looking out for and marking parachute mines. Later, the seven Maunsell forts of two different designs that were bedded way out in the waters of the estuary, operated as forward anti-aircraft batteries, also having a role against surface raiders, and radar extended the cover far out from the river mouth. Radar also operated close in, and a hexagonal brick tower still stands on the foreshore at East Tilbury.

London's Land Defences

Owing to the developments in land warfare that had taken place between the wars, London's land defences during the Second World War were much more extensive and more complex than previous systems. From a national perspective, they were part of a complex defence system with many components. The Coastal Crust, consisting of batteries of heavy guns, minefields, beach obstacles, concrete defence positions with light guns and automatic weapons, fieldworks and mobile light artillery, was designed to slow down the process of landing enemy troops and supplies until the Royal Navy's capital ships could travel south from their Scottish bases to disrupt seaborne reinforcements. Further inland was the GHQ Line, a continuous AT obstacle reinforced by concrete emplacements for AT guns and automatic weapons and field artillery, which ran from the Bristol Channel eastwards to Reading, curving around to the south of Aldershot and London itself to reach the Medway at Hoo. Crossing the Thames at Canvey Island, it ran northwards past Chelmsford and Cambridge and on up the east of the country. The few existing armoured and mechanised units were located some distance behind this line, their tanks on flatbed railcars, awaiting appropriate deployment. Other intermediate defence lines were inserted behind and between these two main barriers. The Coastal Crust defences were continuous around the south and east coasts of Britain, extending into the Thames and Medway estuaries, linking with the Medway towns' designated defended area, and the all-round defences of London. All this was constructed during the latter half of 1940, when there was little alternative to linear, static defences, and an invasion was perceived as both inevitable and imminent. By spring 1941 however, with the defeat of the Luftwaffe, and the German invasion of Russia, the picture had changed, and the new defence policy switched to a system of defended points rather than lines, with many of the defences further north consisting only of planned demolitions of bridges to create AT obstacles, and nodal points turned into AT islands with all-round defences, but by autumn 1940 London had already become one enormous AT island.

The Air Defence of London

The most important lesson of the First World War related to the successful integration of all the elements of an air defence system: the fighters to intercept and hopefully despatch incoming bombers, the AA guns, the searchlights and the barrage balloons, all with their own operating space, and controlled centrally, acting on information supplied by the radar network and observers. Central Control was Bentley Priory in Stanmore, north London, the HQ of Fighter Command, AA Command occupying 'Glenthorn', a house in the grounds, and the (Royal) Observer Corps. The IAZ of AA guns consisted of three groups of HAA batteries. The eastern area (ZE) stretched from Cheshunt and Chingford to Hackney Marshes, and consisted of twenty-two, mainly four-gun, batteries. In the south (ZS) twenty-seven similar batteries extended from Wimbledon to Dartford. From Enfield and Mill Hill down to Wormwood Scrubs and Gunnersbury were the fourteen batteries of ZW. These batteries were all controlled from the London AAOR on Brompton Road. To the east of London, the Thames and Medway GDA included fifty HAA batteries, half of them north of the Thames. Other clusters of batteries contributing to the defence of the London area included twelve centred on Slough, controlled from the TA drill hall and newly built in 1939 on the Uxbridge Road, protecting Windsor, the Iver area with its ground defences and Admiralty laboratory, the factories on the Great West Road, and RAF Uxbridge and Northolt. Additionally, there were four batteries at Brooklands aircraft factory, and others protecting the fighter airfields at Biggin Hill, Redhill, Kenley, Northolt, Hornchurch and North Weald.

The guns were thus one element in a system that deployed three belts of searchlights, put 1000 barrage balloons into the sky and processed information from the increasingly effective radar sites, largely replacing the ineffective sound location apparatus, and the spotters of the ROC, organised in area groups across the country. The II Group and Fighter Command Operations Rooms, located at RAF Uxbridge and Bentley Priory respectively, ensured that all this data actually informed the activity of the fighter squadrons tasked with stopping the bombers.

The Defences of London in 1940

The London defences would ultimately comprise three concentric lines of fixed fortifications, but this system was only developed over a period of twelve months. The immediate fear after Dunkirk was that an airborne invasion, using London's airfields as landing grounds for transport aircraft, and green spaces for glider-borne troops or parachutists, would be mounted before proper measures could be taken to defend the capital. Priorities therefore centred around the notion of denying landing grounds to the enemy, and erecting obstacles to his advance in the event of successful landings. The first aim was achieved by covering every open space with obstructions: permanent ones such as scaffolding poles and wires, heaps of rubble and rubble-filled oil drums, stakes, felled trees, or trenches; and temporary ones such as old vehicles filled with heavy material. These measures were applied to any space 500yds long by 100yds wide, this being the size of field in which, it was calculated, the German Junkers transport aircraft could operate. Even St James's Park was obstructed. Arterial roads with straight stretches 500yds long by 30yds wide were obstructed with either overhead hoops, as on the Caterham bypass, or vertical pillars along the verges. Other roads obstructed in such ways included Western Avenue, westwards from Greenford, and the bypass roads around Sidcup and Kingston. To save on scarce materials, it was decided that around 10 per cent of obstructions could be dummy ones: timber posts, for instance, could stand in for steel rails. Heathland was often seeded with dummy bushes made of timber and canvas in order to dissuade gliders from attempting a landing. Operational airfields were obstructed in ways that imposed only minimal restrictions on their legitimate users. Landmarks were disguised; the northern exit of one of the railway tunnels at Crystal Palace was covered over using a naval anti-submarine net. Guns were mounted to command the Thames, and reservoirs were guarded. Stretches of water were seen as vulnerable to landings by seaplanes, and a total of thirty-nine reservoirs received obstructions of some kind in the end, including the King George VI at Staines, those at Barnes and Ruislip and the Welsh Harp at Neasden. It was even proposed that large ponds, such as Pen Ponds in Richmond, should be drained, until it was realised that this would deprive the fire fighters of water in the event of bombing raids. The second aim sought to ensure that any landings in the east would be blocked by defences ranged along the River Lea, from the Thames to the King George reservoir at Chingford. On the west, from Mill Hill, these interim defences followed the River Brent and the Grand Junction Canal down to the Thames at Hammersmith, then turned west as far as Kingston Bridge. On the south, the Thames itself, from Hammersmith Bridge to the Blackwall Tunnel, was the only real barrier, so all its bridges were defended. Experience in France had highlighted the problems that demolitions and permanent roadblocks could cause for the defenders' mobility, so an element of caution came into play. Protocols relating to demolitions, the destruction of munitions, the closure of road and rail blocks, the immobilisation of vehicles, and the jamming of railway points were all worked out to define the criteria to be met before irreversible decisions might be taken by panicked junior officers on the spot.

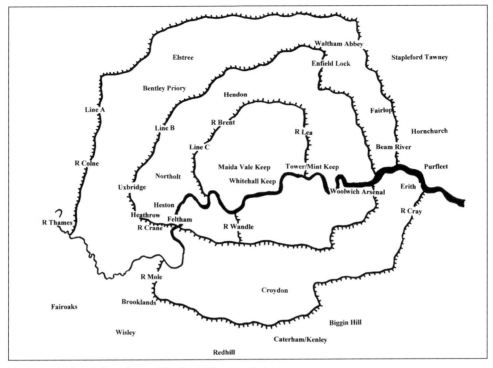

Figure 5 London defence lines with selected key installations

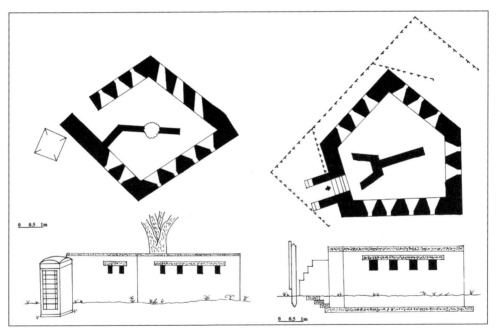

Figure 6 Defence works in Palmers Green, Southgate. These two defence-works, along with others, were designed in the office of the Borough Engineer at Southgate Town Hal in July 1940, before a real defensive strategy for London had been planned. That on the left, a section-post for twelve riflemen, stood on an island at the junction of Hedge Lane and Green Lanes. It was open-topped and built around a tree. That of the right, another section-post for twelve rifles, was a more conventional pillbox with a concrete roof and built on a concrete raft. It was disguised by advertising hoardings which could be dropped flat 'in an emergency'. Owing to their irregular form, neither could benefit from pre-fabricated parts or programmed construction. *With grateful thanks to Jeff Dorman for the original plans*

As well as these improvised outer defences, there was a concentration of resources to secure the heart of government. The area around Whitehall and the Palace of Westminster was ringed by sandbagged Bren posts, while windows in the tall ministry buildings that might enjoy commanding views were earmarked for occupation by their potential last-ditch defenders. Early additions to the defences were four lines of obstructions centred on Barnet, Perivale, between Brentford and Egham, and Foots Cray and Dartford. The main element of these positions was the roadblock, made of knife rests, moveable obstacles, and protected by fieldworks. Dumps of the necessary materials for the construction of these roadblocks were established by the Royal Engineers. There were even initiatives where local councils undertook the construction of often improvised defence works. All the defences we have looked at were manned by Household troops, the depots and training cadres of London regiments, and, as they came on stream, the LDV/Home Guard. The three main Infantry Training Centres – Hounslow for the Royal Fusiliers, Mill Hill for the Middlesex Regiment, and Kingston for the East Surreys – all had roles in providing garrison troops, backing up locally deployed battalions of their parent regiments. The East Surreys guarded Kingston, Richmond, Kew and Barnes bridges; the 13 Bn Royal Fusiliers looked after the Rotherhithe Tunnel; and the 2/8 Bn Middlesex Regiment was responsible for the Blackwall Tunnel and London Docks, with HQ at the Commercial Road Gate of the West India Docks. Battersea and Blackfriars bridges were overseen by 12 Bn the Queen's. Sometimes an air of desperation is discernible in directives put out by the different HQs. In one communication from Horse Guards in the summer of 1940, outlining the chain of command and defining local commanders' responsibilities, attention is drawn to the troops available at AA gun and searchlight sites, and to the use of AA weapons in an AT role, even without armour-piercing shells. In emergencies, local commanders could divert troops from one task to another. It is further pointed out that, although troops on AA sites would have rifles, and possibly Lewis guns, their transport provision was often limited to bicycles. Once this emergency network was in place, then work could begin on a stronger, more extensive and more coherent system to protect the capital, comprising three concentric lines of permanent armour-resistant works.

Line A: the Outer London Defences

Line A roughly corresponded to the course ultimately followed by the London Orbital motorway (M25) and was 120 miles (192km) long, much of it out in the countryside, skirting the built-up areas. Starting in the east, Line A left the Thames via the Beam River, which then formed the eastern boundary of the Ford works at Dagenham (built in 1929–31 and the biggest plant in Europe, employing 40,000 workers). At Dagenham East station (TQ504851) a long line of AT blocks runs alongside the railway continuing through to the Pumping Station at Dagenham Beam Bridge, with a pillbox, now partially buried, on the elbow at TQ512850. There is also a long line of AT blocks along the south side of the Chadwell Heath to Romford railway line at Crow Lane (TQ487877). The line follows the River Rom to Dog Kennel Hill, around Chigwell Row, and up Pudding Lane past Fulhams Farm and Pettitt's Hall to Rolls Park, and on toward Debden Station, crossing the River Roding some way to the north-east. These last few miles represent what is referred to in contemporary documents as the Fairlop Loop. In the cuttings, and against the eastern face of the railway embankment from Newbury Park past Barkingside and Fairlop underground stations as far as Hainault, are lines of AT blocks and

94 Dagenham East Station, AT blocks on Line A, the Outer London defences (TQ504851).

at least one FC Construction-type pillbox (TQ450909). It would appear likely that this original line hit the River Roding and then followed its course past Debden station. The extra 5000yds enabled Fairlop airfield, a fighter station, and the higher ground to the north-east that overlooked it, to be brought within the defences. Minefields are recorded at Hainault Station, Fairlop and Barkingside. From north-east of Debden station, a stream probably marks the course of Line A as far as Centenary Walk in Epping Forest. Near Jack's Hill the AT ditch is still visible as it heads off past Ripley Grange, to cross the Epping road (TL432001 and 431006) south of Amresbury Banks, and then follows the stream east of Copped Hall. This next part of the line is marked by large, octagonal Type FWD3/27 pillboxes, spaced every half-mile or so, and crossing points on the ditch marked by AT blocks and hedgehogs of AT rails set in concrete. Line A curves around through farmland, past Nazeing Gate to Bumbles Green and then on to Nazeing Marsh and the River Lea at Kings Weir (TL373053). Between Copped Hall and Kings Weir, there survive around a dozen of these octagonal pillboxes. The rail crossing, here representing the county boundary, is defended

95 Nazeing, AT block and AT rails, known as 'hairpins', on Line A (TL382053)

by a heightened pillbox (TL368052) and AT blocks, and it must be noted that at the next crossing north at Broxbourne (TL373070), there are loopholes in the parapet of the B194 bridge over
the railway and river. West of the River Lea, the line follows the New River towards Cheshunt
Park, north of Cuffley, along the Ridgeway, down to Boltons Park and across the golf course to
the railway north of Potters Bar where there are AT blocks on the embankment each side of the
tracks (TL249024). In the farmyard at Tanfield Stud (TL324050) there is a long, low bunker with

96 Batchworth, Type DFW3/27 octagonal pillbox on Line A (TQ076940). It had an open central
platform for mounting an LAA light machine gun.

97 Batchworth, Type DFW3/27 octagonal pillbox showing the chamfered roof and three of the eight
loopholes

machine-gun loops dominating the lower ground to the north. This section of line contains a mixture of Type FWD3/27 and FWD3/24 pillboxes. There are large numbers of AT blocks, particularly where the road runs under the railway east of Newgate Street (TL307046), and in the old Cuffley Scout Camp, where there are two sets of roadblocks with sockets for horizontal lengths of RSJ to be inserted. The line then runs on to South Mimms and Shenley, following streams until it joins the River Colne south of London Colney. Again, there is a mix of pillbox types with assorted AT obstacles down to the A41 at Watford. A rectangular pillbox is sited under a railway viaduct at Oxhey (TQ119995), and a half-hexagonal pillbox built onto the end of a factory building. From Watford, Line A continues along the River Colne past Merchant Taylors' School where a rectangular pillbox was built onto a porch overlooking the river. The school building is the largest structure in Europe to be built of 2" bricks, and it is noteworthy that even in the rush of the invasion crisis, it was felt worthwhile to build the pillbox out of these rare bricks. There are further pillboxes in Batchworth. The line runs on past Uxbridge, where two bridges over the Grand Union Canal have pillboxes built into their abutments, down to Iver, where a cluster of pillboxes guards a particularly vulnerable point where the canal crosses the River Colne on an aqueduct (TQ045806), and the main-line railway crosses the defences. Line A followed the Colne Brook to the Thames at Egham, turning east via Staines, Chertsey Mead and Shepperton toward Sunbury where it crossed the river.

South of the Thames, Line A followed the River Mole down to West End Common, Esher, before turning east to Chessington Zoo and heading for Epsom. At the point where the railway crosses the Mole (TQ132658) a solitary AT block remains. Near Kingston Bridge, not technically on the line itself but nevertheless a key point in the defences, pillboxes were built into shops, one a greengrocer's on the corner of Eden Street and Market Place, and another nearby. From Epsom station, the line ran south from the college to Epsom Downs station, along the railway and defended by AT blocks and pillboxes, some of which survive, eventually crossing Longdown Lane (TQ225596) through an existing gap in the houses, before turning north-

98 Uxbridge, pillbox built into a bridge abutment on the Grand Union Canal (TQ050838), here forming part of Line A.

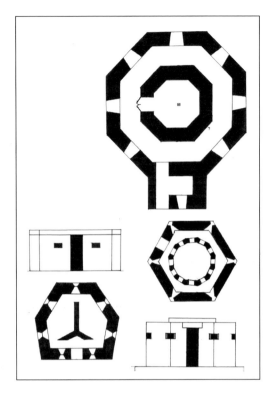

east to zig-zag its way to Drift Bridge (TQ231601). Each turn was defended by a pillbox, and, along the foot of the railway embankment either side of Drift Bridge, the AT ditch was reinforced by lines of AT blocks. Around the bridge, some of these AT blocks, two octagonal pillboxes, and a Type DFW3/24 pillbox all survive, if hidden. It is known that there was at least one fortified house in the area. A house at 55 Winkworth Road, the A2022, had its ground floor reinforced to carry a concrete, loop-holed wall in the front bedroom. The windows, complete with curtains, were left in place as camouflage. Near Banstead (at TQ249604, 248598 & 275583 among others) were some of the biggest block-houses so far found in Britain, suggested as built to house the old 3.7in howitzer, eight of which were known to have been made available to troops in this area. Line A then crossed the Brighton road and the railway at Coulsdon with a rail block (TQ303601) following the railway through Purley, then heading off via Sanderstead to Combe House (TQ347644), and then more or less due east to West Wickham station via Shirley golf course, one of whose tees is said to stand on a buried AT blockhouse. This southern section of Line A was manned by 20th Guards Infantry Brigade, equipped with ex-naval 3- and 12-pounder lorry-mounted QF guns to defend the

principal roadblocks on the arterial roads into London, and laying AT minefields. A correspondent to the Defence of Britain Project described building a pillbox on the upper floor of a pet shop on Portland Road, overlooking Goathouse railway bridge in South Norwood (approx TQ341684), but hidden behind a hoarding with hinged sections. The road outside had sockets made of lengths of drainpipe into which bent rails could be slotted to block the road, and there were more of these sealing off the railway embankment. A little way to the north, on Croydon Road, this procedure was repeated where the road was narrowed by AT blocks. This position would appear to occupy an intermediate point between Line A and Line B. In addition, the railway embankment between Coulsdon and East

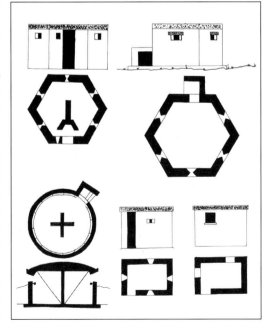

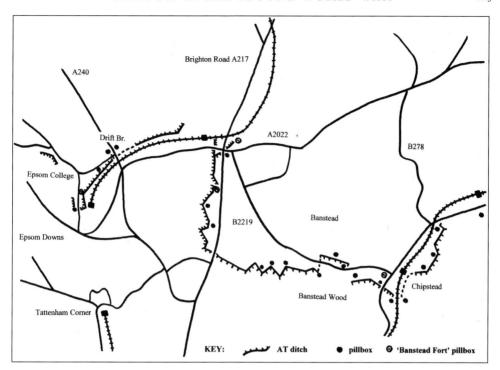

KEY: 〜〜〜 **AT ditch**   ● **pillbox**   ⊖ **'Banstead Fort' pillbox**

Opposite Above: Figure 7 Pillbox types.
[Top] Type FWD3/27 octagonal pillbox
for Bren lmgs and rifles.
[Bottom left] A standard FWD3/24
splinter-proof pillbox for five lmgs.
[Bottom right] A unique pillbox at
Brooklands aircraft factory.

Opposite Below: Figure 8 Pillboxes and
guard posts.
[Top left] A standard Type 22 hexagonal
pillbox.
[Top right] Another hexagonal pillbox,
slightly larger than the Type 22. This
example is one of two defending the
HAA site at Slade Green.
[Bottom left] FC Construction, or
Mushroom pillbox. Also known as the
Oakington or Fairlop pillbox.
[Bottom right] Police posts provided at
ordnance factories, depots and dumps.

Above: Figure 9 The defences of Drift
Bridge and Banstead. *Compiled from
information provided by Mike Shackel and
William Foot*

Right: Figure 10 Banstead Fort. This
is the largest pillbox built on inland
defence lines, with perhaps half-a-dozen
being built around the Banstead area.

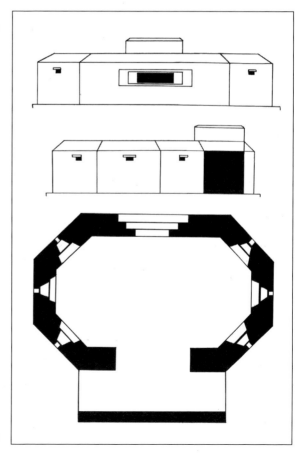

Croydon was protected by continuous lines of AT blocks along the ends of all the gardens backing on to the railway line. The line ran across Bromley Common, over the railway south of Petts Wood station to St Mary Cray, following the River Cray to its confluence with the Darenth (TQ536760). This short, final stretch brought Line A to the Thames at Crayford Ness, opposite the Purfleet magazines and rifle ranges. A number of pillboxes have been recorded in this area: on Crayford Marshes, along the Darenth and either side of its outfall into the Thames at TQ528751, 534774 (several), 536770, 537754, 540781 and 543779, all now demolished, but two defending the Slade Green HAA site survive at TQ530774 and 532773.

Line B: the Middle Defence Line

The middle Line B started at Barking Creek and ran north up the River Roding to the City of London Cemetery and Wanstead Park. Numbers of AT obstacles have been reported, especially at the rail crossing (TQ435848) and along the eastern edge of the cemetery. A pillbox still marks the course of the line as it crossed the A12 (TQ416884) to continue north as far as South Woodford, where it turned west to gain the River Lea. Two pillboxes have been reported in Woodford (TQ394907 and 400908) east of Highams Park, through which the line appears to have run prior to running up the Lea to the top end of King George's Reservoir, where it then turned west again. Following streams and cuts, it ran to the north of Forty Hall and Clay Hill, Chase Side, over the railway near New Barnet and then Whetstone stations, and on to Mill Hill Barracks (TQ240920). Line B then ran to Stanmore, before dropping southwards through Harrow to Sudbury, where it picked up the Grand Union Canal, following it as far as the junction with the Paddington Arm at Bulls Bridge. The line then continued south along the River Crane, joining the Thames at Eel Pie Island, in one version, or at Twickenham Bridge, in another. It either followed the Thames to Putney Bridge, where it transferred to the River Wandle before turning east through Tooting Bec, Streatham and Crystal Palace, then via the Pool River to Catford. Alternatively, from the Thames, it crossed Richmond Park, Wimbledon Common and Wimbledon Park to reach the same spot on the Wandle. There are reports of AT blocks across Roehampton golf course, so there may have been a defence line along the Beverley Brook from the Thames, across Barnes Common to Richmond Park. However it reached Catford and then ran east and north to meet the Thames at Woolwich Arsenal. There is a pillbox near an important rail junction in Beckenham (TQ367702), another at the rail crossing of the A20 (TQ413738), and a spigot mortar pedestal behind the police station at Shooters Hill (TQ430766), where AT walls have recently been excavated, these probably marking points along the line. Two more pillboxes have been reported along the railway line between Well Hall and Blackheath (at TQ405759 and 413758). Line B anchored itself on Woolwich Arsenal, a self-contained fortress with its own all-round defences, including 75mm field guns in emplacements, and pillboxes. The Arsenal Home Guard, formally 22nd Bn Kent Home Guard (RA) and numbering 1350 men at its greatest strength, managed to acquire odd weapons that had been made or tested on the premises, and were the proud owners of an 1893 Maxim 0.45in gun on a Fort mounting, the whole ensemble weighing in at 150kg. Arsenal personnel also reactivated ex-aircraft Browning machine guns for LAA use on homemade quadruple mountings. At stand down, they were overstocked to the tune of 50 Brownings and a Matilda tank that had been sent for use on the testing ranges. Pillboxes have been recorded east of Woolwich (TQ467798) and at Erith Pier (TQ517780).

Line C: the Inner Defences

This close-in defence system ran in an arc from Bow Creek (the outfall of the River Lea) in the east, to Grove Park, on the Thames between Kew Bridge and Chiswick station. Line C followed the River Lea northwards to Hackney Marshes, with AT blocks where the Central Line crosses the Lea east of Bromley-by-Bow station. Further north, a roadblock comprising four concrete blocks with sockets for horizontal steel joists, along with a covering pillbox, survives where the Sewer Outfall, now a greenway, crosses the river on the very edge of the Olympic village. At South Tottenham the line swung west to join the New River at the reservoirs south of Seven Sisters Road, following it to Alexandra Park. Here, there are what appear to be two Home Guard explosives stores (TQ299905 and 305903) and also AT blocks on the railway embankment at Alexandra Park Station (TQ302905). The Wood Green tunnel on the LNER was defended by 62nd AT Regiment. The line continued north till it met the Strawberry Vale Brook, which it then followed westwards, past the St Pancras and Islington Cemetery. As the line crossed the railway south-east of Finchley Central, a house on Rosemary Avenue, backing onto the railway cutting, has been identified as having a reinforced rear wall with a loophole inserted at first-floor level replacing a window, with AT blocks in the next-door garden. It would appear that these defences were part of Line C, and representative of many similar constructions that have neither survived nor been recorded. The line continued to follow the brook towards its confluence with the River Brent at Mutton Bridge, and thence on to the Welsh Harp Reservoir, the Brent forming the line until it cut westwards to take in the buildings around Wembley Stadium. There are reports of rooftop pillboxes on the GPO building, formerly the Hall of Trade in the Exhibition complex and more at ground level on the railway. Line C appears to have followed railway

99 Bow, a roadblock comprising four large concrete blocks slotted to receive RSJs, covered by a Type DFW3/22 pillbox (TQ373838 astride a Greenway). (Photograph: Adrian Armishaw)

100 Putney Bridge station, a pillbox of a lozenge-shaped design commonly used on Southern Region railway sites. Here the location, high up on a raised plinth at the end of the platform overlooking the river, forced it to be built in a truncated form (TQ245758).

lines from Wembley Central, past Stonebridge Park, turning southwards at Harlesden, and incorporating the London Underground's Acton depot, itself defended by numerous pillboxes and AT obstacles. Two pillboxes guarded a rail bridge at Old Oak Road (TQ213820), from whence the line continued down to the Thames at Grove Park, running along the river back to Bow Creek, with most of the bridges across the Thames defended. Beside All Saints' church on Putney Bridge was a hexagonal pillbox with stone quoins and merlons looking perfectly in place in a churchyard. In Wandsworth Bridge Road was a pillbox disguised as a builder's hut, and at Chelsea Bridge, a pillbox was made to look like a refreshment kiosk with timber panels and gabled roof. Machine guns were mounted on the roof of the power station in Fulham's Townmead Road, midway between Wandsworth and Battersea Bridges, as early as September 1939, presumably in a dual role with air defence in mind as well as enemy landings on the Thames. At the foot of Big Ben, a camouflaged pillbox commanded the exit off Westminster Bridge, with others along the Embankment towards Waterloo Bridge. A pillbox at the bottom of Kingsway was the first to be demolished in 1945. The Thames railway bridges were defended by lozenge-shaped pillboxes, with a raised, open platform either at one end or in the middle where a LAA machine gun could be mounted. There are examples of such pillboxes on Barnes Bridge, and at each end of Kew Bridge, one of which is visible from the road at its north end (TQ196776). Another, overlooking the river at Putney station, is built up on a pillar at the end of the high-level platform. The restricted site necessitated it being truncated, with only one pointed end. At the other end of the platform is a defensible signal box. Kew Bridge also has a spigot mortar emplacement. At the eastern end of the river line there is a pair of canopied structures, probably mine-spotting posts, near the locks forming the entrance to the former West India Docks and, still on the Isle of Dogs, the HAA battery approach road, now the access to the City Farm in Mudchute Park, appears to have sockets for AT rails.

London's Innermost Defences

All cities had drawn up defence plans by early 1941, and each plan provided for a last-ditch defence based on the 'keep': often a single building such as a drill hall or police station or sometimes a small city block. London had at least three such sites earmarked for the final stand, each on a scale befitting the size of the city. The first was the Tower of London, surrounded by

101 Whitehall, the Admiralty Citadel, opened just before the outbreak of war, providing a shelter for Admiralty staff, and a defence position on the corner of the Whitehall 'Keep'.

vegetable gardens in its moats, and with a rectangular pillbox on its esplanade that was incidentally not demolished until 1959. The tower functioned as a prison and a military HQ, but was also one of the final fall-back positions at the heart of a complex of defended buildings that included the Royal Mint, three schools, factories and warehouses. Many of these buildings were steel-framed and deemed fireproof. The largest of the 'keeps' had at its heart the Admiralty Citadel, purpose built in 1939 to provide both a bombproof haven for staff directing naval operations, but also a capability for defending the north-west corner of Whitehall. Its monolithic concrete construction integrates built-in weapons positions, and shelter, providing a dominating presence over Horse Guards Parade. It is linked to other strengthened government buildings such as Montague House, the then War Office, with access to some of the many tunnels beneath Whitehall. The third 'keep' was in Maida Vale where the BBC studios formed the central core of a defended block. The BBC had its own Home Guard company of nearly 200 men, which manned four guard posts that controlled access to the building through steel doors with spy holes. The studios were in a steel-framed building with a concrete roof, constructed to provide protection against bombing in order that transmissions could continue even under attack. These three 'keep' locations were designed to be held to the last against ground attack by an invading force, and were quite distinct from the numerous 'citadels', which were intended to provide shelter from air attack and are therefore considered elsewhere. In addition to the 'keeps', other locations such as the barracks of the regular army and defended airfields such as Northolt would have been expected to hold out to the last man and the last round against ground attack. A number of institutions had their own Home Guard units, such as the LCC's County Hall, next to Westminster Bridge, where enterprising members of staff converted some of their Rolls-Royce official limousines into very robust armoured vehicles, equipped with Vickers machine guns in revolving turrets. The home guardsmen of the American Embassy in Grosvenor Square were fortunate to benefit from weapons and equipment unavailable to other units. With the problems caused by refu-

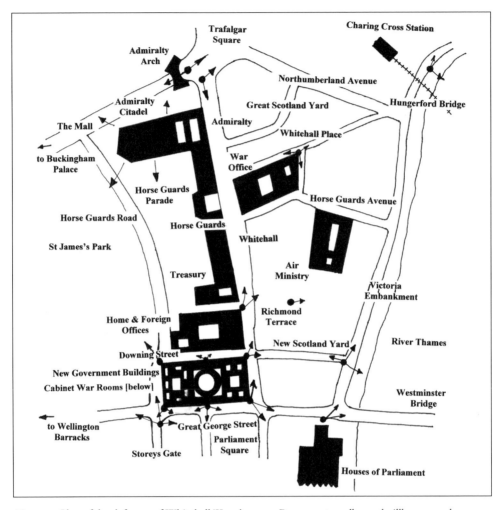

Figure 11 Plan of the defences of Whitehall 'Keep', c.1941. Permanent sandbagged pillboxes are shown with indications of their fields of fire specified in the Defence Plan, published through London District Operations Orders and Instructions, noted in Horse Guards War Diary.

gees clogging up the roads in France and Belgium in 1940 in mind, the official line was always to tell people to stay put in the event of an invasion. However by 1942 this had changed. Despite all the indications to the contrary, the government continued to warn of the possibility of invasion, but the new message from Sir Ernest Gowers, London's Commissioner, was that people should have a go, using the depth and complexity of the completed defence lines as the basis for resistance. Sir Ernest, however, failed to mention the enemy's likely response to an attack by *franc-tireurs*.

Whitehall, at whose heart, of course, was Horse Guards, where the whole plan was masterminded, was given special attention with regard to anti-invasion defences. In May 1940, what we might now call a risk assessment was carried out, as it was decided that the area around the seat of government must have contingency plans in place, not only in the event of a full-scale invasion, but also against a raid by up to 500 enemy troops with only light equipment and arriving by parachute, glider or transport aircraft. As a result, a number of pillboxes, listed in an order of 16 May 1940, were built to supplement the earlier sandbagged positions and knife-rest roadblocks and barricades were added. Small parties of troops were held in reserve to respond to the ever-present fear of raids: a Royal Marine guard of twenty in the Admiralty, a platoon of Grenadier Guards on fifteen minutes' notice in Wellington Barracks, and the King's Guard at Buckingham Palace. The permanent guard of Whitehall, with a strength of three officers and 158 guardsmen of the Grenadiers, stationed in Horse Guards, were to hold out until reinforced by the remaining 750 Grenadiers from Wellington Barracks, the 200 Household Cavalry at Knightsbridge Barracks and the local Home Guard units, commanded from 179 Queens Gate initially, and later, as Zone B, from 107 Sloane Street. These essentially makeshift arrangements were constantly under review. In August 1941, for example, it was decided to site a new pillbox in Trafalgar Square, because the plinth, built facing down Whitehall to protect the bronze equestrian statue of King Charles I, had obstructed the field of fire of the existing pillbox under Admiralty Arch, and the sandbagged post at the corner of Whitehall had collapsed. Finally, by March 1942 a Fortress HQ had been set up in Room 70A of the basement of the New Government Offices. Now known as the Treasury, these had been built between 1899 and 1915, occupying a site between Great George Street and King Charles Street with, from 1908, a bridge linking them to the Foreign Office. Also in the basement, reinforced in 1938, were the Cabinet War Rooms. Contemporary plans of the ground floor show pillboxes at each corner manned by either guards or RAF personnel, also manning daytime sentry posts at the entrances. Also part of the defensive cover, outside the main entrance from Horse Guards Road, was Rance's Guard, consisting of twelve guardsmen under George Rance, the resident Office of Works administrator co-ordinating use of the Cabinet War Rooms. Individual government departments were responsible for the defence of the different parts of the building that they occupied. The Air Ministry's new building, shared with the Board of Trade, had only been started in 1939 behind the old Banqueting Hall, and was not finally completed until 1959. It became the Ministry of Defence in 1964.

The Defences of the Thames

The river between Tilbury and the Port of London was the country's lifeline and it was imperative that aircraft or surface craft were prevented from laying mines in this narrow and congested shipping lane. At Purfleet the machine-gun training section of the Middlesex Regiment manned nine section posts against mine-laying aircraft. Other such posts were manned by the 7th (Home Defence) Bn Essex Regt on the north bank, and the 16th, 17th and 18th Bns Kent Home Guard on the south. Many of the industrial and commercial concerns lining the banks of the Thames such as the Tunnel Portland Cement Works, and many of the numerous wharves and jetties, were ordered to make available the guns of any ships loading or unloading. On the south bank of the Thames, east of Woolwich, are two defensible mine-watching posts. Between Woolwich and Stone Point, Dartford, there were at least twenty light automatics mounted on the bank or on moored barges, plus four pairs of Lewis guns on AA mountings. The river itself was patrolled by ten motorboats of the Thames Auxiliary Patrol (which had absorbed the River Emergency Service), with its HQ, HMS *Tower*, nominally the accommodation barges *Hilda* and *Yeoman*, moored at Tower Pier. A further fourteen boats, with a depot ship, HMS *Worcester*, mounting a 12-pounder and several AA machine guns, and a repair craft, the *Melissa*, were based at Greenhithe, with five more boats at Cliffe and six at Dagenham. At Tilbury, there were nine patrol boats, plus craft for operating the balloon barrage and minesweeping. These patrols were

102 Woolwich Reach, a defensible mine-watching/mg post with an open compartment at the back possibly for a LAA machine gun (TQ454810).

operated as far as Southend, from where more substantial craft, converted drifters of the Naval Control Service, took over. A fleet of small craft, tugs, drifters, and motorboats carrying out minesweeping and bomb-disposal duties, was based on Gravesend. The tugs carried 6-pounder Hotchkiss guns, while most of the other craft were armed with machine guns. There were also a number of merchant ships moored in the river, forty at any one time according to the defence plan, between Woolwich and Dartford alone, armed with a mixture of guns, supplementing the AA defences and combating mine-laying aircraft or motorboats. Activity also extended upstream from the Pool of London. The stretch from London Bridge as far as Teddington Lock was patrolled by 34 County of London Bn, and above Teddington by 31 Middlesex Bn Home Guard. There were standing patrols along the towpath to guard locks and weirs, and a water-borne Home Guard unit in motor launches, commanded by a retired rear-admiral, patrolled along the river.

A Defensive Strategy Develops

These London defence lines were part of a fully integrated system of anti-invasion defences, designed to delay an invasion force. The general consensus of modern opinion seems to accept that a German invasion would have been able to establish bridgeheads on the coast and maybe even further inland through the use of airborne forces, but the problems of resupply and reinforcement would ultimately have defeated them. Initially, General Ironside's strategy was to put as many obstacles in place as possible, in order to restrict the use of those *Blitzkrieg* tactics employed in continental Europe. However, as resources became available, attempts were made to inject some element of mobility into the defences. As early as 15 May 1940, the CO of the 8th Bn Royal Tank Regiment, based in Wanstead, was under orders to carry out a sequence of reconnaissance patrols along the roads eastwards to Romford, Barking and Dagenham; through the Blackwall Tunnel and out to the airfields of Biggin Hill, Croydon and Kenley; and around the North Circular road, to the airfields of Hendon, Northolt and Heston. The purpose of these patrols was to ensure that any enemy landings by troop-carrier aircraft would be summarily dealt with. There were other mobile elements in development. Fleets of buses were assembled to rush troops to hot spots. The Irish Guards at Wellington Barracks had seventeen buses, the 590 men of the 2 Bn Queen's Westminsters at Old Hall, Paines Lane, Pinner, were provided with nineteen, and the 330 men of the 2 Bn London Scottish had a further twenty at Monkseaton, Northgate, Northwood. In support of these mechanised infantry was a rudimentary mobile AT battery formed by the Royal Navy with two 12-pounder guns, and two 3-pounders, probably out of stores at Woolwich Arsenal, and based at the, hopefully evacuated, children's home in Norwood. Alanbrooke took over responsibility in August 1940, introducing more fluid defence systems, establishing a more effective mobile strike force than the one he inherited while retaining most of the earlier components. His London District Field Force comprised three infantry brigades: 20th, 24th and 30th Guards Brigades with associated artillery and engineers. In total there were eight guards battalions plus one each from the Royal Warwickshire Regiment and the Royal Norfolks. Additionally, the Household Cavalry contributed two motorised companies. This force was under twelve hours' notice to move, and would occupy the outer London anti-tank defences, Line A. As new units arrived, amendments to Operation Instructions noted their deployment, hence 456 Battery RA with its eight 3.7in howitzers to the Banstead area. A pool of transport was assembled, adding some forty-two 38-seater buses contributed by the London Passenger Transport Board to the lorries of 920 Coy RASC. Private companies also did their bit, as can be seen by the promise of the Metropolitan Transport Supply Company of Bow to provide twenty to thirty lorries with full fuel tanks at three-quarters of an hour's notice. The RN mobile AT battery, now designated C1, had moved to the drill hall at Wallington with two further batteries – C5 at 42 Foxgrove Road, Beckenham, and 120 Field Bty RA – each of these units armed with four ex-naval 4in guns. To support these units in the field, and the Home Guard in rural areas, ordnance stores were established at local distribution depots such as the Highbury Corner Motor Co. at 114 Canonbury Road, N1. Fuel was made available at emergency depots such as Farnborough Garage on Farnborough Hill and Whitehouse Garage at Keston Park. The mobile columns were equipped with SYKO Cipher (*sic*) machines (codeword 'Beetle') and carrier pigeons. There were facilities for ammunition replenishment from the magazines in Hyde Park, or from its two sub-depots in the racing stables at Alexandra Palace, and in Dulwich.

Other Defences Outside the London Lines

From no point of landing on the south or east coasts would an invading force have had fewer than five defence lines to negotiate, and virtually every important road, rail and waterway junction had all-round defences provided, particularly just outside the outer defences of London. The obvious nodal points such as Dorking and Reigate were defended in conjunction with the GHQ Line, but smaller places, well inside the GHQ Line, also received defences. Limpsfield, for instance, was defended by concentric lines of barbed wire and roadblocks, and was supported by a half-dozen or so spigot mortars with their magazines.

Major road and rail routes, important waterways, strategic bridges and other vital crossing points were generally incorporated into the defensive master plan. However this still left dozens

103   Roehampton Lane, a loop-holed wall guarding the approach to the Thames bridges (TQ221752). (Photograph: Adrian Armishaw)

of other minor road junctions and bridges, which, probably at a local level, were deemed worthy of defences. In-between the London Lines A and B, numbers of nodal points were defended. The roundabout on the A3 at Tolworth was prepared as a roadblock, the level crossing at New Malden station was protected by a camouflaged pillbox, and there were road and rail blocks at Norwood Junction. The simplest of all defences was the loop-holed wall, an example of which can be seen in Roehampton Lane (TQ221752) covering the southern approach to road and rail bridges over the Thames.

The Defence of Vulnerable Points

Invasion was regarded as a certainty well into 1941, so within the system of linear fortifications there were many potential targets in need of local protection. These installations, generally referred to as Vulnerable Points (VPs) included airfields, munitions factories and depots, communications centres, and HQs. Where these coincided with the wider defences, as did Woolwich Arsenal, RAF Northolt, or Crayford ammunition depot in the London lines, for instance, then they would be integrated into them. Where they were isolated, they would receive their own local defences.

Airfield Defences

The London Area HQ at Horse Guards recorded in its war diary unconfirmed reports of paratroop landings in London on 20 May 1940. Throughout the Second World War a belief in the strong possibility of airborne landings was maintained in official thinking until after the Battle of the Bulge near the end of the war in Europe. Specifically, there was a fear that airfields, of which there were over 700 in Britain by 1944 with three dozen in greater London, would provide convenient landing grounds for enemy airborne forces that had previously been successful in Belgium, Holland, Norway and Crete. Those responsible for the defence of the UK were not to know that the level of casualties sustained in 1941 by the German parachutists in Crete was so unacceptable to Hitler that he forbade any repeat of such an operation. The defence of airfields was, therefore, seen as a priority, but scarce resources meant that not all could be provided with defences to the same level. The task of deciding relative priorities was given to Major-General Taylor, Inspector General of Fortifications at the War Office, who recommended a system based on location rather than function. Those airfields near ports or other especially vulnerable installations that might figure in enemy invasion plans, would receive the highest level of defences. Strangely, while one might expect to see all of London's airfields deemed at risk by virtue of their collective proximity to the very bull's-eye of an invasion target, only Biggin Hill, Hornchurch and Fairlop qualified as Class I airfields to be defended by twenty-four to thirty-two pillboxes, a trio of Pickett-Hamilton Forts, and a garrison of 274 regular troops. Taylor directed that some pillboxes should face outwards to counter enemy attacks from outside the perimeter, and others should face inwards to oppose enemy landings on the flying field. Although all other airfields were classed as of lower priority, North Weald, Kenley and Stapleford Tawney were subsequently brought into the Pickett-Hamilton programme but, as late as February 1941, they were still without dates for scheduled installation, and Fairlop, included in the initial top-priority list but still under construction, appears to have been omitted altogether.

There were a number of complementary elements to airfield defence, the HAA and LAA guns often being supplemented by barrage balloons and parachute-and-cable devices. The hardened defences on the ground were usually pillboxes, but invariably supported by fieldworks: trenches, weapons pits, mines and barbed wire. Given that airfields covered large areas of land, there was a need for a mobile element, made up of conventional armoured vehicles where available, but more commonly made up of improvised ones; the Armadillo, for example, was a flat-bed truck 'armoured' by stacking wooden boxes full of pebbles around the edge, thus contriving a minimally protected cabin for a Lewis gun crew but still lacking the overhead protection crucial against aerial attack. The defence force of an airfield usually included regular, but probably only recently enlisted and relatively untrained, troops and also details of RAF ground personnel, seldom adequately trained. In September 1939, Kenley was defended by troops of the 12th Bn Royal Fusiliers, and of the Honourable Artillery Company. Control of such forces ideally rested with an officer of the regular army but very often was given to an inexperienced and supernumerary RAF officer. The formation of the RAF regiment in 1941 with the defence of airfields as one of its primary tasks, at least brought some professionalism to the situation, but that was after the immediate crisis of autumn 1940 had passed. A permanent garrison at the height of the invasion scare might be quite substantial. The airfield at Northolt was defended by a garrison of six officers and 276 men of the Coldstream Guards, and five RAF defence officers with 253 other ranks. The Coldstream Guards manned three Bedford trucks, one Armadillo, and a Peerless car, while RAF personnel manned two further Armadilloes. Heston, Hanworth and Heathrow were defended by men of the 10th Bn Middlesex Regiment, supported by Home Guardsmen in Beaverettes, the other most commonly improvised armoured vehicle. Initiated specifically for the defence of airfields by Lord Beaverbrook, Minister for Aircraft Production at the time, they were based on the chassis of the Standard 14hp. The body was of 8mm mild steel, backed by 75mm of oak planks. Armament was usually a Bren and/or a Boys AT rifle. Hornchurch was protected by two companies of the 70th Bn Essex Regiment, AA gunners with 4.5in and Bofors guns, four Armadilloes, and RAF ground crew manning LAA machine guns. The 700 men of the 10th Bn Essex Regiment lay in reserve at Hacton House, a grand Palladian house on the eastern edge of the airfield.

The defence of an airfield was to be directed from the Battle Headquarters (BHQ). In the early days, this was an extemporised or adapted structure. At Hornchurch (TQ533840) what appears to be a semi-sunken hexagonal pillbox, with an underground entry tunnel, was most

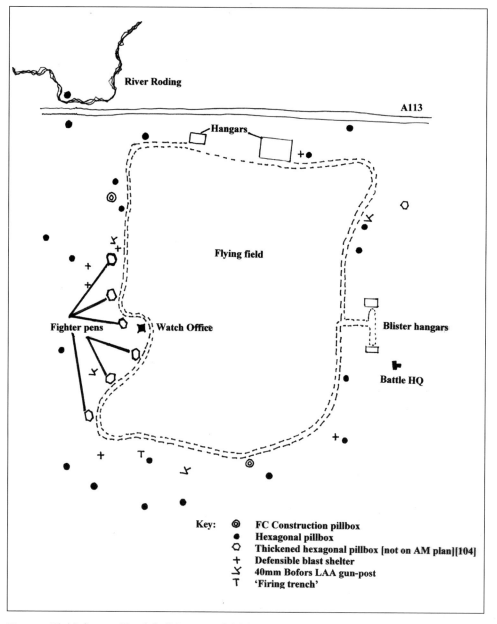

Figure 12 The defences of Stapleford Tawney airfield, from the 1945 Air Ministry plan.

probably a prototype BHQ. It has a raised hexagonal chamber with all-round observation, and an armoured slit in each face. At Redhill (TQ303482), a hexagonal cupola is located over an underground chamber, in a complex of structures that includes a separate shelter. In August 1941 a standard design for a BHQ was issued by the Air Ministry (11008/41). This was a large underground chamber with telephone exchange (PBX) and messengers' room, over which was mounted a square cupola with a horizontal, 360° observation slit. There were two entrances: one was a trapdoor with vertical ladder next to the cupola, and the other a sunken flight of steps leading into the messengers' room at the opposite end. One of this type was built at Stapleford Tawney but at Hendon the garrison commander had to make do with an improvised structure perched on top of the station HQ.

Pillboxes, built to defend airfields, were of a number of different styles. The early ones at Stapleford Tawney (TQ491975), North Weald (TL494046 & 493051) and Hornchurch (TQ535840, 536843 and 536848) were standard, hexagonal, bullet-proof Type FWD3/22, constructed of poured concrete with timber shuttering, and were very different to the weak brick pillboxes put up at Redhill (TQ296484 and 296482) and Biggin Hill (TQ415619). A more substantial type of pillbox commonly found on airfields is shellproof and hexagonal, with a sunken entry, allowing six loopholes for light machine guns on Turnbull mounts. Examples can be seen at North Weald (TL489036, 492500 & 495041). Alec Beanse has pointed out that some of the North Weald examples received additional outer skins at some time, apparently conforming to the Air Ministry instruction that new builds should have thicker walls, and fewer loopholes. An example at Stapleford Tawney (TQ499974) exhibits these features, as does another at Uxbridge, guarding the underground ops room

In 1941, another innovation from the Air Ministry was the FC Construction pillbox (9882/41), variously referred to in official documents as the Oakington, the Fairlop, or the Mushroom pillbox, this latter epithet probably being the most useful as it best describes its

104 Stapleford Tawney airfield, a hexagonal pillbox built with thickened walls and, as can be seen, a reduced number of loopholes (TQ499974).

105 North Weald Airfield, an FC Construction cantilevered roof pillbox at TL486037.

appearance. It had a cantilevered domed roof over a circular, concrete-lined pit, leaving an all-round, horizontal firing embrasure, served by two lmgs clamped to a continuous tubular mounting, capable of being traversed around the circumference. There are examples at North Weald (TL487037 and 495045) and Fairlop (TQ450910). Whereas the accent had previously been on perimeter defence based on a linear model, it now switched to point defence, involving the construction of strongpoints capable of all-round defence. This switch in tactics can be observed at Hornchurch, where by autumn 1941 the defences had been reorganised with fifteen discrete but interdependent defence sectors ringing the flying field. Seven were manned by the army, six by RAF ground defence units, one by the Home Guard, and one by the HAA battery, and the pillboxes seem to have been relegated on the plan as 'dummies'. In June 1941 a number of armoured units received new Cruiser tanks, permitting the release of eighty-seven light tanks for airfield defence. Of the twenty-eight airfields chosen as beneficiaries of this windfall, ten were in the London area, including Croydon, North Weald, Fairlop, Kenley, Northolt and Biggin Hill. The Hornchurch defence plan shows one of these light tanks at a fixed point, plus the location of a Troop HQ suggesting that two more were deployed as a mobile reserve. It was not until 1942 that it was deemed safe to remove any of the permanent garrisons, and only in 1943 were eleven Beaverettes of 2741 and 2801 Squadrons RAF Regiment redeployed from Northolt down to Devon.

Other defensive structures employed on airfields included, the Allan Williams Turret, a rotating steel dome with weapons mountings in hatches, sitting on a circular track over a concrete trench, with room for two men to operate lmgs against aircraft or ground targets, seventy-five of which, out of the available 200, were allocated to London District. An example remains *in situ* on the edge of the former Radlett airfield, beside the A414 road (TL157048) with two more at North Weald Redoubt. The most ingenious but possibly least practicable, was the Pickett-Hamilton Fort. Designed in 1940 by Donald Hamilton, a London architect, it consisted of two concentric concrete cylinders buried in the ground. Pneumatic pressure supplied by

106 Radlett Airfield, Allan
Williams Turret at TL157047.

107 North Weald Airfield, a
Pickett Hamilton 'disappearing'
fort at TL487047.

108 Hornchurch Airfield, a Tett Turret, one of two at TQ535842.

compressed air enabled the inner cylinder to rise above ground level, enabling its crew of two to engage the enemy with lmgs through the loopholes provided. They were usually deployed three to an airfield, and were sited to cover the runways or landing field. When flush with the ground, only a hatch in a circular concrete apron was visible, offering no obstruction to friendly aircraft. The loop-holed inner ring of one of these survives in its raised position outside the clubhouse at North Weald. A third construction was the Tett Turret, not designed specifically for airfield defence, but found to be useful in that role. Like the previous two installations, it was manned by a crew of two, and consisted of a buried concrete cylinder with a revolving collar incorporating weapons mountings. Two surviving examples can be seen at Hornchurch (TQ535842) and recent investigations for a TV feature revealed the existence of several more there.

The Defence of Depots and Industrial Sites

Some sites were so important to the war effort, either as centres of production, or as stores, that they merited their own defences, often manned by Home Guard units raised from their own work force. The London Underground depot and works at Acton, which carried out all sorts of engineering tasks, was defended by pillboxes, and the Woolwich Arsenal is recorded in 1940 as being provided with twelve pillboxes and two emplacements for 75mm guns. Waltham Abbey was defended by pillboxes and one, of a type that can be seen at other ordnance factories, still remains at Enfield Lock, the small arms factory, where there were once more. Also at Enfield is a small, rectangular, brick pillbox with a concrete roof, sometimes described as a police post, or guard post, and apparently developed for the exclusive use of ordnance factories and depots. Other examples can be seen at the Purfleet magazine. At Dawley ROF (TQ0879),

109 Enfield Lock (TQ378994), a standard Royal Ordnance Factory guard post, also found at Purfleet magazine, and Dawley ROF.

now redeveloped, there were formerly at least four of these brick police posts, a gatehouse and four concrete hexagonal pillboxes, and on Croydon's Purley Way, near to the airfield and the complex of factories, a pillbox, only recently demolished, was built at first-storey level to improve visibility for its defenders.

Other Vulnerable Points

Owing to the sensitive nature of the work carried out on them, a number of sites were given fixed defences. Garston Manor, north-east of Abbots Langley, was an experimental site, heavily defended by a screen of half-a-dozen pillboxes, which may also have been intended to afford some protection to the aircraft factory at nearby Leavesden, since this complex lay outside London Line A. At Dollis Hill (TQ222863) is a loop-holed wall defending the secret site known as 'Paddock'. Just as many of the road and rail crossings of the major defence lines were defended by AT obstacles, so were many

110 A Bren gun showing the mounting generally used in pillboxes.

other minor routes whose denial to the enemy was seen as necessary. Odd clusters of AT blocks can still be seen as well as rare survivals such as the caltrop, located on the B556 at South Mimms (TL218015), an obstacle, mediaeval in origin, scaled up to delay the passage of vehicles so that an ambush might be sprung. Even larger versions can be seen on the Normandy beaches. Some important sites, such as Whitehall, were so obviously vulnerable and well known to the enemy that saturation defences were provided.

The Home Guard

The direct descendants of the VTC of the First World War and the later National Defence Companies were the Local Defence Volunteers, soon renamed the Home Guard. By stand down in 1944, there were 151 battalions in the Greater London area, by then constituting a highly trained, professional force that had taken over many of the regular army's commitments, particularly AA defence. In the early days however, activities were low-key, requiring the minimum of equipment and organisation. The Selsdon Mounted Platoon of the 59th (Addington) Bn Surrey Home Guard, for instance, had an observation post on the top floor of the Selsdon Park Hotel and stables at Selsdon Park and on Chelsham Common, enabling three-man overnight patrols to be carried out in the surrounding open countryside. One expectation of the Home Guard was that in the event of an invasion they should operate as urban guerrillas, so much of their early training was organised to that end. Under the leadership of Tom Wintringham, who had led the British element of the International Brigades in the Spanish Civil War, a Home Guard training school was set up at Osterley Park, to teach the relevant techniques and principles. Sadly, Wintringham's politics proved inimical to Churchill and the school was closed down, but his mission was continued by local Home Guard schools such as those operating in Richmond Park

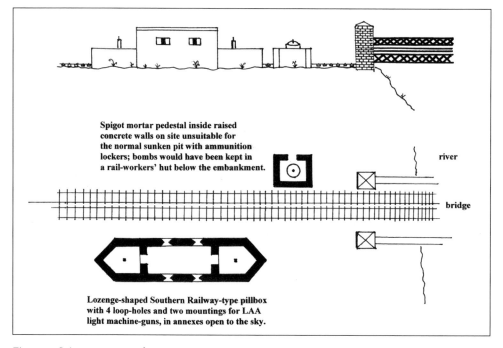

Figure 13 Spigot mortar emplacement.

and the grandstand of Epsom Racecourse. The scarcity of weaponry, particularly light artillery, was a real problem for the Home Guard until well into 1942, and it became necessary to invent cheap and easily manufactured pieces such as the Smith Gun, the Blacker Bombard and the Northover Projector. The Smith Gun fired a 3in shell and could be towed behind a small car. It was manufactured by TRIANCO Ltd of East Molesey, who ran training courses at Imber Court. The Blacker Bombard or spigot mortar fired a 20lb (9kg) anti-tank projectile, or a 14lb (6kg) anti-personnel bomb, and was effective only at short range. It was mounted on a concrete pedestal the size of an oil drum sunk into a pit along with lockers for the bombs. A domed surface containing a vertical stainless-steel pintle, on which the mortar sat, is often all that shows above ground. Where it was impossible to dig a pit, the pedestal was placed in a small enclosure of concrete walls; several such structures may be seen on Thames bridges, notably Kew and Barnes.

London District was divided into four sub-districts made up of a total of eighteen sectors including the Westminster Garrison, and premises were required for their HQs. Some were accommodated in drill halls as in Ealing, Brixton, Eltham, Bermondsey and Hampstead, for example, with overall operational Battle HQ in Offord Road, Islington by 1941. Latymer School provided suitable Hammersmith premises, as did the Surrey County Hall in Kingston. Other zones made use of private houses, which were often the homes of their commanders; this was something that happened all over Britain. Many HG battalions were recruited corporately, six of them exclusively from LPTB staff, for instance, and eight more from GPO staff. The Upper Thames Patrol consisted of 116 boats crewed mainly by uniformed staff of the Thames Conservancy. Two of the fifty-nine County of London battalions were converted to HG Transport Columns with HQs at South Kensington, while a third became the London HG Taxi Column at St Marylebone. Additionally, there were Auxiliary Bomb Disposal squads based on factories and affiliated to the Home Guard proper. London provided three ZAA regiments at Victoria Park, Bromley and Chelsea, and two HAA regiments at Hampstead and Bickley. There were also troops of LAA covering the aircraft factories at Hayes, Cricklewood and Langley, the Vickers plants at Crayford and Dartford, and the experimental establishment at Fort Halstead, as well as other important industrial sites.

In March 1943, General Pile, the AA supremo, speaking at a rally at the Albert Hall, predicted that the Home Guard would assume the major responsibility for crewing the capital's AA defences. Little did he or his audience realise that the V1 and V2 onslaught would accelerate this process.

The Defence of the London Area Against Air Attack

Civilian war deaths due to bombing in the LCC and city area alone reached almost 20,000, and the politicians' fatalism seems to have been justified. However, the planning of the previous few years was to pay off, and the combination of active and passive defence went some way to limiting the number of casualties, even if it cannot have felt like it at the time.

Anti-aircraft artillery

A typical HAA gun site occupied quite a large piece of land, its battery of guns being emplaced in a semi-circle of four octagonal concrete pits with ready-use ammunition lockers built into their sides. Behind the guns was a command post containing the sound location and predicting apparatus, telephones and plotting table. Behind that were magazines and a gun store, while some way further back were living huts, workshops and garages. The whole was surrounded by a wire fence with a guardroom and caretaker's bungalow near the gate. Sites in locations perceived as vulnerable to enemy attack were often provided with close-defence pillboxes. Battery commanders, incidentally, were reminded that in the event of an invasion, their gun sites were to be regarded as strongpoints, and held to the last round. Prior to its issue to units, the equipment was kept in a network of mobilisation stores located in convenient places across the country. The 4.5in guns for the Chadwell Heath (ZE1) HAA battery (TQ488897) would have been kept in the mobilisation store on Colliers Row Lane, prior to issue to 155 Bty 52 HAA Regiment RA, TA, fully operational on site by January 1940. The neighbouring battery at Lippitts Hill (ZE7) was equipped at this date with four 3.7in guns, while nearby Buckhurst Hill (ZE4) still had four old 3in guns until May 1940. Even these old guns were not easily obtained. In August 1939, of the two 3in guns assigned to RAF North Weald, one came from the TA drill hall at Whipps Cross, where it had been used for drill, and the other came from the Imperial War Museum, where it had been an exhibit. The sole 40mm Bofors LAA gun in the hands of the TA on the outbreak of war was defending the small-arms factory at Enfield Lock. Despite the discovery that Poland had a licence for producing the Bofors gun, and was exporting surplus production, the build-up was painfully slow. In September 1939 the majority of the LAA weapons defending airfields, factories, ports and other vulnerable communications centres, were old First World War Lewis guns, singly, or in pairs, often on makeshift mountings. This reliance on light automatics for AA defence is underlined by the instruction in the 1940 defence plans that all pillboxes should have an external mounting for an AA light machine gun so that, providing the garrison was not engaged in fighting enemy ground forces at the time, they might contribute to the anti-aircraft operation. It is worth noting here, that the Type DFW 3/27 pillbox, which only appears in large numbers on the outer London defence Line A, has an open pit in its centre to accommodate a Lewis or a Bren on a high-angle tripod mounting. Clearly every little helped in the fight against the bombers.

111 Purfleet, the main London AA magazine opened in 1939. Each of the eight separate magazines comprised nine pairs of back-to-back sections each accessed by two entrances.

While the HAA batteries were tasked with breaking up the massed concentrations of bomb-ers, it was equally important to provide local protection against low-level attack by lone bombers, dive-bombers or ground-strafing attacks. This is where the lack of suitable LAA provision was most keenly felt. Munitions factories, stores and depots were seen as priorities, but so were airfields and aircraft factories, and in the early months of the Second World War the cover was spread, but thinly. Waltham Abbey and Enfield Lock were each initially defended by forty-eight Lewis guns, with a solitary Bofors at Enfield. By 1943 they each had a dozen 40mm Bofors guns. Purfleet started the war with one quadruple Vickers gun, later receiving five batteries of Bofors, which was just as well considering that the magazines for the entire supply of AA ammunition for the London area were here. Incidentally the original location for the ADGB magazines had been Banstead, but this was seen as too vulnerable in the event of an invasion, so the stocks had initially been transferred to Mill Hill and then on to Purfleet. Ultimately, hundreds of guns would be emplaced, but the conflicting demands of the regular army, the navy, merchant ships, and the ports, factories and communication centres in the rest of Britain and the empire, made logistical planning a nightmare. Gaps in the HAA cover were gradually plugged as the new LAA guns became available. Kingston-upon-Thames, with its aircraft factories, eventually got four 40mm Bofors guns in 1943, as did Radlett, Langley and Hatfield. Ironically, given the demand for AA guns and, at the same time, the disappointment in their performance, a detachment of the 54th (Chislehurst) Bn Kent Home Guard, manning a roadblock in St Paul's Cray in August 1940, took exception to being strafed by a Dornier bomber, and brought it down with just 180 rounds of well-aimed rifle fire.

There are meagre remains on the ground of this extensive AA provision. At Chadwell Heath (ZE1) much of the HAA battery survives; the guardroom, cottage and magazine now form part of a garden centre, while two of the gun pits with associated structures occupy a fenced enclave in the middle of gravel workings. On the Isle of Dogs, some of the emplacements of ZE8 (TQ382788), a battery of four 4.5in HAA guns, are now used as pens for the pigs and chickens of Mudchute city farm. South of the river, ZS1 Slade Green [TQ531775] retains its four octagonal pits for 3.7" HAA guns, its central command post, and a magazine, all defended by two hexagonal pillboxes. No doubt other odd remnants remain, hidden away, but possibly not for very much longer. Some sites remain but in barely recognisable form, such as the AA mobilisation centre in Colliers Row Lane, now disguised as a furniture factory.

Necessity, as ever, mothered a profusion of ingenious solutions in the struggle against the air assault. Fort Halstead, one of the old London Mobilisation Centres, near to Sevenoaks, had become a defence laboratory in the interwar years, and it was here that the 3in Unrotated Rocket Projectile was developed. Better known as Z-Batteries, these provided a flexible and relatively cheap complement to conventional AA artillery. They were essentially close relations of fireworks, needed only rudimentary mountings on small concrete plinths, and could be fired in salvoes to the same height as AA shells. In retrospect, they also probably caused far less damage to the people they were meant to protect than did the fragmenting spent shells of the HAA batteries. These Z-Batteries often had as many as seventy-two rocket projectors, and were manned by the Home Guard. The fourteen Z-Batteries defending London tended to be sited in open spaces such as Victoria Park (19Z) in Bethnal Green, or Battersea Park (9Z). Towards the end of the war, many conventional AA batteries were manned by the Home Guard, and many were also mixed, with women of the ATS serving in them, so it was not only technical conven-tions that were challenged. In the early days of the Battle of Britain, when the fighter airfields were under constant attack, improvisation was vital. One example was the parachute and cable launcher (PAC). The idea was simple. The line of eight or nine launchers would fire their cables up to 600ft (183m) in the air, where small parachutes would open to keep the cables vertical. This would provide a barrier into which low-level enemy raiders might fly, thereby slicing off their wings. RAF Kenley was one of those targets, and was provided with twenty-five of these devices; in a raid by nine Dornier 17s in August 1940 they brought down at least one German aircraft and damaged others. A combination of ground fire, fighter action and PAC installations accounted for four of the attacking aircraft. One of the problems faced by AA crews, especially in built-up areas, was that of visibility, as they were unable to see attacking aircraft from ground level when surrounded by tall buildings. Most of the HAA batteries were therefore located in open ground: parks in the centre of London, heaths, open spaces such as golf clubs, and marshes on the outskirts. Hyde Park (ZW5), Finsbury Park (ZE13), Richmond Park (ZS20) and Shirley Park golf-course (ZS13) are all typical examples of battery locations in open spaces. LAA guns, however, were meant to protect against closer encounters. Some could be mounted on the tops of buildings, as they were, for instance, on top of the former Wembley Exhibition buildings. Where this solution was not practicable, towers were sometimes built specifically for mounting LAA guns. There is one such tower on the River Lea, guarding Waltham Abbey ammunition works, and others at Ruislip Manor, Erith, Iver, Brooklands and by Dagenham East station. They usually consist of twin platforms rising from a common base but not quite touching, in order that the vibration of the gun mounted on one would not affect the sensitive height-finding instruments mounted on the other. Some, as at Brooklands, were skeletons of concrete beams, others were solid brick and concrete structures. There was even a rail-mounted gun on the line between Bowes Park and Palmers Green stations, kept in a shelter on a siding, and thought by locals possibly to have been a 4in naval gun. The most important development, of course, was Radar, providing the controllers at Bentley Priory with invaluable early warning of aerial attack, enabling the fighters to be off the ground at the critical moment, and the guns to be manned

112 Ruislip Manor, the Bofors LAA tower (TQ099868) which defended the nearby RAF depot and RAF Northolt.

and pointing in the right direction. The CH stations around the south and east coasts provided cover on all the routes to London. As the war progressed, gun-laying (GL) radar shortened the hitherto impossibly long odds against hitting the target.

Bentley Priory itself was absolutely vital to the successful prosecution of the Battle of Britain. By September 1940, sandbagged and wired gun-posts had been established around the house, camouflaged with green paint with its windows permanently blacked out with paint. Huts were constructed in the grounds, fifteen by the end of 1939, as overspill for messing and accommodation facilities. There was also a Cypher Section in a hut on the east side of the house. Ground defence was the prime responsibility of 'backers-up', groups of battle-trained airmen that later became defence squadrons, and then in 1941 the RAF regiment, and a holding battalion of the Guards Brigade. The RAF Wireless Intelligence 'Y' Service at Cheadle (Cheshire) contributed signals intelligence. In March 1940 the underground block, known as 'The Hole', came into service, housing the Ops Room, Filter Room, plus departments for Intelligence, Home Office (Air Raid Warnings Section), Code and Cypher Section, and the Type X coding machine, along with offices and services. The Defence Teleprinter Network was powered by underground cables in steel pipes carrying 167 phone lines into the Ops Room. An additional seventy outside lines and 250 extensions, were all routed through interconnection panels protected by reinforced concrete and capable of prompt rerouting if bomb-damaged. The estate's Harrow Road entrance lodge provided a home for the station commander and The Cedars with its swimming pool was requisitioned from the Maclean (toothpaste) family as No. 2 Mess. Food rations were stored at The Rookery in Stanmore village, and Rosary Priory, a Catholic convent in Elstree Road, was a hostel for the WAAFs who worked in the ops rooms.

Other dimensions of the anti-aircraft system

As well as the AA guns there were the barrage balloons and searchlights, in three deployments. An outer belt of thinly spread lights acted as an early warning on the Kent coast. Next was a belt of lights 16 miles (25km) deep, designed to illuminate targets for night fighters to engage. The final layer was about 6 miles (9.5km) forward of the GDA to help gun crews identify targets. Early in the war, lights tended to be assigned fixed positions, hence the line of ninety-six sites between Gerrards Cross and Thame, planned to be taken up on the outbreak of war. Similarly there were existing locations around the south-west approaches to London, earmarked for occupation by the sixteen troops of 35th (1st Surrey Rifles) S/L Regiment formed from the 21st Bn London Regiment in 1935 at their drill hall in Flodden Road, Camberwell. Within a short time it became clear that much more flexibility was required as experiments in clustering or dispersal were carried out, and the lights needed to respond to tactical changes in the operations of both fighters and guns. The early permanence of S/L sites with living huts and even concrete pillboxes, soon gave way to more ephemeral scatterings of tents and sandbagged emplacements that could be moved at very short notice. S/L regimental HQs tended to be in requisitioned houses, centrally placed to control their scattered and itinerant units. RHQ of 93 S/L Regiment was at Moor Park, Rickmansworth, from whence seventy-two individual sites were controlled, twenty-four of them belonging to 495 Battery with HQ in Swakeleys House, Ickenham. Barrage balloons, on the other hand, were only effective if maintained in permanent deployments. Over 1000 balloons took to the sky, and, in London, they were maintained from four major depots at Chigwell, Hook near Kingston-upon-Thames, Kidbrooke near Lewisham, and at Stanmore Park. These depots were large camps accommodating hundreds of personnel, their vehicles, workshops, gas storage, fabric stores and so on. In the early days at Chigwell,

400 men slept in two old hangars, but in time, hutting was provided for them. In September 1940, a new balloon squadron was formed, dedicated to the defence of the Brooklands factory, with sections based in Byfleet and Cobham with HQ in St Georges Avenue, Weybridge. This unit deployed a total of twenty-five barrage balloons around the factory and its approaches. Major repairs to balloons were handled by the depot at Hook. Expected by the public to pump an unending stream of shells into the air, the AA guns were entirely dependent on a regular supply and a magazine for AA ammunition had been established at Purfleet in 1939. Eight magazines, each consisting of nine pairs of back-to-back storage bays, were built in concrete with asbestos sheeting covering their roofs, outer concrete blast-walls, and loading ramps for lorries working round the clock. On the night of 11/12 September 1940, London's thirty-five HAA batteries fired over 13,000 rounds. The development of proximity fuses and the special powder that enabled consistency of rate of burn had been carried out at Waltham Abbey.

A few survivals remind us of these operations. Odd concrete blocks with threaded screws in the top often represent balloon anchorage points. An octagonal one survives at Gerrards Cross (SU998885), but the four balloon depots have all gone, mainly under housing. A few remnants may survive at the Metropolitan Police sports ground in Chigwell, and there is a hut at Kidbrooke that may represent the depot. Stanmore is still in RAF use so may have remains. At the time, the barrage balloons offered some comfort to vulnerable Londoners going about their everyday business, and two tethered over Chelsea were affectionately known as Flossie and Blossom. One precaution that could be taken at ground level was sandbagging doors and windows. Few, however, took this to the lengths of Pruniers restaurant, whose exterior décor was matched by blue-painted sandbags.

The ROC in the Second World War

The Battle of Barking Creek highlighted the shortcomings in the system that had been set up in the interwar period but was yet to be tested for real. On 3 September 1939 reports of enemy aircraft over the Thames Estuary prompted the scrambling of three flights of fighters from RAF North Weald. Only after the ensuing dogfights had resulted in the loss of two Hurricanes, did it become apparent that no enemy aircraft had been involved at any stage. This debacle caused a complete rethink of the reporting and control systems, fortunately leading to greater effectiveness.

Bromley's ROC HQ was in Church House, itself destroyed by incendiary bombs in April 1941, forcing a move to alternative premises in the Masonic Hall in Masons Hill. It was felt necessary by this time, to provide purpose-built accommodation for Group HQs, and Watford's, in Cassiobury Drive, was the prototype. The Ops Room was placed in a horseshoe of buildings containing rest rooms, canteen, offices and segregated dormitories. Some posts were also improved, with brick structures, often mounted on stilts and covered at one end, being substituted for the old sheds. In the almost wholly built-up areas of London, posts were constructed on rooftops, often on top of telephone exchanges as at Gresham Road, Brixton, the Laburnham Exchange at Winchmore Hill, Crouch End, Harrow, Uxbridge and Hounslow. Other such rooftop sites included the Ministry of Pensions building in Bromyard Avenue, Acton, the London University Senate House on Gower Street, the Mount Pleasant GPO Parcels Office, Highpoint Flats in Highgate, and Haberdashers' Aske's GS, Hatcham. The post on the roof of New Cross telephone exchange was destroyed by enemy action, necessitating a move to Robinson's Flour Mills, Deptford. From 1943, the four London Air Raid Reporting Districts: Central, East, South and Croydon, were all brought under Bromley (Group 19) until the final V2 incidents. Bromley liaised with Wartling (Sussex) radar station in order to coordinate information going to the fighter airfields of Biggin Hill, Redhill, North Weald and Kenley via the Ops Room at RAF Uxbridge. The ROC was stood down after a rally and fly-past at RAF North Weald in June 1945.

Fooling the enemy: decoys, deception and camouflage

There were, of course, other ways of thwarting the bomber besides shooting it down. One course of action was to persuade it to drop its bombs somewhere where little damage might be done. Hence the bombing decoy, which was designed to replicate a genuine target, but at some distance, and in open country. Most of the airfields in operation in 1939 were given decoys. The K site was a daylight decoy with fake buildings and aircraft, often fabricated by technicians from the film studios at Shepperton, which successfully tendered for the work. A certain amount of daily activity was maintained in order to sustain the pretence. The Q site was for use at night, and relied on simulated runway and taxiing lights. On hearing the sound of approaching enemy aircraft, the RAF crew would (not too) quickly dowse the lights from the relative safety of their concrete control bunker. Preventative measures are always difficult to evaluate, but most decoys received bombs, and we must assume that otherwise these would have been directed at the real target. Cities and factories also had decoys. Some of these were Starfish sites where on the approach of enemy aircraft large fires were lit to burn fiercely in braziers, suggesting to the oncoming bombers that this, the real target, had already been located by earlier bombs. Some of the early Q sites were subsequently adapted as Starfish sites when the pattern of bombing and target priorities changed. There were local Starfish sites covering Slough, Hatfield and the munitions works at Waltham Abbey. In such a densely populated area as the metropolis it was difficult to find sites that could safely absorb enemy bombs, and it would sometimes appear that the location of decoys merely substituted one target for another, but five sites including Lullingstone and Rainham Marshes were identified in an attempt to provide some protection for London. Most of the airfield decoys were deactivated by 1942, but there was still a need for protection for towns and factories. Little was visible on the ground of any of these decoys. The most one might expect to see was the control bunker, an above-ground structure in brick and concrete, sometimes incorporating a short, Nissen hut-like tunnel, with at least one ground-level entrance, and, usually, a chimney-like hatch in the roof. The decoy blockhouse for RAF Hornchurch survives in fields at Bulphan (TQ654861). RAF Northolt's was on the Shire golf course in Barnet (TQ23498). Biggin Hill's decoy at Lullingstone (TQ526648) was later converted into a Starfish site, hoping to attract bombers approaching London over the Darenth valley. Smoke and fire were not only used as bait in decoys, but also to mask targets, as at Slough, which was often obscured by a controlled oil smokescreen. Airfields were generally camouflaged to blend into the surrounding countryside by painting buildings in brown, black and green paint, and by drawing in fake hedges across the flying field, but at Northolt the surroundings were urban, so the field was painted as streets of terraced houses.

Defending against the V-weapons

By 1944, Londoners must have felt that they had endured all that was to be thrown at them for long enough, but the worst, in some ways, was still to come. The arrival of the first V1 flying bombs coincided with the celebration of the success of the D-Day landings. The response, known as Operation Diver, was immediate. The AA guns were pushed out to the coast as the Coastal Gun Belt; between that and London was the Kentish Gun Belt extending in depth from Crawley to Chatham; the Thames Estuary was covered by the Diver Box, a quadrilateral defined by Chelmsford, Clacton, Canterbury and Chatham. The guns were free to operate above these three defined areas, while fighters patrolled the rest of the airspace and the Chain Home Radar cover once again came to the assistance of both the gunners and the pilots. The associated barrage balloon operation was controlled from Biggin Hill. As the direction of attack altered so the gun lines were extended, first up the east coast to the Great Yarmouth (Norfolk) GDA, as the Diver Strip, and then further north as far as Filey (North Yorkshire), known as the Diver Fringe. Despite these defences with hundreds of HAA, LAA, Z-Batteries, and every conceivable type of AA weapon, the impact, on London especially, was enormous.

Civil defence

At the time of the V-weapon offensive, Londoners had access to many more shelters than during the Blitz. The whole question of passive defence against aerial attack, or civil defence, as it was called, had presented problems since the early planning of the Air Raid Precautions (ARP) organisation before the war started. Official policy was that public shelters were only provided for the 10 per cent of the population who at any one time might be caught out in the open during an air raid. The majority of people would either be at home, in which case they would have their own cellar, Anderson shelter, or communal street shelter, as refuge, with indoor Morrison shelters later being added to the list of options. Alternatively, they would be at work, in which case their employer would provide shelter. The general public, however, took shelter wherever they could. At the height of the Blitz, 7500 people lived in Chislehurst Caves, and the platforms of London Underground stations were regarded as ready-made shelters, regardless of official policy. While there had never been any intention on the part of the authorities for the underground system to provide shelter to the public, the Tube did have a part to play in ARP. First, there was a danger that bomb damage might cause the train tunnels to flood, so twenty-five steel floodgates, each 13in (33cm) thick and weighing 6 tons, were installed at strategic points, particularly near the Thames Embankment, to seal the system as necessary. The control centre for these was initially at Leicester Square Underground station, but later moved to Bull and Bush, the disused station under Hampstead Heath. The tunnels under the Thames itself were furnished with hydrophones in order that the London Transport chief engineer's office at South Kensington station might monitor the riverbed for delayed action mines that had been parachuted into the river. Tunnels under Exhibition Road linked this office with the London CD HQ under the Natural History and Geological museums. There were a number of other unused Underground stations, and these too received new roles. Down Street, between Hyde Park Corner and Green Park, became HQ of the Passenger Transport Executive Committee. Here offices, sub-station, telephone exchange, living accommodation and rest rooms were all built along the platforms. Ventilator shafts were fitted with baffles to stop bombs entering, and a small lift was installed inside the spiral staircase. The street-level door, used by workers, was given a spy-hole. Short lengths of platform were left accessible to Executive members who travelled by Tube train, controlled by manually operated signals. Dover Street housed London Transport's emergency HQ, while the British Museum station became an administrative HQ for the Brigade of Guards, and temporarily, an emergency HQ for London Military District, prior to the opening of the Rotunda. Disused sections of the Underground at Piccadilly and Aldwych provided temporary homes for art treasures prior to their removal to more remote locations.

By 1942, under the pressure of public opinion, and in view of the reluctant official acceptance of public use of Tube stations throughout the Blitz, the policy on deep shelters for public use

was reversed. In 1943 ten public shelters, deep below existing stations, were nearing completion. In the end, not all were ever available. Work at St Paul's was stopped when it seemed to
be threatening the Cathedral's foundations, and an underground river at the Oval forced the
engineers there to abort. Chancery Lane and Clapham Common were earmarked by the government for future official use, in the meantime being used to billet troops in transit through
London. Stockwell lodged 1000 US servicemen, and Goodge Street, given a new, high-speed
lift, became Eisenhower's HQ. The onset of war in 1939 had forced the abandonment of the
Northern Heights Project to extend underground services to Alexandra Palace and Bushey
Heath. The tunnels through Brockley Hill were used as a rifle range, and the Aldenham Depot
became an aircraft factory. Only Belsize Park, Camden Town, Stockwell, Clapham North and
Clapham South were ever officially allocated to the general public, with total provision for
around 40,000 people; the first, Stockwell, opened in July 1944. At each site, twin tubes, 16ft
6in (5m) in diameter and 1400ft (430m) long and constructed of reinforced concrete and cast
iron were built parallel to the station platform. Each tube had two floors with bunks for 8,000
people. Given the time it had taken to build these shelters it is as well that earlier initiatives took
up some of the slack. St Mary's, Whitechapel Road, closed in 1938 to be replaced by Aldgate
East nearby, and it was agreed that the disused platforms could be used as air-raid shelters, but
bombing twice destroyed the entrances. King William Street station, Stockwell, had been closed
for some years by the time an office block called Regis House was built in 1933. During the
war, the underground tunnels were leased temporarily as an air-raid shelter for employees, prior
to its later general use. South Kentish Town was adapted for use as a shelter in 1940 with bunks
and a first-aid post. Independent of government policy, some local authorities had dug air-raid
shelters, such as the deep shelter for 12,000 people at Finsbury, later an underground car park.
By the time of the V1 and V2 onslaught several more public air-raid shelters had been provided.
One, in a 70ft (22m) deep tunnel of the old City & South London Railway provided 10,000
places for the inhabitants of Southwark. In the east end, where shelters were most needed, one

113 Holborn, 39 Furnival Street, the entrance to the air-raid shelter.

was built in Bethnal Green for 7000 people and another at Liverpool Street with 10,000 places. There survives at 39 Furnival Street, off Holborn, the entrance to a public air-raid shelter built in 1942–43 but maintained into the Cold War period.

London's ARP Region 5 extended into Hertfordshire and included ninety-six separate local authorities, all of whom, with their varying levels of provision, had to be integrated into a single consistent system. London suffered 30,000 deaths, constituting fully half of the national total, including 1400 in a single night on 10–11 May 1941. Around 2350 V1s fell on London, killing 5000 and injuring 15,000 followed by a further 2724 deaths caused by 518 V2s. By the end of the war 1–1.5 million homes had been destroyed or damaged, the Port of London had been reduced at times to 25 per cent capacity, and there had been 53 million attendances in underground tunnel shelters. A V1 landed at Grove Road, Mile End, E3 on 13 June 1944, the first of some 963 across the LCC area and the city, with the Tower of London taking three direct hits. The Guards Chapel at Wellington Barracks was hit by a V1 on 18 June 1944, causing 121 deaths. Between 15 June and 16 August 1944, over 140 V1s fell on the borough of Croydon, causing over 2000 casualties including 211 dead. If the V1s seemed bad, then the follow-up V2s were even worse as nothing could be done to stop them until ground operations on the Continent pushed their mobile launch-sites out of range. Woolwich Arsenal took seven hits from V2s in a single week. Just four V2s in Croydon destroyed or damaged 2000 homes.

Bomb disposal

Unexploded bombs caused a disproportionate amount of disruption as areas had to be evacuated for the time it took for the bomb to explode, for its fuse to expire, or for the RE's UXB teams, based on CD areas, to defuse it, successfully, or not. In the early days 5BD Coy RE was based at Chelsea Barracks with just twelve sections totalling 180 men to cover the whole of London. By the end of 1940, this had expanded and No. 1 BD Group had its HQ at Princes Gate, South Kensington. The whole operation came under General Taylor's Fortifications and Works Department of the War Office with its HQ at Romney House, Marsham Street, Westminster. There was an experimental centre for BD in Richmond Park, at Killcat Corner, between the Roehampton and Robin Hood gates. Here, new techniques were developed to counter the measures taken by German bomb designers to prevent their bombs being defused. The navy also based BD teams in London; their HQ was HMS *Firework* in Vintry House, Upper Thames Street, with out-stations at 81 Ashley Gardens SW1, and in Forest Gate. Personnel included mine-disposal teams, BD officers and Making Mines Safe parties, particularly concerned with parachute mines dropped into the river.

Government shelters

Alongside shelter provision for the public, there were also underground shelters for officials dating back to 1933, when an extensive programme of construction had begun. The Admiralty had an underground citadel in Cricklewood, in the grounds of the Admiralty Charts Depot at 403–5 Edgware Road; the Air Ministry had another in Harrow, beside the HMSO works in Headstone Drive, Wealdstone; the Treasury had the 'Hole in the Ground', under Storey's Gate, and the Cabinet Office had 'Paddock' under the Post Office Research Station in Brook Road, Dollis Hill, designed to accommodate 200 staff in bomb-proof vaults. The area around Whitehall was already an underground warren, with the Admiralty Citadel connected to the War Office in Montague House, and a secure telephone exchange, 'Federal', in the basement of the Old War Office on Whitehall. Churchill built the Cabinet War Rooms between Downing Street and Parliament Square, connecting them by more tunnels to the Hole in the Ground, and to a new citadel in Marsham Street, and also excavating new quarters, such as the Rotunda under the gas-works in Horseferry Road. The Rotunda was built in three sections to house Air Ministry staff, the Home Security War Room, and Army HQ London District – nearly 1000 staff in all. The Post Office's Faraday House underground telephone exchange, misleadingly named 'Kingsway', was actually near St Paul's. Many of these installations went on to have extended, but fortunately undistinguished, careers through the Cold War, and some are now open to the public, either regularly, like the Cabinet War Rooms, or intermittently, like Paddock. Goodge Street and many of the other dual-use Tube stations are easily recognisable by their drum-shaped concrete entrances and distinctive ventilators. It must be remembered that the construction of these underground installations was only part of a bigger scheme that also involved decentralisation. 'Yellow Move' saw the Admiralty ship out much of its staff to the requisitioned Empire Hotel in Bath, the Air Ministry take flight to Harrogate, and the BBC transmit itself to Wood Norton near Evesham. 'Black Move' would have seen more central government personnel reforming in Worcestershire, and the communications infrastructure for all these moves was in place prior to the outbreak of war. The basement shelter in the MI5 building in Curzon Street was allocated to the royal family, replacing provision in the north terrace of Buckingham Palace.

Military aviation

One function the capital was admirably equipped to fulfil was recruit reception. The RAF set up a reception centre at Lord's Cricket Ground in St John's Wood. Recruits moved on to RAF Uxbridge to be assigned to training facilities. Although much had been accomplished in the 1930s to modernise the RAF by providing more up-to-date airfields, the demands of war meant that many more were still needed. Given the pressure on land in the London area there would be no wholly new stations, but hitherto civilian sites such as Croydon, Redhill and Stapleford Tawney were requisitioned and expanded, quickly becoming front-line stations in the Battle of Britain.

114 Stapleford Tawney Airfield, the civilian pre-war structure, modified in c.1940, as a hangar/armoury.

115 Biggin Hill, a T2 hangar, possibly one of those which replaced the earlier hangars destroyed by enemy action.

116 Redhill, one of this pre-war airfield's original timber buildings adapted for RAF use, in this case, the equipment store/crash crew-room

Application of the twin principles of dispersal and utility meant that buildings, particularly those housing aircraft, were scattered around the airfield perimeter, and communal sites, that is living accommodation, were located off-site. Virtually all buildings were timber huts or of temporary brick. The hangars were T2 transportable hangars on concrete bases, or Blisters. All the building types were standard, the stores, for instance, would be a pair of Romney huts linked by a corridor roofed in corrugated iron, or else two tb huts with a taller fabric store in-between. Water towers were cast-iron Braithwaite tanks on girder towers, and watch offices were rendered brick cubes.

The fighter stations made do with utility model watch offices: Stapleford Tawney and North Weald (17658/40), Fairlop (14483/40) and Biggin Hill (7335/42), all of them simple, single-storey tb huts with small windows overlooking the flying field. Like Stapleford Tawney, Redhill retained many of its pre-war timber buildings but received new hangars and some tb structures. (See Appendix 6.)

The Royal Navy

On the Thames, HMS *President*, moored off the Victoria Embankment, served as depot of the London Division of the RNVR with HMS *Chrysanthemum* next door from 1939. One of the navy's wartime tasks was to provide guns and gun crew for merchant ships sailing from the Port of London. This DEMS programme had its office in Albert Dock until bombing in September 1940 forced a move to 2 Newell Street, Limehouse, an eighteenth-century detached villa, converted *c.*1850 by the British and Foreign Sailors' Society as a boys' training centre. The actual gunnery training took place aboard ships. HMS *Copra*, Chelsea, was the London's RN pay and drafting office. The WRNS had its HQ in Great Smith Street, with its main recruiting base HMS *Pembroke III*, centred on HMS *President*. Accommodation for new Wrens was provided by hostels at Mill Hill, Golden Square (Soho), Crosby Hall (Highgate), Barkestone Gardens (Earls Court), Woodford Green, and Westfield College, Kidderpore Avenue, NW3. There was a training and drafting depot at Mill Hill, which had moved into the former National Institute of Medical Research at Cannons Corner, Stanmore, by the end of 1942, a site later used as a satellite of Bletchley Park (GC&CS). Newly commissioned WRNS officers received their three weeks' training at Greenwich. Foots Cray Place became the temporary home for the duration of HMS *Worcester*, the training ship previously moored at Greenhithe. A number of other establishments were based in London, including *Caserne Surcouf*, the Free-French Navy barracks on Clapham Common; HMCS *Niobe*, the depot in Canada House prior to its move to Greenock in 1941; and HMS *Evolution* in Chelsea Court, SW3, the special operations base, later renamed HMS *Odyssey*. There was also a naval contribution to the capital's air defence organisation. HMS *Golden Eagle* was one of three Eagle-class paddle steamers that replaced the Queen-class boats as floating AA batteries in the Thames Estuary, later serving as a barrage balloon vessel, then reverting to an AA ship alongside HMS *Plinlimmon*. As bomb damage increased and living space became ever less obtainable, accommodation ships such as the sailing barges and houseboats *Dorothy*, *Gypsy*, *Hilda*, *Monarch* and *Pilgrim*, an ex-powder hulk, found berths on the river. By 1942, HMS *Exmouth*, dating from 1905, was serving as HQ ship for the River Thames Fire Floats.

Preparations for the Normandy Landings

London Docks was central to both the planning and the implementation of Operation Neptune, the naval element of Overlord. It was accepted that while the success of the Normandy landings would depend on the continuous passage of supplies and reinforcements across the Channel, it was unlikely that a suitable port in northern France would easily be captured. Therefore, artificial harbours, code-named Mulberry A and B, would be necessary. Scientists and engineers at the National Physical Laboratory, Teddington, and at the RN Laboratory, based for the duration in Grosvenor Hotel, Mayfair, were given the task of designing the combination of block-ships, artificial breakwaters, pontoons, floating dock caissons, ramps and roadways that would comprise Mulberry. Port Engineering was the responsibility of the new Department 5 of the Directorate of Transportation at the War Office, with a base on Northumberland Avenue, and much of the Mulberry operation was run from offices in County Hall. In London Docks, the East India Import Dock of 1833–34 was pumped dry in 1943, and Surrey Commercial Dock was drained for the construction of Phoenix Caissons, built by a number of firms including Oscar Faber, Sir Alexander Gibbs & Partners, WT Halcrow & Partners, Sir Cyril Kirkpatrick, Rendell, Palmer & Tritton, and Robert White & Partners. Additionally, eight B1 Caissons, built by Mowlems, were floated out through the King George V and Greenland docks to be towed to their embarkation assembly points off Weymouth. Other firms such as Green & Silley Weir, Harland & Wolff, J. Russell & Co., and the London Graving Dock Co., were all employed both on repairing civilian and naval craft and, from 1942, on the construction of landing craft. Pontoons were fitted out at Woolwich. A Mobile Landing Craft Advanced Base (MOLCAB) Assembly Depot was set up in 'B' Shed, West India Docks. Experimental work was undertaken by the Royal Navy on the Queen Mary Reservoir at Staines, with indoor work being carried out in the United Dairies premises at Wembley. Vehicles were waterproofed at the White City vehicle depot.

Merchant ship operations
Only docks the size of London's could cope with the sheer volume of materiel necessary to sustain the D-Day landings. On D-Day itself, Force L3 of twenty-eight LSTs left London heading for Sword beach. A convoy (ETM1) of eleven Liberty ships, all bearing 'SAM' names – *Samark, Sambut, Samos* etc. – sailed from London Docks on 7 June 1944 mainly carrying vehicles and their attendant troops. A fleet of over 120 coasters was loaded with cased petrol in the Thames, and sailed for France in the days following the initial landing, along with some larger freighters carrying Royal Engineers with bridging equipment, which left from King George V Dock. Other ships carrying supplies were loaded at Millwall, Royal Victoria, Royal Albert and the South West India Docks. The *Sambut*, carrying vehicles and over 500 men, was headed for JUNO Beach when it was hit by shells from a German shore battery in the Straits of Dover, and had to be abandoned where it sank east of the Goodwin Sands. Fortunately, the following convoy of troopships carrying over 9,000 men passed unmolested through the Straits. The remaining ten ships of *Sambut*'s convoy discharged their cargo on the beaches, returning to London Docks on 9–11 June. Further convoys of Liberty ships continued to load up in London Docks to leave for Normandy, including one (ETM4) of twelve ships, with five Empires and three Forts among them, which sailed on 10 June. These convoys continued until the end of June, by which time Neptune was reckoned to have achieved its object, but in terms of the Merchant Marine this operation represented just one peak in a continuous process. Between January and March 1944, 6626 ships were loaded and unloaded in London Docks; between April and June, 10,609; and between July and September 11,024.

PLUTO

From 1941 there had been a pipeline from Avonmouth (Gloucestershire) to Walton-on-Thames (Surrey), with a spur from Aldermaston (Berkshire) to Southampton's Fawley refinery, from June 1942. This had a capacity of 120,000 tons of fuel per month. This became the basis for the PLUTO operation, which would sink two permanent pipelines under the English Channel, and thus deliver a constant supply of fuel to the Allied armies fighting in Europe. Some of the production work was carried out in London with the Siemens factories in Harden's Manor Way, Charlton, and in Woolwich producing PLUTO pipeline lengths that were stored in London Docks, and also the cabling necessary to install the system. Pipe-handling equipment was developed by Johnson and Phillips of Dupree Road, Woolwich.

Munitions Production in the Second World War

There can hardly have been a single business concern that did not contribute to the war effort in one way or another. There were 33,000 factory operations involved in munitions production in the Greater London area alone, and their half-million workers used the transport system daily. A few random examples convey the range and diversity of these operations. Esavian sliding doors for aircraft hangars were made by the Educational Supply Company, whose offices were at Esavian House in High Holborn, WC1. Some of the ubiquitous huts were built by Laings of Elstree, ORLIT of West Drayton, and the Romney hut was named after the Air Ministry offices in Romney House. Packards marine engines were made in a factory on the Great West Road, hit by a V2 in 1945. Heal's furniture shop in Tottenham Court Road became a parachute factory. The escalators ordered for St Paul's and Holborn Underground stations were diverted to underground munitions factories in the disused quarries at Corsham near Bristol. An unused stretch of the London Underground's Central Line between Gants Hill and Wanstead was taken over by Plesseys as an aircraft components factory. Mollins, whose core business was making cigarette machines but had become manufacturers of feed mechanisms for Hispano-Suiza AA cannon, planned to convert a disused quarry in Dartford into an underground factory but were allocated space at Corsham (Wiltshire) instead.

Aircraft factories

Aircraft manufacturers had a pretty lean time of it between the wars. The stop-start expansion plans of the RAF did little to help, and there was little incentive to invest in research and development. Fortunately, some did, and one of the successful results was Hawker's Hurricane developed at Kingston-upon-Thames, previously Sopwith's, and built there, at Hawker's new Langley factory near Slough, and at Brooklands from 1935, the three factories together employing 4000 workers by 1939. During the course of the Second World War, some 15,000 were built in Britain and in Canada, with Typhoons, Tempests and Sea Furies appearing in numbers later on. In 1920, de Havilland, formerly Airco, had moved from Colindale up the road to Stag Lane, but quickly outgrew this new site too and, from 1930, began to establish a factory and flying school at Hatfield. The outbreak of war saw the factory producing Rapides, to be followed by their military version, the Dominie. The aircraft they wanted to build, the Mosquito, had been rejected by MAP, and was developed privately at nearby Salisbury Hall. When, in 1941, official production finally got under way, the factory worked flat out to make up for lost time. Handley Page were forced to move their flying field to Radlett in 1930, but retained their factory buildings. The two sites built Halifax bombers throughout the war, with more built under licence by London Passenger Transport. Radlett was extended at the Park Street end to accommodate the output from Cricklewood. This wartime expansion also saw the acquisition of the Leavesden site by MAP, where an aircraft factory was built, and a 3000ft-long runway was laid to be leased to companies building aircraft, some under the direction of de Havilland's. Over 4000 Mosquitoes were assembled here, along with Halifaxes. Brooklands was used by Hawkers and Vickers throughout the 1920s and 1930s and by 1939 was working at full capacity producing Hurricanes and Wellingtons. The Warwick was developed for use by Coastal Command, since it had been overtaken as a bomber by the four-engined Halifax and Lancaster. Another aircraft production centre was Martin-Baker's at Denham. Heathrow had been set up by Fairey in 1929, for flight-testing their Battles and Hendons, but in 1942 the Air Ministry requisitioned it as a heavy bomber station to open in 1944, so Fairey finished the war based at nearby Heston.

117 Salisbury Hall, the de Havilland premises where the Mosquito was developed as a private venture prior to its acceptance by the Air Ministry.

118 Elstree, the R–Type hangar built by MAP at this aircraft repair facility. When Redwing were evacuated from Croydon to run their operation repairing damaged Blenheims in Odhams printing works in North Watford, Fairfield Aviation at Elstree, carried out test flying, also handling Wellingtons and Lysanders. Repaired aircraft were flown out by women pilots of the ATA from Hatfield, and mobile gangs with the motto 'Ubendum wemendum' went all over the country carrying out repairs in situ.

At Elstree, a former aero club, Fairfield Aviation repaired aircraft for MAP who provided an R Type hangar. The widespread operations of MAP were directed from their HQ at Thames House, Millbank, renovated in 1990 for use by MI5.

Shipbuilding

The shipyards of the Thames contributed to the war effort in a number of ways. The Fairmile company, with HQ at Cobham, gathered together parts that had been made for its MLs, MTBs and MGBs at a variety of small commercial factories, together with Packard engines imported from the USA, at a large depot in Brentford. These were despatched to the various east-coast shipyards where the boats would be assembled and launched. Many naval craft were built on the Thames, well above Westminster. James Taylor at Chertsey, Thorneycroft at Hampton, Toughs at Teddington and Watercraft at East Molesey all built MGBs and MTBs. High-speed launches for the RAF search and rescue operations were constructed by Walton Yacht Works, all these vessels requiring sideways launching into the river. The Maunsell AA forts, successors to the old AA paddle steamers, were constructed at Gravesend and towed out into the estuary.

The production of weapons and ammunition

Just as in the First World War, in the Second World War a network of ROFs was set up. In 1939, Waltham Abbey was one of only four propellants factories in operation, and the industry needed expansion. Although the new factories were generally built in traditional industrial areas away from the metropolis, primarily to tap into a skilled workforce, some were built in Greater London. Manufacturing Oerlikon LAA guns was BSA at London Transport's depot in Ruislip. The ROF at Yeading made small-arms ammunition (SAA), and there was another ROF nearby on Bourne Avenue, Dawley. The Woolwich Arsenal continued to develop and manufacture new weapons, good examples being the three generations of AT gun – the 2-pounder, the 6-pounder and the 17-pounder – producing prototypes for mass production at engineering works around the country. Much of this work was almost at the cottage-industry level and often only local knowledge will reveal these sites, as at London Colney (TL176031), where two pairs of large, corrugated-iron-clad sheds, now storage for a car auction, are remembered as the site of a workshop assembling tank-turrets.

Depots and storage facilities in the Second World War

Throughout the 1930s preparations for the outbreak of war had been in hand, and a dispersed network of mobilisation stores was established for storing materiel in readiness for immediate issue to units. The assumption of responsibility for AA defences by the TA provided one specific purpose for these centres. There was an AA Advance Mobilisation Store at Kidbrooke, south-east London, and another mobilisation store at Edgefield Road, Eltham. North of the Thames, there was an AA garage and War Office depot at Colliers Row Lane in Romford. Many of the new TA drill halls were provided with adequate storage for weapons and equipment, but it was necessary to stockpile in these mobilisation centres for immediate issue to gun sites scattered around the capital.

In 1936, the RAF had two stores depots in London: No. 1 at Kidbrooke, and No. 4 at Ruislip. By mid-1941 it had its own hierarchy of depots, known as Maintenance Units (MUs) issuing SAA and bombs, including Air Ammunition Parks such as 11/36/64MU at Ruislip, with an out-station at Hatfield for 11 (Fighter) Group. These were reorganised as Forward Ammunition Depots (FADs) in 1941 in order to limit handling and deliveries, which were for the most part received direct from the factory. Normal capacity of these units was initially set at

750–1250 tons, increasing, after the reorganisation, to 6000 tons. Chessington was the base for 248MU, and there were other MUs concerned with equipment, barrack and clothing (Hammersmith, Wembley, Kenley, Waddington/Coulsdon and Hendon), mechanical transport (Grove Park in south-east London and White City), or Salvage & Repair (50/90MU Kidbrooke). Later in the war, some airfields were chosen as intermediate ammunition depots receiving direct deliveries, with Redhill, 36MU, serving as a satellite for Ruislip. The US Army had an ordnance depot in Gorst Road and Sunbeam Road, near North Acton Tube station. Remains of depots are scarce. Part of the Ruislip complex became a USAF depot, but has now been developed as housing. Two of the original buildings, east of the railway, remain in use by Sea Cadets.

Barracks, Camps and Billets

In wartime, the military's need for accommodation is all but insatiable so, prior to the Second World War lists of houses to be requisitioned in the event of war were drawn up, and allocations were made to the services and government departments, not only for existing bodies that would need to be evacuated or decentralised, but also for new ones thrown up by the war, particularly foreign troops and governments-in-exile and their agencies.

Meeting wartime accommodation needs
In the summer of 1940, when it was becoming apparent that the metropolis would soon have to prepare itself against invasion, it was necessary to find homes for all the troops that would be required to man the defences. Clearly, many could continue to be accommodated in the numerous barracks in and around London: Wellington, Regent's Park, Chelsea, Kensington and Knightsbridge in the centre, and Hounslow, Barnet (Stapylton Road), Mill Hill, Kingston and Woolwich on the periphery. The Guards Depot at Caterham was forced to spill over into Sandown Park, and the Coldstreams took over Elstree School, raising their 4th and 5th Bns there. They also used the clubhouse at Bushey golf club for their royal escort details, which also had a role to play in the defence of Bentley Priory. The 2nd Northamptonshire Yeomanry were billeted in the stables at Windsor Castle while they were on royal shuttle service duties from Buckingham Palace. The Royal Herbert military hospital on Shooters Hill became the base for London's medical units as the RAMC barracks at Millbank had insufficient capacity. New quarters in requisitioned property were found for many units such as the 42nd Bn Royal Tank Regiment at Crewes Place, Warlingham, and the 48th Bn at Llandaff House in Sanderstead. The operational HQ for London District was moved out of Horse Guards to Leconfield House, Curzon Street. In the event of the codeword 'Martello' being used to signal an invasion, all unattached troops in London, on leave or in transit, were to be gathered together at Wembley Stadium prior to being organised into scratch units and deployed to defensive duties.

    The outbreak of war saw those regiments based in London having to increase their office accommodation in order to cope with rapid expansion. While those whose COs had good social contacts might lay claim to prestige premises, as did the Welsh Guards, for instance, taking over 18 Wilton Crescent in Belgravia, most in general had to settle for something less grand. Large complexes like the Bentley Priory estate or RAF Uxbridge were able to expand to provide extra capacity. In 1943 the Advanced Allied Expeditionary Air Force (AAEAF) HQ moved from Hillingdon House to Kestrel Grove, Hive Road, 500yds from Bentley Priory. Later, No. 11 Group Filter Room relocated to Hill House on Stanmore Hill. However the

119 Hounslow, Beavers Lane Camp, the guardroom.

accommodation problem could often only be solved by a repeat of the hutted encampments of the First World War, particularly as D-Day approached and hundreds of thousands of troops awaited the invasion. The existing traditional barrack accommodation had quickly proved inadequate for the army's needs and hutted camps were added to Inglis Barracks, Mill Hill, and to Hounslow Barracks, as Beavers Lane Camp in 1942. Camp Griffiss at Bushy Park near Teddington is a good example of this phenomenon, starting life in February 1943 and being completed in record time. Its purpose was first to house the HQ and associated units of 8th USAAF, and then SHAEF. It was composed of a mixture of hutting – Nissen, Dallas, ORLIT, Ctesiphon and MOW – and some brick buildings, totalling around 150 in all. Some of these 'single' buildings, such as Blocks A–E, however, were complexes of linked units subsuming the equivalent of twenty or so huts, measuring over 400ft by 200ft (120 x 60m), and each covering about 900 sq yds. The contemporary plan from the office of the engineer, Eastern Base Section, SOS, ETOUSA, shows that it was a small town with its own post office, fire station, electricity supply and recreation facilities. It is now totally gone but for a commemorative plaque, just like dozens of similar sites. At Woldingham, the bungalow known as 'Funny Neuk', a survivor of the First World War army camp, was in 1940 a private residence of Admiral Sinclair, a former director of Naval Intelligence, and now head of MI6, and the man who had set up Bletchley Park. Donated to the Czech branch of SOE as a secret radio station, it functioned until 1942 when its operators moved to the Bedford Triangle to be nearer to the other SOE stations.

For many, even hutted camps were unavailable, so billets had to be found. The sheer numbers of US military personnel in London in the months running up to D-Day meant that every available space was occupied. In mid-1942, US troops were billeted in the former Hotel Splendide, in the Badminton Club in Piccadilly, in Shepherd Market in South Audley Street, and in Curzon Street. The former Washington Hotel was a US Red Cross Club, along with about thirty other such premises around the Bloomsbury and Mayfair areas, at least two of them

120 Woldingham Garden Village, Funny Neuk, the much-modernised First World War hut, used by SOE's Czech radio-operators in the Second World War arranging, among other operations, the assassination of Heydrich. The concrete pad for the aerial still exists in the garden.

for women. By June 1944, there were thirty-three officers' billets including twenty-four hotels, and 300 other buildings were used for billeting other ranks. The ballroom of the Grosvenor House Hotel in Park Lane became a US officers' mess, serving 6000 meals a day, and the corner of Shaftesbury Avenue and Piccadilly Circus, previously Del Monico's and the Lyons Corner House, became Rainbow Corner, open to US servicemen night and day. A parallel population was billeted below ground, in the Tube tunnels. Enormous swathes of west-end London's most fashionable residential districts were assigned to the Allied military. The *Stars and Stripes* was produced in the *Times* building in Printing House Square, and the Officers' Uniform Shop was in Selfridges. The WAC detachment had a Beauty Shop at 48 Park Street off Oxford Street.

Corps depots
The army's support services had a number of centralised installations. The RASC depot at Feltham included the Central Ordnance Depot and the Vehicle Reserve Depot. The RASC Heavy Repair Shop, transferred to the newly created REME in 1942, was at Ashford. Another REME workshop and stores depot stood next to Inglis Barracks at Mill Hill from 1943. Prior to D-Day, enormous numbers of vehicles were collected together in parks, ready for shipment from London Docks. Group HQ for this collection and distribution operation was Roehampton. The main AFV depot was Harringay Stadium, spilling over into Finsbury Park, with further detachments at Mill Hill, Willesden, Crystal Palace, Epsom, Staines, Brentford, Kingston, Croydon, Woolwich and Hurlingham. In 1944, the Royal Army Education Corps established a new base at Eltham Palace in the art deco part of the building, which was only recently vacated by the Courtaulds. The Army Tactical School was centred on the golf clubhouse at Wentworth, and the School of Military Administration moved to Wimbledon.

Command and control

By far the greediest consumers of requisitioned buildings were the wartime bureaucracies that were HQs. The basic problem was that there were not enough premises in military hands to satisfy the increased demand generated by fighting a world war. GHQ Home Forces occupied Kneller Hall in Twickenham, built in neo-Jacobean style in 1711, enlarged as a teacher training college in 1848, and now the Royal Military School of Music. HQ Eastern Command was in the dated Hounslow Barracks. The WRNS had its HQ in Great Smith Street. In 1939, the army had requisitioned St Paul's School in Hammersmith, and in 1942 it became the HQ of 21 Army Group and the scene of much of the planning for the Normandy landings. Montgomery, the C-in-C, a former pupil, later joked that it was only once he had become a Field-Marshal that he could gain entry to the headmaster's study. Much of the parallel naval planning for D-Day took place in Norfolk House, St James's Square, prior to the general move to Southwick, above Portsmouth. The Whitehall ministries and the RAF Sector and Command HQs occupied enormous tracts of real estate and the emergency coordinating bodies laid claim to most of the prime underground sites. After 1940, governments in exile, or their representatives, all needed London bases. These included the Belgians in Eaton Square; the Norwegians in Cockspur Street, Trafalgar Square and Knightsbridge; the Dutch at Stratton House, Piccadilly; and the Poles, also at Stratton House, as well as at the Hotel Rubens in Buckingham Palace Gate and properties in Portland Place among other sites. The Free French were based at 4 Carlton House Gardens. The Canadians had established a military HQ in the Sun Life building in Cockspur Street in November 1939, along with a naval HQ at Kings House, 10 Haymarket, but it was the US presence from January 1942 that was to make the greatest demands on space, building to a London garrison of 18,000 troops occupying 10 sq km of office accommodation. The greatest concentration was in Grosvenor Square, around the existing embassy, but Eisenhower's COSSAC offices were in Norfolk House, and, as we have seen, he also had some representation at Bushy Park. Nevertheless, John Reed lists well over 100 addresses, mainly in the Mayfair area, accommodating US army, army air force and naval units, ranging from military police to legal, engineer, signals, supply, medical and finance departments. All needed transportation, administration and other day-to-day functions.

Intelligence gathering in wartime becomes an enormous operation. Such was the volume of traffic generated in the Enigma operation, that bombes were installed at far-flung locations such as Stanmore and Eastcote. The Post Office Research Laboratory in Dollis Hill was used to develop the electro-mechanical computers used at Bletchley Park. While the SHAEF specialist joint services signals operation was at Goodge Street Underground station, the US Signals Security Detachment was based in a Jacobean manor house – Hall Place in Bexley. The US UK Base Counter-Intelligence branch could be found (or not) in the John Lewis building on Oxford Street. The secret intelligence services were based in Curzon Street and at 54 Broadway, backing onto Queen Anne's Gate. The Ministry of Information, as one of the newly created government departments, solved its accommodation needs by taking over London University's Senate House as its offices, also requisitioning Pinewood Studios for the films it would make to inform the public. The Inland Revenue moved to Denham Lodge in 1941, staying until 1947. As the war progressed, even more property was swallowed up by the proliferation of covert organisations such as SOE with all its departments and national sub-sections.

Camps for Prisoners-of-War (POWs) and internees

In the Second World War there was a greater emphasis on dedicated POW camps, designed using standardised layouts and building types, and many of which were built by Italian prisoners in 1942. London's racecourses were used as convenient staging camps, and a wide range of sites was used for the camps themselves. One of the strangest was The Cage, at 8 Kensington Park Gardens, one of London's most expensive addresses, which was set up to hold senior Nazi POWs. Many of these POWs had been processed at the transit and interrogation centre set up for high-ranking captives in Sir Philip Sassoon's former house at Trent Park, usually referred to as Cockfosters. Even royal palaces were not exempt: offices in Saint James's Palace were used for the storage and updating of the dossiers of Allied POWs, in order that families could be informed of the current whereabouts of their loved ones. As well as dealing with obvious captives, there was the problem of accommodating those who were known to be spies, those who were suspected of being spies, and those seeking to prove they were not spies. In January 1941, the Victoria Royal Patriotic School, occupying neo-Gothic buildings near Clapham Junction, opened as the London Reception Centre (LRC), through which would be channelled all foreign refugees entering Britain, stabilising at around 700 per month. An annexe for females was set up in neighbouring Nightingale Lane. A number of premises were used to interrogate those under strong suspicion but still yet to be proven guilty, including the Oratory School, listed in the London HQ War Diary as No. 15 Internee Collection Centre, and it was important to maintain a high degree of secrecy especially if a captured agent was to be turned. Latchmere House, a Victorian house on Ham Common, had been bought by the War Office during the First World War for use as a military hospital, catering for officers suffering from neurasthenia, a higher class of shell shock, in a residential annexe. Now it became Camp 020, with the main house being used for interrogation and administration, and the annexe, with its thirty rooms, by now bugged, for the inmates. Nissen huts were provided for the camp's other needs, and were situated within a compound guarded by military police and surrounded by a wire fence. Some of the guilty became double agents in the XX scheme, some were executed, but others were left in a sort of limbo, too compromised or unreliable to turn, too dangerous to release, and with nothing to be gained by putting them on trial. Many of these prisoners were incarcerated at Camp 020R (Reserve) at Huntercombe in Nuffield (Oxon), to where much of the central operation could have been evacuated in the event of a repeat of the bombing of Ham in 1941. Throughout the war, Camp 020 received suspects from the LRC, and, after D-Day, from forward camps on the Continent. Technically, the whole operation was a civilian one, overseen by the Home Office, and therefore not subject to the Geneva Convention.

nine

London in the Cold War 1946–90

Within a very short time of the end of the Second World War, the country faced an extended period of perceived conflict. There had been occasions when the Cold War appeared to have warmed up, with the Home Guard re-forming in 1951 for a brief period, and V-bombers taking to the skies carrying armed atomic weapons during the Cuban Missile Crisis of 1962. While it eventually transpired that many of both sides' perceptions were misconceived, a quite tangible paranoia had been generated that initiated delusional notions of defence against nuclear attack, including the notorious 'Protect and Survive' campaign. Many of these measures were still being promoted into the mid-1980s, and even after the so-called 'peace dividend' of the 1990s the country's politicians appear still to be equipping the armed forces for cut-price global warfare – Armageddon on a budget.

The Defence of London Against Air Attack

Although the fighter stations of the Battle of Britain era were updated into the jet age, in the air defence field the emphasis was on passive defence. An AA capability based on gunnery was only in existence until the mid-1950s. This was the short-lived ROTOR system, where AAORs such as that at Lippitts Hill controlling fully automated HAA sites, received information from new dedicated GCI radar sites such as Chenies, or Kelvedon Hatch, near Brentwood. The end of 1942 had seen the introduction of new 5.25in HAA guns, some of which were emplaced in twin mountings at Primrose Hill (ZE14), Wimbledon (ZS19) and Coldharbour Farm (ZS27), plus many more as singles. Such upgrading of equipment, added to constant advances in control and detection, produced a formidable organisation, but at the same time as the defence improved, so did the attack methods. The world was moving into the rocket age, and the defences were forced to recognise this, as the early-warning systems, anti-missile missiles, and submarine-borne delivery system for the nuclear deterrent all migrated away from areas of population in the 1960s. In 1955, AA Command was stood down, and surviving AA regiments became part of the field army. The other AAORs in Greater London had been at Merstham, Vange, and, of course, Brompton Road. The ROTOR installation at Kelvedon Hatch is open to the public. Of the other sites, Vange and Chenies are derelict, Lippitts Hill is a police training area and Merstham is reported as being recently demolished.

The ROC was reactivated in 1947, but unfortunately, even some of its surviving posts were not easily reoccupied. The New Cross post (19/Y4) for instance, had been appropriated by Haberdashers' Aske's GS as a weather station, and the locks had been changed. The ROC was to face more serious challenges than this as the pace of change accelerated though. In 1952 it was still charged with identifying hostile aircraft, and Orlit, a firm of concrete building manufacturers on the Colnebrook Bypass near Heathrow, was commissioned to produce a standard post for this purpose. Two designs were put into production, one at ground level, and one on stilts; several hundred were installed by 1954, but it was rapidly becoming apparent that modern aircraft flew too fast to be accurately identified by visual means, and even when successfully identified, their presence could not be communicated quickly enough to a central control for any meaningful action to be taken by interceptors. Among the results of investigations at the time was the recognition that there was a need for a system to monitor nuclear fall-out following an attack, however unthinkable that might be. In 1953 the London Civil Defence Region had begun to identify elevated sites such as Shooters Hill, Crystal Palace and Hampstead Heath for the visual reporting of nuclear strikes. This policy failed to take into account other research that had promoted the use of protected posts equipped with recording instruments. In 1956 the prototype for such an underground post was unveiled at Farnham (Surrey) and, over the next few years some 1500 were installed across the UK and Northern Ireland. Each consisted of a concrete box, 19ft (5.7m) long, 8ft 6in (2.55m) wide, and 7ft 6in (2.25m) high, buried some 8ft (2.4m) below ground and accessed by a vertical ladder reached through a hatch on the surface. Each post, with a crew of four, had bunks, chemical lavatory, food and water for a few days, and work surfaces for processing the data collected by the external instruments for relay to HQ by telephone. Where the water table demanded it, posts were re-sited to higher ground, but without too much disturbance to the established triads. The problem in London was the lack of open space on which to build secure posts. One was built at Heathrow Airport, and others at RAF Chigwell and RAF Northolt. It was also decided that Group HQs would benefit from some greater degree of protection. In 1945, the Bromley centre had been moved to Dura Den, a house in Beckenham's Place Park, but a reshuffle of Groups in 1961 established the HQ of a new 1 Group, merged with 19 Group, in Maidstone. Watford received a standard semi-sunken operations room in 1961. From 1965 a reduced service was proposed with a joint Home Office and ROC HQ at Kestrel House, Stanmore. In 1968 this planned rationalisation of the network was put into effect, with many posts such as Acton, Brixton and Harold Wood being closed down, but ROC HQ remained at Bentley Priory. London's final layout included posts at Billericay, Bowes Park, Chigwell, Elstree, Knockholt, Redhill and Dulwich, each one linked with at least two others. This network of monitoring posts was to last until 1991. A number of

121 Watford, Cassiobury Drive, ROC protected Group HQ, built in 1961, operational until 1968 when 5 Group was dispersed, but retained for training purposes until 1973.

122 Knockholt, ROC underground post installed 1962 at TQ472615, numbered I/A3 and grouped with I/A1 Dartford and I/A2 Borough Green, all three in use until 1991.

posts remain, either as mobile phone masts or as curiosities. The site of Dura Den in Beckenham is now housing, and Watford is a veterinary practice.

While the ROC plotted the ground zero and monitored the levels of nuclear fall-out, the life of both central and local government, the BBC, the armed services, public services, and the utilities, was to continue, with minimal disruption, from the safety of underground citadels not too dissimilar to those constructed during the previous conflict. Many, in fact, especially in central London, were the very same citadels – the Rotundas, Paddock, the Admiralty Citadel – intended to fulfil the same role under nuclear attack as that for which they were originally designed. The Rotundas and Central Government Buildings were all linked to 'Fortress' at Moorgate, 'Bastion' at Covent Garden, 'Citadel' at St Paul's and 'Rampart' at Waterloo. Even in the relatively short duration of the Cold War however, there were several generations of bunker, shelter or citadel. While the ROC/UKWMO Protected Group HQs stayed in continuous service from 1961 until 1991, the AAORs and Radars of the ROTOR system had become obsolete by the early 1960s, and their bunkers became available for new uses, usually just as secret as their original ones. Despite the vast investment in underground shelters for the use of HM government, it was generally recognised that London would not survive a nuclear attack for very long, so arrangements for the operation of regional centres were put in train. Between 1957 and 1963, a network of Regional Seats of Government (RSG) was set up across Britain. Most were semi-sunken bunkers, but that immediately west of London and covering the whole of southern Britain, was a Second World War-era underground aircraft factory at Warren Row, Henley-on-Thames, (Oxfordshire). As part of a national provision of control rooms, four Civil Defence War Rooms were built in London itself in 1955: at Kemnal Manor, Chislehurst; Partingdale Lane, Mill Hill; Northumberland Avenue, Wanstead; and Church Hill Road, Cheam. A fifth was added in 1972 at Southall, alarmingly buried under Hanborough School in South Street. Kemnal Manor was later abandoned for the nearby Pear Tree House, incorporated in a block of flats. The Metropolitan Police were provided with emergency War

123 Tottenham Court Road, the GPO Tower of 1961, one of the microwave towers of the 'Backbone' defence communications system.

HQs at Lippitts Hill and Merstham, both former AAORs. As well as control bunkers, the Civil Defence organisation built training centres, usually simple halls, but at Epsom there was a mock-up of a bombed city block, designed to allow Civil Defence workers to practise rescues and other emergency procedures in an authentic environment.

As well as all this secure accommodation for central government functions, similar provision was made for local government, with building taking place in two main campaigns. The first was in the mid-1960s following the Cuban Missile Crisis, and the second, to the bewilderment of many, was under the Thatcher government during the mid-1980s. The majority of County and District authorities were urged to construct underground bunkers that would be proof against explosion and nuclear fall-out. Structures spanned a wide range of effectiveness. At the luxury end were Epping Forest's Second World War operations block at RAF North Weald, which was converted in 1986 and the bunker built under Thameslink House in 1985–86 for the use of Richmond-on Thames council, both of which offered the highest possible protection factor. At the other end were the bargain-basement models adopted in the 1950s at Bexley, Camberwell, Hackney and Southwark. Despite the logical absurdity of their position, both geographical and political, several local authorities resolutely declared themselves 'nuclear-free zones' and refused to join in the waste of effort and resources defending the indefensible. Ealing opted out of the charade but was allocated space in the Southall bunker. Some authorities, such as Epsom and Ewell, and Malden, felt that their 1950s models were out-dated by the 1980s, and took advantage of government grants to rebuild to higher standards. Since 1991, many of these nuclear bunkers, especially those located in town-hall basements, have provided secure document storage while retaining the option of becoming a centre for coordinating the emergency services in a natural disaster or large-scale accident scenario. Others have been demolished or buried.

Protection against nuclear attack was also sought for communications systems and public utilities. The majority of these structures were outside the London area for obvious reasons, but the Kingsway Second World War telephone exchange was extended and upgraded to be 'nuclear-proof'. Railway control bunkers were built at Knebworth and Brickets Wood near Watford, but were soon replaced by mobile units. The 1961 Post Office Tower in Tottenham Court Road is a very visible element of the defence-based microwave communications network, of which other examples may be seen at Harrow Weald and Kelvedon Hatch. The Central Communications Establishment for the Home Office Hilltop Radio network was at Harrow, with local stations at Kelvedon Hatch and Knockholt Pound.

The Regular Army and the TA

The decades since the end of the war have seen the army in a continuous process of contraction. After the large-scale demobilisation that followed VJ-Day, manpower shortages could only be met by conscription, or National Service, which was already being phased out by the late 1950s. Regiments faced reorganisation, change of role, amalgamation or disbandment. The Royal Fusiliers (The City of London Regiment) was amalgamated with the Lancashire, the Royal Warwickshire, and Northumberland Fusiliers as the new Royal Regiment of Fusiliers within the Queen's Division in 1968. The KRRC joined with the Rifle Brigade as the Royal Greenjackets. Even Household Troops were not immune when the Royal Horse Guards (Blues) combined with the Royal Dragoon Guards to become the Blues and Royals in 1969. Similar exercises were going on in the TA. In 1947, 297 (Kent Yeomanry) LAA Regt was formed, amalgamating with 3rd/4th County of London Yeomanry in 1961 to become the Kent & County of London Yeomanry (Sharpshooters), currently a signals unit.

While many TA units had undergone major reorganisations in the years leading up to the war, some were presented with that particular challenge as they attempted a return to peacetime, volunteer soldiering. One such unit was 7th Bn The Queen's Regiment which was reconstituted in 1947 as 622 (Queen's) HAA Regiment RA, TA. Despite a partial rebuilding of their Braganza Street drill hall in 1938, the premises were far from suitable for a mechanised HAA unit, even had there been any equipment with which to practise. Tyres had to be let down to enable vehicles to traverse the entrance archway, and kerbs had to be recessed and lowered. Only the 3.7in guns with the shortened, weighted barrels could be used indoors, so weekend drills were held on a disused Second World War HAA gun site in Dulwich. When AA Command was stood down in 1955, many local TA regiments were amalgamated, in the ratio of two or three existing regiments to one new LAA Regiment, the 7th Queen's joining with the 1st Surrey Rifles for example, to become 570 LAA Regiment RA, TA.

Regular Army barracks

By the 1960s many of the old Victorian barracks were showing their age at a time when the expectations of recruits were beginning to rise. Chelsea was rebuilt in 1962 to accommodate 1000 guardsmen in a long five-storey block, with married quarters in two fifteen-storey towers. Knightsbridge/Hyde Park Cavalry Barracks, after less than 100 years of use, was rebuilt in 1967–70 to a design by Sir Basil Spence, with a tower 320ft (97m) high. Some rebuilding at St John's Wood in 1972 sent the RHA as lodgers to Combermere Barracks, Windsor. At Wellington Barracks the Guards' Chapel had been rebuilt in 1961 by Bruce George, incorporating some surviving earlier features but taking some inspiration from Coventry Cathedral to present a generally modernist building. New multi-storey accommodation blocks were added in 1979–85. Mill Hill Barracks took on additional roles including that of BFPO in 1962 but has now been redeveloped. Beavers Lane Camp, the hutted addition to Hounslow Barracks, lasted until 1983, occupied by 10 Signals Regiment, but while the barracks survives, the camp site is now covered with housing. Much of the fabric of Caterham Barracks has been converted into dwellings with spaces occupied by sympathetic in-filling. As at Chelsea, the Victorian chapel survives. At Kingston-upon-Thames, the armoury is the only major survivor in an estate of MOD housing. Goodge Street Underground station stayed as a military transit camp until 1956.

124 Wellington Barracks, the new Guards Chapel of 1963 replacing that hit by a flying bomb during a service in 1944, causing great loss of life.

Drill halls of the TA

Several drastic reductions in the size of the TA have meant a minimum of new building, and a wholesale disposal of premises. New uses have been found for some of the older drill halls, but others, including the moderne East Ham, and the neo-Georgian Highwood Barracks have been demolished and their sites sold for development. At 97 Horseferry Road, Westminster, the drill hall built in 1986–88 for the London Scottish, now a company rather than a full battalion of the London Regiment, incorporates the original iron frame moved from their former drill hall at 59 Buckingham Gate. Although reduced from its original size, two upper galleries are suspended from the roof trusses, leaving the maximum area of unobstructed floor space. In Mayfair, 56 Davies Street, the drill hall of the former Queen Victoria's Rifles, was remodelled in 1950–52 for another company of the Londons, and that in Worship Street was extensively renovated in 2001. At least one TAC, at Southall, has been built from scratch to a more modern design. However, form follows function and the function of a TAC is pretty obvious and allows for little latitude, so it is sad to see the rebuild of the former Essex Regiment drill hall on the site of the Cedars at the Portway, Stratford, described in Pevsner as an 'unwelcome intrusion'. The traditions of the TA survive in good health, and 221 Field Squadron, 101 (City of London) Engineer Regiment (EOD), an unusual part-regular and part-TA unit is based at Hudson House, Catford, named for the Second World War bomb-disposal pioneer Professor John Hudson who had joined the RE Bomb Disposal service with a degree in horticulture and ended up playing a key role in the coordination of an organisa-tion with 20,000 operatives.

125 Southall, one of the more modern of the very few recent TA Centres.

126 Biggin Hill, the control tower (5223a/51) identical to that at North Weald, built at the time of the Korean War, when the possibility of a conventional conflict, involving Russian bombers and British jet fighters, was recognised.

Military Aviation

The advent of the Cold War prolonged the active life of some airfields. Biggin Hill and North Weald received runway extensions and modern control towers in order to operate their Vampire and Meteor fighters until 1958. Heathrow had been prepared as a base for heavy bombers – B29s – receiving a new control tower and a long runway, but the bombers never arrived, and the airfield was handed over to the CAA as London's main civil airport. While final adaptations were being made, civil flights used Northolt. Much of the aircraft and guided-missile research and development of this period, took place in Greater London but under the auspices of civilian companies based at Hatfield, Radlett, Kingston-upon-Thames and Brooklands, among others. Their successful products were, for the most part, tested and deployed elsewhere.

By 2000, very few RAF stations were still active, and only at Northolt could military flying still be observed. The old Fighter Command Ops Room is preserved at Uxbridge and replicated in the RAF Museum at Hendon. Stanmore Park continues as part of the control system. Civil flying goes from strength to strength, with many of the former training and club fields flourishing, with Biggin Hill, in terms of flights, reputedly being one of the busiest airfields in Europe.

Command and control

In the years immediately after the end of the war, much of the direction of air forces remained in London. Bentley Priory HQ of RAF Fighter Command in 1946 and of 11 Group, Fighter Command, which had moved there from Uxbridge, until 1987, while Hendon served as HQ No 65 Group RAF Reserve Command from 1946–51. Bushy Park, Teddington, was HQ RAF Transport Command in 1946, but had been reclaimed by the USAF as HQ 3rd Air Division, 1948–62, with HQ US Strategic Air Command Operations at South Ruislip until 1959. HQ US Naval Forces (Europe), 1990s–2000s was in the US Embassy complex at 20 Grosvenor Square. HQ Military Air Traffic Control remained at Hillingdon House, Uxbridge until 2000, moving to MOD land at West Drayton as part of the National Air Traffic Services.

Training

Uxbridge remained an important centre for RAF personnel functions, including selection and training, but other, covert, operations went on elsewhere. Owing to its proximity to London University, premises in Bloomsbury were leased to house the Joint Services School of Linguists throughout the 1950s, spilling over to 'Tin Town', the First World War army camp set up next to Caterham Guards Depot, its entrance by the Old Fox PH. The Central Asian Research Centre, a room over the Kardomah Café in the King's Road, Chelsea, was used as a reading room for translating newspapers. There were other joint-service language schools at Greenwich (Japanese), RAF Kidbrooke (Russian) and at the Admiralty's Benet House in Mount Pleasant (Russian). Most of the students were National Servicemen being trained to eavesdrop on foreign radio transmissions, collecting what was to become SIGINT, and were accommodated in digs all over London.

Supplies and Services in the Cold War

Munitions development and production

The successors of those factories that built the Hurricane and the Mosquito also contributed to the new generation of military aircraft operating in the nuclear age. The first atomic bombs were designed to be delivered by the V-bombers, developed at Brooklands by Vickers, whose Valiant was test-flown from Wisley, and by Handley Page, whose Victors and Victor-conversions were tested and flown from Radlett. De Havilland's at Hatfield built Vampires and Venoms, and their Comet, the world's first jet airliner, provided the basis for the Nimrod AEW aircraft. Leavesden became a factory for the Rolls-Royce Aero division, building engines for successive genera-tions of military aircraft, both helicopters and fixed-wing. Hawker's Hunters and Harriers were produced in Ham. One alternative to delivery by aircraft is the use of rockets, and Fort Halstead, Chessington and Woolwich Arsenal have all been involved in their development at some time.

Services and supplies

The need to safeguard supplies of food, clean water and power to all sections of the community, civilian and military, and to maintain a fluid transport network in times of war, have always been government priorities. This was to assume a greater prominence in Cold War planning, when possible disruptions would be catastrophic in scale and unpredictably sudden. Throughout the 1950s two initiatives were set in motion. Firstly, the control centres for transport systems, as in the Second World War, but now needed for utility supply as well, were moved into hardened bunkers. Secondly, a network of food-storage reserves was established, in order that emergency feeding programmes might be effected in the aftermath of a nuclear attack. In expectation of total devastation in the centre of London, Buffer Depots, dispersed around the outskirts, held general inventories, from eating and cooking utensils to mobile bakeries, from flour and sugar stocks to tinned meat and powdered milk, and would be activated once survivors had exhausted their (notional) personal fourteen days' supplies. The London depots Campbell lists are at Hounslow, Sunbury, Brentford, Walthamstow, and Bermondsey, with others a bit further out at Hatfield, Borehamwood, Westerham and Harmondsworth, all outside the anticipated epicentre. An early identified need was for the road system to be kept open for official traffic, a national network of Essential Service Routes being designated, and in the event of nuclear war, kept clear of civilian traffic, probably by the TA under police supervision. In the London area this included fourteen radial routes and four ring routes such as the North and South Circular roads. This system for use in any type of emergency was still being updated in 1979. Overlaying this civil network were the Military Road Routes designed by the army to get solely military traffic, travelling to and from the ports and military bases, around London. In those pre-M25 days, a rather tortuous route circling London consisted of three legs codenamed 'Fox', 'Cat', and 'Stag'. Given that 'Cat' was the winding A25, and 'Stag' was the single-carriageway North Circular, then the imperative to keep them clear of refugees would have been absolute.

The War on Terrorism

The peace dividend appears to have exchanged the certainties of mutually assured destruction for the unpredictability of terrorism. Although the early 1970s introduced Londoners to this phenomenon when the Provisional IRA exported their campaign to mainland Britain, the

127 Lambeth, Vauxhall Cross, the MI6/SIS HQ opened in 1994.

128 Westminster Bridge, Temporary Vehicle Control Barriers outside Parliament on the approach from
Westminster Bridge.

media miss no opportunity to remind us of events in September 2001 in New York, of July 2005
in London, and of similar tragedies in Madrid, Bali or Paris. One effect of the publicity has been
the employment of publicists by the security services. Whereas in the 1970s we were not really
meant to know of the existence of MI5 and MI6, let alone name their directors or locate their
addresses, such things, if not necessarily more secure, are now more transparent. In 1994, MI5
was able to combine all its departments under one roof at Thames House, Millbank, opening

the Joint Terrorism Analysis Centre there in 2003. Vauxhall Cross, the MI6 building, opened in 1994 on the South Bank opposite Chelsea, variously referred to as 'Babylon' or 'Legoland', is a very visible replacement for Century House. Only a little further west along the river is the site for the new US Embassy, due to open in 2017. An article in the *New York Review of Books* describes it as a fortress. Its twelve floors sit on a bunker-like podium, there are grassy berms designed to foil truck bombers and concrete walls form a fortified perimeter, beyond which is a 100ft (30m) buffer blast-zone. All these features, plus the wet moat, combine to 'make it the twenty-first century avatar of the Tower of London'. The Houses of Parliament have been given their own defences, TVCBs, dubbed the architecture of paranoia by the *Observer* in 2007. These barriers are designed to prevent suicide bombers driving close to the buildings. As part of the security arrangements safeguarding the 2012 London Olympics, batteries of RAPIER ground-to-air missiles are being mounted, in one case, and to the surprise of its occupants, on the roof of the Bryant & May match factory in Bow, now converted into apartments. All these measures represent just the latest solutions to the evolving problems of defending London.

Appendix 1

Prehistoric Camps

National Grid References are six-figure, approximate to 100m, or four-figure, giving the relevant km square.

Barnet, Hadley Wood, univallate camp
Brentwood camp, TQ578945
Carshalton, Queen Mary's Hospital, camp
Caterham, War Coppice Camp
Chobham, The Bee Garden, Albury Bottom, SU974643
Edmonton, Bush Hill camp
Elstree, Brockley Hill, Pear Wood Belgic camp
Epping, Amresbury Banks, plateau camp, TL438004
Ewell, Diana's Ditch, TQ227634
Gerrards Cross, Bulstrode Park Camp, SU995880
Holwood Park, Keston, Caesars Camp, TQ422639
Heathrow, Caesars Camp
Ilford, Uphall Camp, TQ447853
Loughton Camp, TQ419975
Weybridge/Walton-on-Thames, St George's Hill Camp, TQ085619
Wimbledon Common, Caesar's Camp, TQ224712
Woolwich Power Station site, ditches surrounding roundhouses

Appendix 2

Mediaeval Fortifications
and Defensible Sites

1. Castles

Addington Castle Hill	TQ370641
Baynards Castle	TQ319808
Chessington Castle Hill	TQ191635
Cranford motte	TQ102771
Eynsford Castle	TQ541658
Farningham Castle	TQ547670
Godstone, Castle Hill, ring-work	TQ363508
Greenwich, Duke Humphrey's Tower	TQ389773
Kingston-upon-Thames, castle	TQ181693
Montfichet	TQ318811
Ravengers, possible outwork of Tower of London, held by de Mandeville in 1141	
Ruislip, Manor Farm, motte and bailey	TQ090878
St Mary Cray, Mount Way, The Mount, probable motte	TQ474681
Shoreham Castle	TQ523635
South Mimms, motte and bailey	TL230025
Tower of London	TQ335804
Walton-on-the-Hill, motte	TQ222551

2. Mediaeval Strong Houses

This list has been compiled with information from Philip Davis and Charles Coulson.

* Ave Maria Lane, a tower and gatehouse, part of the London residence of the Earls of Pembroke from around 1350
* Baynards Ward, house licensed to John de Molyns, 1338, Treasurer to Edward III
* Bread Street, licensed to John de Wengrave, 1314, Lord Mayor 1316–19
* Coldharbour, La Tour, a property fronting the Thames, possibly with a crenellated tower attached to a hall, owned by Alice Perrers in 1370s and still occupied in 1480s
* Cornhill, licensed in 1337 to John de Cologne, financier of Edward III's wars
* Distaff Lane (near St Paul's) licensed to John de Pelham, in 1311
* Fleet Street, Salisbury Court, licensed to bishop in 1337

* Lombard Street, Bucklesbury, Servats or Sernes Tower, licence to crenellate a turret above the gate of house with the Walbrook forming one boundary; acquired by Queen Isabella in 1317 later housing the Great Wardrobe
* Old Fish Street junction with Lombard St, Bishop of Hereford's house (TQ328810)
* Old Jewry and Ironmonger Lane, the Prince's Wardrobe, passed to the Black Prince from John of Eltham; it included great hall, chamber, chapel and kitchen and, at least in its later life, it had a defensible outer wall and a tower
* Pountney Lane, Candlewick Street, near the Thames waterfront, Manor of the Rose licensed 1341 to Sir John Pultney, Lord Mayor in 1336; four-storey, battlemented tower
* St Mary at Strand, licensed in 1305 to Bishop Langton of Coventry and Lichfield
* Silver Street, licensed to John de Pelham in 1311
* Thames Street, Steelyard, hall of Cologne merchants, by 1275
* Threadneedle Street, Merchant Taylors Hall of 1375, built on undercroft extended to support the chapel; also detached stone kitchen and a Great Gate onto Cornhill
* West Cheapside, licensed to Robert de Kelsey, citizen, lawyer and trader, 1315
* Westminster, Hospital of St John, Thomas Orgrave pardoned for unlicensed tower
* Westminster, Rosemont at Eye, licensed 1308 to John de Benstede

3. Mediaeval Manors and Palaces

Battersea, Bridgecourt Palace
Croydon Palace
Esher, Waynflete's Tower
Greenwich (Placentia) Palace
Kennington Palace
Rotherhithe Palace
Sheen/Richmond Palace
Walton Manor
West Wickham, Wickham Court

Bow, King John's Palace
Eltham Palace
Fulham Palace
Isleworth Palace
Lambeth Palace
Savoy Palace
Stepney Green, Worcester House
Westminster Palace
Winchester Palace, Clink St,
Woolwich, Tower Place

4. Mediaeval Moated Sites

Aldenham Park, Butterfly Lane, moat	TQ167969
Aveley, Belhus Park, Bretts Farm, moat	TQ560820
Aveley, Belhus Park, (Sir Henry Gurnett PH), moat	TQ563818
Banstead, Preston Hawe	TQ236572
Barnet, Monken Hadley, Old Fold Manor, later house in moat	TQ245976
Barnet, Galley Lane, Old Fold Farm, moat	TQ226975
Barnsbury, manor house of the Canons of St Paul's; now Barnsbury Square	TQ311843
Beckenham, South Norwood, double moated site	
Becontree, Valence Park, moat, C13 date, but Valence house in C14	TQ481866
Beddington, Carew Manor	TQ296653
Bexley, Hall Place, possibly moated; rebuilt c.1547; C17 four-storey tower	TQ502744
Bromley, Simpson's Moat or Place	TQ403690
Bushey, Moat Field Recreation Ground	TQ136956

Chertsey, Hamm Court Farm, moat	TQ067655
Cheshunt, Goffs Lane sports ground, moat	TL346025
Chingford, a lease dated 1265 mentions a moated house	
Chiswell Green, Burston Manor Farm, moat	TL135036
Chiswell Green, Holt Farm, moat	TL121036
Crayford, Howbury moated site	
Crockenhill	TQ505674
Datchet, Ditton Park, moat licensed to John de Molyns, 1331	TQ001778
Dyrham Park, moat	TQ224985
Ealing, Down Barns Farm, West End	TQ110838
Eltham, Well Hall, two moated enclosures	TQ424751
Enfield, Camlet, Trent Park	TQ288982
Enfield, fortified house of de Bohuns, Earl of Hereford, licensed 1347	TQ315964
Great Fosters, moat	TQ013696
Greenford, moat alongside Grand Union Canal	TQ168842
Hanworth, Castle Way, Tudor Court, excavated moat	TQ1071
Harefield, Hillingdon, Pynchester; pottery of C14 and C15 found	TQ072868
Harold Hill, Dagnam Park, square moat filled in by 1748	TQ5493
Harold Hill, Cockerels, square-moated site near demolished mansion	TQ550927
Heston, Cranford-le-Mote, site of moated manor under M4	TQ104783
Highbury, Hospitaller manor house, destroyed in 1381	TQ319856
Highgate Wood, moat of palace of bishops of London on golf course	TQ274884
Ickenham, Breakspear Road, Brackenbury, C15 house within a moat	TQ069871
Ickenham, Manor Farm, excavated moat	TQ090879
Ickenham, Swakeleys later mansion on site of earlier house of c.1300	
Kings Langley, Clapgate Farm, moat	TL077017
Lambourne, Bishops Hall, moat	TQ476954
Lambourne, Bishops Moat, moat	TQ484956
Langley, Moat House, moat	TQ016804
Leatherhead, The Moats, moated site	TQ154578
London Colney, Salisbury Hall, moat	TL196029
Merstham, Albury Manor	TQ293527
The More, Rickmansworth	TQ082940
North Ockendon, Hall Farm, moat of the Poyntz mansion	TQ588847
Northolt Manor, excavated moat	TQ133841
Oatlands Palace, Weybridge, moat of late C15	TQ078651
Oxhey Hall moat	TQ104944
Radlett, Battlers Green Farm, moat	TQ152987
Romford, Warren Farm, site of Marks, moated house	TQ485893
Shenley, Wild Farm, moat	TL176011
Shoreham, Filston Farm, moat	TQ516607
Sidcup (Bromley), Scadbury Park, C14 house, C15 moat	TQ459701
Slade Green, Howbury Farm, moated site	TQ527766
Southwark, Copt Hall	
Southwark, Paris Gardens, manor house with banks and ditches	
Upminster, Dury Falls, remains of a possible moat	TQ550873

Upminster, Lilliputs, moated site, probably mediaeval   TQ554884
Waltham Cross, Theobalds Park Farm, moat   TL349003
Walthamstow, Water Ho. (ex-Cricklewoods), Wm Morris Gallery, moat   TQ372901
Wattons Green, moat   TQ529953

Appendix 3

Barracks, Camps and Depots

Barracks 1600–1914

Croydon Cavalry Barracks, 1795

Finsbury: Armoury House (HAC), 1734–36, C19 additions, artillery ground

Holborn, Gray's Inn Road: barracks for London & Westminster Light Horse Volunteers, 1812–28

Hounslow Heath: camp established by James I, 1685

Hounslow, Beavers Road: Cavalry Barracks, 1793 and 1871

Hyde Park Barracks, c.1800, behind Park police station

Knightsbridge Cavalry Barracks, established 1792 (infantry barracks demolished)

Pimlico: Ordnance Office, 1907

Regent's Park, Albany Street: Cavalry Barracks, 1820s

Romford, between Waterloo and London Roads, Cavalry Barracks, 1795

St James's: St George's Foot Guards Barracks, 1826, now National Gallery

St James's, Birdcage Walk: Wellington Barracks, Foot Guards, 1834

St James's, Buckingham Palace: proposed barracks for Foot Guards, 1834

St James's, 23 Carlton House Terrace: Guards Brigade Office, early 1900s

St James's, Royal Mews, now National Gallery site: Horse Grenadiers, 1683–1788

St Johns Wood: Cavalry/Infantry/Artillery Barracks, 1812

Tower of London: Irish Barracks, 1669–70, rebuilt 1755

Tower of London: Waterloo Barracks and Officers' Quarters, 1855

Victoria, Buckingham Gate: Orderly rooms for Grenadier/Coldstream/Scots Guards

Victoria, James St (now Buckingham Gate): temporary stabling for Horse Guards

Westminster, Stretton (now Strutton) Ground: Artillery Grounds, 1600s

Whitehall, Scotland Yard: quarters for New Model Life Guard of Horse, 1660s

Whitehall, Horse Guards Tiltyard, corps-de-garde built 1641

Whitehall, Old Horse Guards and Foot Guards' wing to south, open by summer 1664,

Whitehall, New Horse Guards: completed 1760 for Life Guards, Royal Horse Guards and three
   Guards regiments

Whitehall, New Horse Guards: Foot Guards' orderly rooms 1880–1901

Woolwich Dockyard: Army Service Corps Depot, 1905

Woolwich, Frances Street: Cambridge (New Royal Marine) Barracks, 1847

Woolwich, Frances Street: New [later Red] Barracks [RM Infirmary], 1858

Woolwich New Road: Connaught ASC Barracks, conversion of 1780/1806 hospital

Woolwich New Road: RE Barracks, 1803

Woolwich, Royal Artillery Barracks, from 1775

Woolwich, Royal Military Academy, 1805

Barracks, Camps and Depots: First World War

Alexandra Palace: cavalry barracks, 1915

Battersea, Town Hall: recruiting office and HQ 10th Bn Royal West Surreys, 1915

Battersea, Latchmere Road Baths: used for drill 10th Bn Royal West Surreys 1915

Belgravia, Belgrave Square: 49 Auxiliary MT Coy ASC, ceremonial duties

Blackheath, Concert Hall: Royal Artillery Pay office, Dependants' section

Blackheath: 2 Reserve (HT) Depot, 665 Coy. ASC, 1916–19

Blackheath: No. 1 (HQ) Coy (HT) ASC Train, 73 Division (Home Forces)

Blackheath: Local Auxiliary HT Coy ASC, West Lancashire Reserve Bde TF

Camden Town, Regent's Park: 5, 6, 22, 27 & 35 Park Crescent & 36 Chester Terrace used as billets for ASC drivers at postal depot

Caterham (Tin Town) next to Guards' Depot, Infantry Camp

Chelsea: 75 Local Auxiliary MT Coy ASC AA Defence, 1918–19

Deptford: ASC Supply Reserve Depot, Light Railway & Crane detachment (MT)

Deptford: 1162 & 1163 Horse Transport Coys ASC

Epsom Downs: Infantry Camp, University & Public Schools Bde

Fulham: 10 Auxiliary [later 12] MT Coy, 1915–22

Grove Park SE12, Marvels Lane, ex-Greenwich Workhouse, ASC Depot: 3rd & 4th (Auxiliary) Omnibus Coys MT, 1914–19

Holborn, Newton Street: 36 Local Auxiliary (MT) Coy ASC, 1916–18

Hurst Park: assembly point for 16 (Public Schools) Bn Middlesex Regt

Kempton Park: assembly point for 16 (Public Schools) Bn Middlesex Regt

Kensington Palace Barracks: 793 HT Coy ASC, 1916–21

Kenwood House: RNAS AA unit HQ

Mill Hill, Inglis Barracks: Middlesex Regiment depot

Park Royal: 1 Reserve (HT) Depot, 661–664 Coys ASC, 1916–19

Plumstead: ASC Driver Training Centre, 1915–19

Purfleet Barracks: tented camp for 10,000, plus 160 huts on Rainham ranges

Regent's Park & Kensington Barracks: No. 28 Local Auxiliary MT Coy ASC, 1915–19

Romford, Hare Hall: Infantry Camp, 28th Bn London Regt (Artists' Rifles), and 24th (2nd Sportsman's) Bn Royal Fusiliers; then OCTU run by 2/28th Artists' Rifles

St John's Wood Barracks: 'B' Reserve Brigade, RHA, 1915–18

Shepherds Bush: 23 Local Auxiliary MT Coy. ASC, 1915–19

Wandsworth, Buckhold Road: drill field, 13th Bn East Surrey Regt 1915

Wandsworth, Buckhold Rd: Young's Brewery, parade yard, 13th Bn East Surrey Regt

Wandsworth, High Street, Town Hall: recruiting office

Whitehall, Great Scotland Yard: Central Army Recruiting Office

Willesden: 2 Reserve (HT) Depot, 666 Coy ASC, 1916–19

Woldingham: Infantry Camp, 11th (Public Schools) Bn Middlesex Regiment

Woolwich: 1163 Horse Transport Coy and 'F' Supply Coy ASC

Woolwich, Herbert Road, Royal Arsenal Co-op Store: Royal Artillery Pay Office

Barracks, Camps and Depots: Second World War

Ascot, Royal Hotel: Horse Guards mobilisation centre, 1939

Ashford: RASC workshops

Bushey Golf Club-house: royal escort details, RASC & 2nd Northants Yeomanry

Caterham Barracks: Guards' Depot and Officers Brigade Squad, 1939

Chelsea Barracks: Guards' Holding Battalion and BD unit

Chelsea, Duke of York's HQ: RAMC, Yeomanry HQs and BD unit

Ealing, Churchfield Road drill hall: 1/8th Bn Middlesex Regt, 1940

Elstree School: depot for 4th/5th Bns Coldstream Guards, raised 1940–41

Eton, Crewer, Old Etonians Club: Horse Guards mobilisation centre, 1939

Feltham: RASC Depot

Finsbury Park: No. 11 Armoured Fighting Vehicle Depot, pre-D-Day

Harringay Stadium: No. 11 Armoured Fighting Vehicle Depot, pre-D-Day

Hounslow, Beavers Road: barracks and hutted camp

Knightsbridge Barracks: Household Cavalry depot

Laleham (Queen Mary Reservoir): No. 1 Vehicle Reserve Depot, pre-D-Day

Lippitts Hill: militia camp, then 184th AA Bty US Army, 1942–45

Mill Hill: Inglis Barracks, Middlesex Regiment depot and hutted camp

Northolt, Manor House: 2nd/8th Bn Middlesex Regt, 1940

Northwood, Monkseaton, Northgate: 2nd Bn London Scottish, 1940

Pinner, Old Hall, Paines Lane: 2nd Bn Queen's Westminsters, 1940

Regent's Park Barracks: Guards' Holding Battalion

Richmond Park: East Surrey Regiment camp, 1941

Richmond Park: ATS barracks, then GHQ Liaison Regiment (PHANTOM)

Rickmansworth, Moor Park: 1st SAS Brigade Tactical HQ

St John's Wood Barracks: London District Signal Troop, 1939

Sanderstead, Llandaff House, Sanderstead Hill: 48th Bn Royal Tank Regiment

Sandown Park Racecourse: overspill for Guards' Training Battalions

Theobalds Park: RA barracks for AA personnel

Twickenham, Kneller Hall: RHQ GHQ Liaison Regiment (PHANTOM) to Richmond

Wanstead Flats: D-Day marshalling camp for transport units

Warlingham, Crewes Place: 42nd Bn Royal Tank Regiment

Wellington Barracks: Westminster Garrison, 1943

Whitehall, War Office: Army Bureau of Current Affairs

Woolwich, Royal Military Academy: 2nd/7th Bn Middlesex Regt, 1940

Regimental Depots: post-1945

Caterham Barracks: Guards' depot
Chelsea, Centre Block, Duke of York's HQ: Special Air Service Regiment
Eltham Palace: Royal Army Education Corps
Hammersmith, Empress State Building, Lillie Road: Army Legal Corps
Hammersmith, Empress State Building, Lillie Road: Military Provost Staff Corps
Regent's Park Barracks, Albany Street: Queen's Royal Irish Hussars
St John's Wood Barracks: Kings Troop RHA
Tower of London: HQ Royal Regiment of Fusiliers
Wellington Barracks: HQ Grenadier, Coldstream, Scots, Irish and Welsh Guards
Westminster, 56 Regency Street: HQ Royal Signals
Whitehall, Horse Guards: Life Guards, Blues and Royals
Woolwich New Road, Government House: Royal Artillery

Appendix 4

Some Drill Halls and TACs of the Volunteer Forces

(**Bold** type denotes structures that are still surviving at the time of compilation)

1. Drill Halls of the London Regiment, 1914

1st Bn	**Handel Street**, Bloomsbury: in use by London Universities' OTC
2nd Bn	**9 Tufton Street**, Westminster: now offices
3rd Bn	21 Edward Street, St Pancras: redeveloped
4th Bn	112 Shaftesbury Street, Shoreditch: site backs onto **Wenlock Street** (qv)
5th Bn	130 Bunhill Row, Finsbury: demolished and redeveloped
6th Bn	**57a Faringdon Road**, Finsbury: archway with crest; hall behind and garages used by OTC from **Saffron Hill TAC**
7th Bn	24 Sun Street, Finsbury Square: demolished and redeveloped
8th Bn	130 Bunhill Row, Finsbury: demolished and redeveloped
9th Bn	**56 Davies Street**, Mayfair: rebuilt post-Second World War, active TAC
10th Bn	**Hillman Street**, formerly 49 The Grove, Hackney: council offices/depot
11th Bn	17 Penton Street, Finsbury: demolished for Public Carriage Office
12th Bn	**Chenies Street**, Holborn: converted to arts centre
13th Bn	**Iverna Gardens**, Kensington: hall in mews off High Street
14th Bn	59 Buckingham Gate, Westminster: redeveloped, part of hall re-erected at the new London Regt (London Scottish) TAC on **Horseferry Road**
15th Bn	**Somerset House**, Strand: between main building and West Wing
16th Bn	**58 Buckingham Gate**, Westminster: frontage remains as offices
17th Bn	66 Tredegar Road, Bow: demolished for Post Office sorting office
18th Bn	**Duke of York's HQ**, Chelsea: luxury apartments, Saatchi Gallery and TAC
19th Bn	76 High Street, Camden Town: demolished and redeveloped as shops
20th Bn	**Holly Hedge House**, Blackheath: active TAC
21st Bn	**4 Flodden Road**, Camberwell: rebuilt *c*.1980s on same site, active TAC
22nd Bn	**2 Jamaica Road**, Bermondsey: active drill hall for Royal Marine Reserve
23rd Bn	**27 St John's Hill**, Battersea, active TAC
24th Bn	**71–73 New Street**, (now Braganza Street), Southwark, active TAC
25th Bn	**Fulham House**, **87 High Street**, Putney Bridge, active TAC
28th Bn	**Dukes Road**, St Pancras: now The Place Theatre

2. Drill halls of the inter-War years: 1919–39

Barnet (London EN5) St Albans Road, active TAC
Brixton (London SW2) Upper Tulse Hill, active TAC
Catford (London SE6) Hudson House, Bromley Road, active TAC
Clapham (London SW4) Kings Avenue, active TAC
Coulsdon (London CR5) Marlpit Lane, active TAC
Croydon (London CR0) Mitcham Road, active TAC
Dulwich (London SE22) Highwood Barracks, Lordship Lane, demolished
East Ham (London E6) Vicarage Lane, demolished
Edgware (London HA8) Deansbrook Road, active TAC
Ewell (London KT17) A240 Ewell Bypass, active TAC
Finchley (London N12) High Road, North Finchley, demolished
Grove Park (London SE12) Napier House, Baring Road, active TAC
Hackney (London N1) Wenlock Street, now printing works
Heston (London TW5) Vicarage Farm Road, active TAC
Holloway (London N7) Parkhurst Road, active TAC
Hornsey (London N8) Priory Road, active TAC
Kingsbury (London NW9) Honeypot Lane, active TAC
Kingston-upon-Thames (KT1) Portsmouth Road/Surbiton Road, active TAC
Romford (London RM7) London Road, active TAC
Tottenham (London N17) Tottenham High Road, now sports centre
Whipps Cross (London E17) Lea Bridge Road, active TAC

Appendix 5

Command and Control

Government, Civil Service and Armed Services: 1600–1914

Hounslow Barracks: Cavalry HQ London Garrison, 1800s

Mayfair, 3 Grafton Street: official residence, First Lord of the Admiralty, 1767

St James's, Carlton House Terrace: Horse Guards annexe, early 1900s

St James's, 80–91 Pall Mall Cumberland & Buckingham Houses: WD offices, 1850s

Somerset House, Strand: Admiralty Board and later Navy Office, 1776

Tower Hill: Navy Board, 1620–1788

Westminster, 10 Parliament Street: Office of the Commissary General for GB, 1798

Whitehall, Cockpit (now Downing St complex): Cromwell's military administration

Whitehall, Horse Guards: C-in-C's HQ 1663

Whitehall, Scotland Yard: War Office 1675–83

Whitehall, Little Wallingford House: War Office 1689

Whitehall, Admiralty Building, 1693–94

Whitehall, 7 Whitehall Gardens: offices for army's civil staff from 1710

Whitehall, Horse Guards: War Office from c.1760, with barracks

Whitehall, Horse Guards: C-in-C's departments from 1854

Whitehall, Old Admiralty (now Ripley Buildings), 1723–26

Whitehall, Admiralty House, 1786–88

Whitehall, Old War Office: built 1899–1906 on Whitehall Gardens site

Government, Civil Service and Armed Services: Second World War

Belgravia, 37, 103, 105, 106, 115, 117, 118 Eaton Square: Belgian government in exile

Belgravia, Kingston House, Knightsbridge: Norwegian government in exile

Belgravia, 16/19 Lowndes Square: Air Ministry offices

Bloomsbury, British Museum Underground station: emergency HQ London District Military Command and Brigade of Guards offices

Bloomsbury, Goodge Street Underground station: emergency ETOUSA joint-services communications centre, 1942–6

Bloomsbury, Goodge Street Underground station: War HQ for Chiefs of Staff Strategic Allied Command (COSSAC), 1944–45

Bloomsbury, Percy Street, The Manor: Air Ministry offices

Bloomsbury, 19–9 Woburn Place: Air Ministry offices

Chelsea, 14–16, 29–33, 42–46 and 50 Draycot Place: Air Ministry offices

City, Barbican, 30 Moorgate: Air Ministry offices

City, Carter Lane, Faraday Building: Post Office trunk exchange

City, Upper Thames Street, Vintry House: HQ Reserve Fleet

Cricklewood, 403–5 Edgware Road: Admiralty Chart Depot, RN War Room

Dollis Hill (PO Research Centre) Cabinet citadel 'Paddock'

Hammersmith: St Paul's School, GHQ Home Forces, then HQ 21st Army Group;

Hampstead, Finchley Road, Wendover Court: HQ RN Coastal Forces, 1941

Harrow: NW Suburban relocation plan for Air Ministry departments included schools:
     Harrow County Boys, Gayton Road; Harrow County Girls, Lowlands Road;
     Eastcote Lane Girls; The Belmont; Wealdstone Bridge, Station Road;
     Hibbert Road and Priestmead, Hartford Avenue, Wealdstone

Hayes, 234, 238/9 Nestles Avenue: Air Ministry offices

Holborn, Aldwych, Bush House: Air Ministry offices, NE Wing, AMWD Drawing Office, 1944

Holborn, Aldwych House: Air Ministry offices

Holborn, Chancery Lane Underground Station: HQ for resistance in the event an attack on
     London, then shelter against V1 & V2 rockets

Holborn, 5–6 Clements Inn: Air Ministry offices

Holborn, Houghton House and annexe: Air Ministry offices

Holborn, Kingsway, Adastral House & Alexandra/York House: Air Ministry offices

Holborn, 11 Kingsway, Awdry/Imperial House: Central Medical Establishment

Holborn, 32–34 Kingsway, Victory House: Air Ministry offices

Holborn, Kingsway, Princes House: MAP offices

Holborn, Pen Corner, 41 Kingsway: RCAF offices

Holborn, 8 New Court: Air Ministry offices

Holborn, Victoria House and 17 Southampton Row: Air Ministry offices

Holborn, Theobalds House, Ariel House: Ministry of Civil Aviation

Kensington, 206 Brompton Road, ex-Underground station: AAOR London GDA

Kensington, Cromwell Road, South Kensington War Room: London Regional Home Security
     (Civil Defence)

Kensington, 26–40 Kensington High Street (Barkers store): Air Ministry offices

Kensington, Princes Gate Court: Air Ministry offices

Kilburn, 16 Randolph Gardens (Convent Buildings): Air Ministry offices

Lambeth, Waterloo Road, Cornwall House and annexe: Air Ministry offices

Maida Vale: BBC Studios

Marylebone, Baker Street, Abbey House: Air Ministry offices

Marylebone, 4–7 and 9–14 Bryanston Square: HQ US Strategic Air Forces (Rear)

Marylebone, 15 Bryanston Square: HQ US Air Technical Services Command (Europe)

Marylebone, 20 Bryanston Square: HQ US 1st Army Group & US 1st Army

Mayfair, 9 Albemarle Street: Air Ministry offices

Mayfair, 40 Berkeley Street and 42 Berkeley Square: Air Ministry offices

Mayfair, Berkeley Square House: Air Ministry Departments of Planning, Production and
     Research, 1939

Mayfair, Bruton Street: Air Ministry offices

Mayfair, Curzon Street House (MI5 building): citadel for use by royal family

Mayfair, Down Street ex-Underground station: Emergency Railway Committee

Mayfair, 15 Grosvenor Place: Air Ministry offices

Mayfair, 15 Grosvenor Square: HQ US Naval Forces in Europe (deputy commander)

Mayfair, 20 Grosvenor Square: HQ ETOUSA and US Naval Forces (COMNAVEUR)

Mayfair, 28 Grosvenor Square: Public Relations Office ETOUSA

Mayfair, 41–43 Grosvenor Square: HQ US Army Quartermaster Corps

Mayfair, 47 Grosvenor Square: HQ US Forces UK Base Organisation and staff

Mayfair, Marble Arch, 1 Great Cumberland Place: HQ US Army Quartermaster Corps

Mayfair, North Row: HQ Royal Netherlands Navy

Mayfair, Oxford Street: scrambler machine in Selfridges basement, 1943

Mayfair, 73–77 Oxford Street (Drages store): RCAF offices

Mayfair, Oxford Street, Selfridges store: HQ US Army Quartermaster Corps

Mayfair, Park Street, Fountain House: Office of President of Poland

Mayfair, 19–20–22 Upper Brook Street: HQ 5th AACS Wing, 89th Base Unit USAAF

Mayfair, 25 Savile Row: Air Ministry offices

Mayfair, 28 Wimpole Street: HQ Polish Navy

Northolt: Sector HQ and Operations Room 11 Group RAF Fighter Command, 1940

Piccadilly, Dover Street Underground Station: emergency HQ London Transport

Piccadilly, Stratton House: Netherlands government in exile

Piccadilly, Stratton House: Polish government in exile main offices

St James's, 55 Broadway: London Transport HQ above St James's Park Tube station

St James's, 2 Cockspur Street (Sun Life): HQ Canadian Forces UK, 1939–45

St James's, 4 Carlton House Gardens: Council of Defence of the Free French Empire

St James's, Millbank, Dean Stanley St, Westminster Ho: HQ Petroleum Warfare Dept

St James's, Norway House, 21 Cockspur Street: Norwegian Ministry of Defence

St James's, Kings House, 10 Haymarket: Navy Office of Canada

St James's, St James's Square, Norfolk House: SHAEF & COSSAC

St Pancras, 194 Euston Road: Air Ministry offices

South Ruislip: HQ 3rd Air Division 8th USAAF

Stanmore, Bentley Priory: RAF operational HQ and emergency HQ for Army and ARP

Stanmore, Bentley Priory: HQ RAF Balloon Command, 1940

Stanmore Hill, Hill House: No. 11 Group Filter Room, 1945

Stanmore, Hive Road, Kestrel Grove, Advanced HQ Allied Expeditionary AF, 1943

Stanmore: HQ RAF Transport Command, 1943

Stanmore: Air Traffic HQ, 1944

Swiss Cottage: Northways House, flats, HQ for Rear-Admiral (Submarines) 1940–45

Teddington, Bushy Park, Camp Griffiss, Station 586: HQ (overall), 8th USAAF, 1942–44, then to High Wycombe

Teddington, Bushy Park: SHAEF HQ *Widewing* D-Day planning HQ

Teddington, Bushy Park: HQ US Strategic Air Forces in Europe (USSAFE) 1944–45

Twickenham: Kneller Hall, GHQ Home Forces

Uxbridge: HQ and Filter Room 11 Group, RAF Fighter Command

Uxbridge, Hillingdon House: Advanced HQ Allied Expeditionary Air Force, 1943

Uxbridge, Combined Control Centre, HQ Advanced Allied Expeditionary Air Force

Uxbridge: HQ 9th Tactical Air Force, 1944

Uxbridge: HQ 2nd Tactical Air Force, 1944

Uxbridge: HQ 85 Base Group, Allied Expeditionary Air Force, 1944

Victoria, Queen Annes Gate: Air Ministry offices

Wealdstone, Headstone Drive/Hailsham Drive: Station Z underground citadel for Air Ministry,

1938; Reserve Fighter Command HQ, ('The Manor'), 1942

Westminster, Victoria, Ashley Gardens: Air Ministry offices

Westminster, Victoria, 8–9 Buckingham Gate: Air Ministry offices

Westminster, Victoria, Buckingham Palace Gate, Hotel Rubens: C-in-C Polish Forces

Westminster, Horseferry Road: 17 and 18–19 Monck Street, 'The Rotundas', built under disused gas holders to house parts of Air Ministry Intelligence Dept, COSSAC and HQ Home Forces; (along with Montague House, Faraday Building and Curzon Street House all code-named 'Anson')

Westminster, Horse Guards Parade: Admiralty Citadel

Westminster, Marsham Street, Romney House: War Office, Directorate of Fortifications and Works (DFW3), 1940

Westminster, Millbank, Thames House: HQ Ministry of Aircraft Production (MAP)

Westminster, Broad Sanctuary, 4 Central Buildings, Matthew Parker Street: citadel for government use, possibly SIS/MI6

Westminster, Parliament Square House: Air Ministry offices

Whitehall, Storeys Gate: Cabinet/Central War Rooms and Number 10 Annexe under New Public Offices at junction of Great George Street, opened 27 August 1939

Whitehall: Cabinet/Central War Rooms, six rooms allocated to GHQ Home Forces

Whitehall, Montague House: Old War Office citadel

Whitehall, King Charles St, New Public Offices: Air Ministry offices

Whitehall, Northumberland Avenue: War Office Department of Transportation (Tn5)

Whitehall, Richmond Terrace: offices of Defence Staff

Whitehall, 2–8 Richmond Terrace: Air Ministry offices

(Whitehall Gardens: planned War Emergency HQ with room for 1000, not built)

Whitehall, West Court basement, New Public Offices: Operational HQ Home Forces

Appendix 6

Military Airfields
and Aviation Sites

The sites listed here include military airfields and aircraft development, production and flight-testing sites, often working alongside operational units, all being integrated into one unified list, the numbers referring to Figure 14.

Drawing or Type Numbers used in several of these appendices show the sequence and year of production. For example, the Watch Office for All Commands was built to the 343rd design from the Air Ministry drawing office in 1943 – hence 343/43.

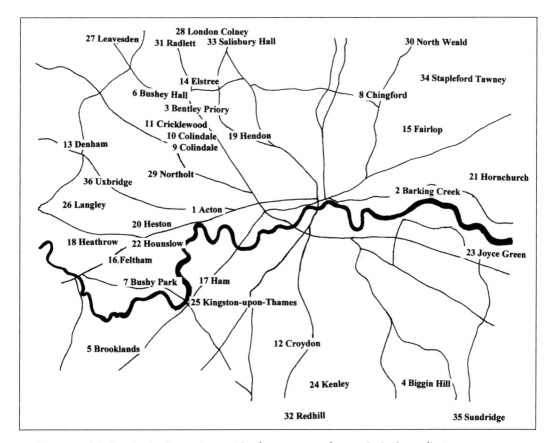

Figure 14 Aviation sites in Greater Lonon. Numbers correspond to entries in Appendix 6.

1 ACTON Unsatisfactory location used pre-First World War and in the early part of the war for training, then as the Alliance Aeroplane Company's factory, closing in 1920. During the Second World War, the hangar was used by MAP making parts for de Havilland's at Leavesden.

2 BARKING CREEK Handley Page works 1909–1912; moved to Cricklewood

3 BENTLEY PRIORY (Stanmore Park) Established in 1926, in the C18 house, as a control centre for aspects of Britain's air defences, it became HQ Fighter Command in 1936. In 1968 it became HQ of the fighter element of Strike Command. The house was restored after a bad fire in 1979. RAF **Stanmore Park** was adapted as a Balloon Centre in 1938, and given high storage hangars and two Bellmans. The site has now been redeveloped as the support facility for the Priory.

4 BIGGIN HILL Opened in February 1917, it shortly became part of LADA, operating Bristol Fighters, and remained in sporadic use until 1929 when a programme of new building to establish an AA training establishment and an operational airfield with two squadrons. A prototype AA Trainer was designed and installed in 1926. Further construction took place in 1938, and the next year a tarmac runway was laid, followed by two more. As a Sector Station in the Battle of Britain, Biggin Hill's Spitfire squadrons were in constant action, and the airfield was virtually destroyed by enemy bombs. During the V1 attacks it functioned as the regional base for Barrage Balloon operations. RAF operational flying ceased in 1958. Surviving buildings include the Officers' Mess, built *c.*1930 in neo-Baroque style, the 5223a/51 (Revised type) Control Tower, and most of the 1920s and '30s North Camp buildings including Station HQ, guardroom, Type C Barrack Blocks (548/28), and extensive 1920s married quarters; later there were also T2 hangars on two sites. It has deservedly been designated as a Conservation Area by Bromley Council.

5 BROOKLANDS (Weybridge) Aircraft manufacture began in 1910 and flying training in 1912. During the First World War, as well as operational squadrons, Sopwith, Vickers and Martynside carried out aircraft construction, with eight large sheds accommodating No. 10 AAP. Hawkers and Vickers-Armstrong built aircraft here between the wars and in 1932 the Flying Club built its Clubhouse/Control Tower. The factory was heavily bombed during the Second World War. Aircraft manufacture continued up until 1970. Surviving buildings include the clubhouse/control tower, an AA tower, a pillbox, and a Bellman hangar.

6 BUSHEY HALL (SE of Watford) From 1942–45 this neo-Jacobean house of *c.*1880 on Aldenham Road, was HQ US 8th AAF Fighter Command.

7 BUSHY PARK (Teddington) Home to HQ US 8th AAF, then HQ US SAFE and many support units from 1942–45. Camp Griffiss, codenamed Widewing, consisted of over 400 buildings, mainly huts.

8 CHINGFORD Used mainly for training throughout the First World War, becoming No. 207 TDS; it closed in 1919.

9 COLINDALE (Edgware Road, opposite the end of Colindale Avenue) Airco's First World War factory incorporated A-frame sheds, and three-storey neo-Georgian offices. Completed aircraft were pushed along Colindale Avenue to Hendon for flight testing.

10 COLINDALE (Stag Lane) Built as an aircraft factory by de Havilland's in the early 1920s and a flying field operated here until the move to Hatfield in 1934. The site continued in use until 1971, when the original buildings were converted for use by BACS (banking) organisation. In 2005 they were demolished for housing.

11 CRICKLEWOOD A Handley Page factory from 1912, increased demand made an expansion to Radlett necessary in 1929. Although flying ceased the next year, production carried on into the 1960s. The site has been cleared and redeveloped.

12 CROYDON Established in 1915 for training and as a defence landing ground, it was also later the site for the short-lived No. 1 National Aircraft Factory. After the First World War, it quickly established itself as London's civil airport, and in 1928 the old aerodrome with its wartime Belfast truss hangars was demolished, and new airport facilities opened in 1928. These consisted of a control-tower/terminal building, hotel, and extensive aircraft sheds including gabled hangars. The Second World War brought RAF units back, and the airfield was extensively damaged by bombing. Flying ceased when Heathrow became London's official airport in 1946. Surviving buildings include control tower/terminal, hotel, and a hangar; the gate lodge of 1928 is apparently based on the RAF Guardhouse, type 166/23.

13 DENHAM Opened in 1917 to house schools of military aeronautics, it became the factory of Martin of Martin-Baker in 1929. In 1939, Bellman and Blister hangars were erected and it became a relief landing ground for Booker. Surviving buildings include two side-opening sheds, a double-gabled hangar and an over blister hangar.

14 ELSTREE (Aldenham) Opened as a flying club in 1935, with two hangars and a clubhouse; within two years it was being used by Hendon, and a year later by Northolt. It was used throughout the Second World War by Fairfield Aviation to test, repair and modify RAF aircraft in new hangars provided by MAP for this purpose. Surviving buildings include a MAP R-type hangar, a pair of joined Super Robins, and a Blister.

15 FAIRLOP (Hainault Farm) Established 1915 as a Home Defence fighter airfield, continuing as such, and as a sub-station of No. 207 TDS at Chingford, until it closed in 1919. Having been earmarked in abortive plans for a City of London airport in 1930, it was rebuilt as a fighter station in 1940, serving as such until 1944 when it became No. 24 Balloon Centre, closing in 1946. Surviving buildings include twin Aeroplane Sheds (56/17), and two groups of 1855 farm buildings, used as accommodation and messes.

16 FELTHAM (Hanworth Park) Used during the First World War as an AAP with large storage sheds. Behind it was the Whitehead's aircraft factory, and a new aerodrome was started in 1929 with clubhouse in the eighteenth-century Hanworth Park House. A FTS began in 1935, and there were firms manufacturing aircraft on the north-west edge of the airfield, much of it contracted to Hawkers, mainly repairing Hurricanes. In 1940, the FTS moved to Meir (Staffordshire) and the production of gliders became the major activity. Most traces have now disappeared, and the First World War AAP is the site for a 1930s RASC Depot incorporating Feltham House.

(HAINAULT FARM *see* **FAIRLOP)**

17 HAM This aircraft factory, in the angle of Richmond Road and Dukes Avenue, now demolished, was operated by Sopwiths in the First World War and by the Leyland Motor Company until after the Second World War when Hawkers moved here from Langley. It appears to have consisted of a solid block of thirty-six GS Hangar-type structures, with additional, possibly end-to-end Robins hangars. The 1958 office block has been demolished.

18 HEATHROW From 1930–44 this private airfield was Fairey Aviation's flight-testing ground, and in 1944 it was requisitioned by the Air Ministry as a base for B-29 heavy bombers. Unused, uncompleted and handed to the CAA on 1 January 1946 as the new London Airport, a control tower (type 294/45 for Very Heavy Transport Stations) was one of the few RAF structures actually built on site.

19 HENDON From 1909 this was established as a premier showcase for flying, the manufacture of aircraft, innovation and display. In 1914 the Grahame-White factory and flying field were requisitioned as a RNAS flying school and as an AAP. Until 1916 the airfield was operating fighters defending London against bombing raids. A large number of storage sheds were built, and in 1925 the RAF took over the airfield as a fighter station. It operated until 1949, and has provided a home to the RAF Museum since 1963. Surviving buildings include GS hangars, integrated into later exhibition halls with only their roof trusses visible. The Grahame-White factory building has been re-erected on the museum campus near to the parachute store (2355/25) main stores (840/30) and workshops (814/30). Other buildings on Aerodrome Road, including the Belvedere, or control tower, and the RFC officers' mess of 1916, are likely to be incorporated in a housing development. At the end of Aerodrome Road stands the London Aerodrome Hotel, dated 1917, which also became an officers' mess. Aeroville is a square of neo-Georgian housing built for 300 aerodrome workers in 1917, and is still occupied as private dwellings.

20 HESTON Opened 1929 as an aero club, it had a clubhouse, a concrete apron, floodlights, and the surviving revolutionary all-concrete hangar, the forerunner of the Lamella. It operated as a satellite of Northolt throughout the First World War, pioneering night-flying techniques and PR, closing as Heathrow opened.

21 HORNCHURCH Known as Sutton's Farm in the First World War, it operated as a base for a Home Defence squadron, and was demolished in 1918. Rebuilt from scratch in 1928, as a fighter station, some distance to the west of the earlier airfield, with A- and C-Type hangars, it operated into mid-1944. Its final role was training and aircrew selection until 1962. Surviving buildings include the officers' mess (Astra Close) similar to that at North Weald, extensive housing and married quarters, and fighter pens and defences around the airfield perimeter. It is now a country park.

22 HOUNSLOW Taken over by the RFC in 1914 as a training depot, it was part of LADA by 1916. Returned to civilian flying in 1918, it was taken back by the army in 1920, when flying ceased.

23 JOYCE GREEN Begun by Vickers in 1911 as a test field, in 1914 it was taken over for RFC training, and in 1915 it housed a flight of fighters. After the war, Vickers returned, soon transferring their operations to Brooklands, and the site reverted to agriculture.

24 KENLEY Started as an AAP in 1917 with fourteen large hangars, it was chosen as a permanent RAF station with some new building taking place in the 1920s. It was a Sector HQ for the Battle of Britain and suffered much damage in air raids, losing three hangars and other buildings. Further damage was sustained when flying had stopped during the V1 offensive. The RAF ceased regular flying in 1966 but retain much of the site for gliding. Surviving buildings include the officers' mess, married quarters of 1928–30, the main stores, and a barrack block.

25 KINGSTON-UPON-THAMES Built in Canbury Park Road 1913–18 as a Sopwith factory fronted by offices; they survive as Sopwith House.

26 LANGLEY Operated as a Hawker factory with grass field from 1936–50, producing and testing Tornado and Typhoon prototypes there in 1939–40.

27 LEAVESDEN Bought by the Air Ministry in 1940 in order to establish an aircraft factory administered by de Havilland's of Hatfield. Hangars and workshops were built, and a 3000yd runway was laid. After the Second World War the site stayed in MoD hands but was leased to Rolls-Royce to build aero-engines. Flying ceased in 1994 and the site now operates as film studios.

28 LONDON COLNEY A landing ground was developed into a training station in 1916, and was provided with timber aircraft sheds and huts. It closed in 1919, and was not used in the Second World War, possibly owing to the close proximity of Salisbury Hall and Radlett. A brick-built First World War plane store and workshop, and a Second World War MT shed used by CD survived until very recently.

29 NORTHOLT Established early in the First World War as a purpose-built home defence night-landing ground. Six flight sheds and a double hangar were built along with workshops and hutted accommodation. RAF use continued after the First World War, and in the mid-1920s new buildings, including an A-Type hangar were constructed, followed ten years later by a C-type, and brick H-blocks, most being camouflaged as rows of suburban houses in 1939. Throughout the Second World War it was mainly occupied by fighter squadrons, and still operates as London's military airport. Surviving buildings include the officers' and sergeants' messes, barrack blocks, two C-type hangars, ops room, guardroom, and station workshops, all from the 1920s and 1930s, and another operations block, decontamination centre etc. from the Second World War. The off-site Second World War operations room at Eastcote House survives as flats. EH recently listed the main site.

30 NORTH WEALD It started life as a home defence station throughout the First World War, lying dormant until its complete rebuilding in 1926. Ad Astra House, built in 1908 and requisitioned as Station HQ in 1916 was one of the few survivors from the early days, with new buildings including two A-Type hangars. It operated as a Fighter Sector station in the Battle of Britain and suffered bomb damage. In c.1952, a new control tower was added, but flying ceased in around 1965, and it was finally disposed of in 1979. Surviving buildings include Ad Astra House, the officers' mess, one A-Type hangar, the 5223a/51 control tower, and the operations block, which has been updated for use as a nuclear bunker.

31 RADLETT The aerodrome opened in 1930 with test-flight hangars, which were soon expanded on the Park Street site to accommodate the large Handley Page aircraft being built throughout the Second World War. In 1952 the main runway was extended for the Victor programme. With the demise of Handley Page in 1969, the airfield closed, and the main site was demolished. The Park Street flight test sheds and offices survive.

32 REDHILL RAF use began with an EFTS in 1937. It housed fighter squadrons throughout the Second World War, and then reverted to Reserve Flying training until its closure in 1954. Surviving buildings include a range of gabled hangars including a MAP A1 hangar, several timber buildings including messes, crew room and stores, a tb guardroom, squash court and offices, Nissen hut workshop and Blister hangars.

33 SALISBURY HALL (Shenley) The Tudor house within its moat, was the secret workshop where de Havilland developed the Mosquito. It is now an aircraft museum housed in hangars imported from other airfields.

34 STAPLEFORD TAWNEY Opened in 1934 as a base for civilian services, and was taken over as an ERFTS in 1938, becoming a satellite for North Weald's fighters in 1940. Late in 1943 it was transferred to US 2nd TAF, who carried out much demolition when they left in 1953. Since then it has reverted mainly to club flying.
Surviving buildings include the large steel and asbestos hangar, and the smaller hangar/armoury office, officers' mess, NAAFI and a few other huts.

(SUTTONS FARM *see* **HORNCHURCH)**

35 SUNDRIDGE A rare survival of three linked 1910 aircraft sheds, listed by EH, re-clad in corrugated iron, but appearing to preserve their original roof timbers. They are used to store animal feed at Dibdale Farm on the B2211 north of the village (TQ484558). However, there appears to be no record of an airfield here.

36 UXBRIDGE Hillingdon House was destroyed by fire in 1844 and its plain replacement, along with the surrounding estate, was bought by the government in 1915 with the intention of using it as a POW camp. Instead it became a convalescent hospital and then, in 1917, the RFC Armament School, transferred from Perivale. In 1918 it was reorganised as the RAF Depot, receiving permanent barrack buildings through the 1920s. The next twenty years were concerned with processing recruits, a wide range of administrative, medical and training functions, and demobilisation, and since then, such similar activities have continued. Surviving buildings include the officers' mess in Hillingdon House, barrack blocks and the Battle of Britain Ops Room, recently listed by EH.

Other Sites Used for Military Aviation Activities 1925–45

Hendon: HQ 116 Wing in Hendon Hall, 1944
Highgate, Athlone House (built 1871): RAF intelligence school
Mayfair, 18 Old Quebec Street: USAAF Air Transport Command passenger terminal
Northwood, Eastbury Park: Coastal Command HQ from 1938
St John's Wood, Lord's Cricket Ground: Aircrew Reception Centre 1939–46
St John's Wood, Lord's Cricket Ground: Aircrew Allocation Centre, 1944

St John's Wood Aviation Candidates' Reception Centre, Lord's Cricket Ground: HQ, officers' mess and WRAF billets: Abbey House, Park Road Bentinck Close and Viceroy Court, Prince Albert Road, Avenue Road and 6 Hall Road (NW8): candidates' billets; London Zoo: recruits' mess (*sic*)

Stanmore, Bentley Priory: HQ Inland Area 1926–36, then HQ Fighter Command

Stanmore, Bentley Priory, Harrow Road Lodge: Station Commandant's house The Cedars, No. 2 Mess; The Rookery, rations store; Rosary Priory, Elstree Road and The Warren, Bushey Heath, WAAF hostels

Stanmore, Wood Lane, Stanmore Hall: Allied Expeditionary Air Force Mess, 1944

Uxbridge, Hillingdon House: HQ 11 Group Fighter Command

Uxbridge: No. 1 Personnel Despatch Centre

Appendix 7

The Militia in 1850

20th (1st Royal Surrey) Regiment of Militia: HQ Richmond
    became 3rd Bn East Surrey Regiment
3rd Royal Surrey Militia, revived 1852
    became 4th Bn East Surrey Regiment
55th Royal Westminster Middlesex Regiment of Militia: HQ Hammersmith
    became 3rd Bn The Royal Fusiliers (City of London Regt), 1881
    then 5th Bn + 6th Bn Royal Fusiliers (City of London Regt), 1898; (NB 4 regular Bns)
Royal South Middlesex Regiment of Militia, raised 1853
    became 7th Bn
58th Royal West Middlesex Regiment of Militia: HQ Uxbridge
    became 1852 Light Infantry, then 1854 Edmonton Royal Rifle Regiment, then 1881, 7th Bn
King's Royal Rifle Corps
65th Royal East Middlesex Regiment of Militia: HQ Hampstead
    became 6th Bn Duke of Cambridge's Own Middlesex Regiment
83rd Tower Hamlets Regiment of Militia: HQ Bethnal Green
    1874 split into King's and Queen's Own Royal Tower Hamlets Militia
    Queen's became 5th Bn and King's became 7th Bn Rifle Brigade
97th King's Own Light Infantry Regiment of Militia: HQ Stoke Newington
106th Royal London Regiment of Militia: HQ Euston Square
Royal Elthorne Regiment of Militia Light Infantry formed 1853 in Uxbridge
    became 3rd then 5th Bn Duke of Cambridge's Own Middlesex Regiment

Appendix 8

Intelligence and Communications 1939–45

(No. 80 Signals Wing RAF was known as the 'Beam-benders')

Aldenham, Wall Hall: SOE Training School STS 39

Aldersgate, St Martin's-le-Grand: Marconi HQ with RAF No. 80 (Signals) Wing

Barnet, Arkley View: HQ Radio Security Service, clearing house for intercepts from amateur 'hams' for onward transmission to GC&CS Bletchley Park

Bexley, Hall Place: US Army 68th Signals Security Detachment

Bloomsbury, Bedford Square (Erno Goldfinger's offices): Industrial Camouflage Research Unit

Bloomsbury, Senate House, London University: offices of Ministry of Information and Ministry of Economic Warfare

Borehamwood, The Thatched Barn (Barnet bypass): Station XV SOE camouflage

Brixton Prison: housed internees

Brookmans Park: BBC transmitter

Chelsea, 22 Pelham Cres.: Belgian ex-patriate Comet group, MI9 (Escape and Evasion)

Clapham, Victoria Royal Patriotic School: London Reception Centre (MI5 B1d) 1941

Clapham, Nightingale Lane: female annexe, London Reception Centre

Cockfosters, Trent Park: Combined Services Detailed Interrogation Centre

Denmark Hill: Metropolitan Police intercept site

Dollis Hill: GPO Engineering Branch Research Establishment working with RAF No. 80 (Signals) Wing

Dollis Hill: GPO factory produced prototype Colossus for GC&CS at Bletchley Park

Elstree: repeater station linking GPO research department transmitters and receivers

Elstree-Harpenden: paired Meacon jammer stations of RAF No. 80 (Signals) Wing

Garston Manor: Road Research Laboratory, RAF No. 80 (Signals) Wing HQ, 1940

Ham Common, Latchmere House: Second World War Camp 020, interrogation of spies/suspects

Hampstead, Parliament Hill: BBC receiver involved in Meacon with RAF No. 80 (Signals) Wing moved from Swains Lane

Hendon: 35 Crespigny Road, site of transmitter for Arabel/Garbo XX agent

Heston airport: Radio Counter Measures out-station of RAF No. 80 (Signals) Wing

(RAF) Heston: RAF Photographic Development Unit, 1939 (PR)

Highgate, Athlone House: RAF intelligence school

Highgate, Swains Lane: BBC receiver involved in Meacon with RAF No. 80 (Signals) Wing moved to Parliament Hill

Holborn, Kingsway, Bush House: HQ Political Warfare Executive from late 1942

Holborn, Adastral House (Kingsway/Aldwych): RAF camouflage design section

Holborn, Kingsway, Bush House, opposite Adastral House: Dept Z (Claude Dansey)

Hounslow: Bromide set up by RAF No. 80 (Signals) Wing to combat X-Geraet

Kensington, 8 Kensington Park Gardens: The Cage Interrogation Centre (Nazi VIPs)

Marylebone, 64 Baker Street/Michael House (M&S office): SOE HQ
Norgeby House, Room 52, HQ Signals office 1942; from 1 January 1944, all foreign sections including RF (from Dorset Square) under one roof

Marylebone, Montagu Mansions (block of flats off Baker Street): new home for SOE Signals section heads of department, from 1 January 1944

Marylebone, 9–14 Bryanston Square: US Strategic AF (Rear) Intelligence Directorate

Marylebone, Chiltern Court: SOE Norwegian and Danish sections

Marylebone, 1 Dorset Square: HQ RF Signals section in Bertram Mills Circus HQ

Marylebone, Duke Street: RF/Free French/de Gaulle's HQ

Marylebone, Orchard Court: SOE Briefing rooms

Marylebone, 5 Sussex Gardens: Services language school – Chinese & Japanese, 1945

Marylebone, 32 Weymouth Street: hostel for France-bound SOE agents

Marylebone, 59 Weymouth Street: US Army Signal Intelligence Section

Mayfair, Berkeley St: HQ diplomatic and commercial code breaking, GC&CS, 1941

Mayfair, 4 Cadogan Place: OSS enlisted men's billets

Mayfair, Curzon Street House: HQ of SIS/MI6/'C'

Mayfair, Crewe House, Curzon Street: office of Lord Northcliffe's Propaganda in Enemy Countries organisation

Mayfair, Devonshire House: HQ MI8 Signals Unit, from 2 Caxton Street

Mayfair, 18 Grosvenor Square: US Navy Intelligence Division & Secret Mail Centre

Mayfair, 18 Grosvenor Square: OSS HQ

Mayfair, 59 and 72 Grosvenor Street: London office of OSS, 1942–45

Mayfair, Oxford Street, John Lewis building: Room 102, US Counter-intelligence

Mayfair, 49 Upper Brook Street: OSS WAC personnel billets

Muswell Hill, Alexandra Palace: BBC transmitter involved in Meacon with RAF No. 80 (Signals) Wing

Potters Bar: Radio Counter Measures out-station of RAF No. 80 (Signals) Wing

Radlett, Aldenham Lodge Hotel: RAF No. 80 (Signals) Wing RCM HQ with Ops Room at 'Newberries' on Radlett golf course from late 1941

Radlett: RCM HQ billets in 'Tintern', 'Lamorna'; 'Heathwood', The Avenue: WAAF hostel; 2 Beech Avenue: sick quarters Howards Garage, Watling Street: RCM HQ MT section

Radlett Hall, Watling Street: RCM HQ services canteen

Radlett, Watling Street, The Houseboat (ex-nightclub): RCM HQ Ops Room

Richmond Hill Hotel: first depot GHQ Signals Liaison Regiment – 'Phantom', 1940

St James's, Ryder Street; HQ Section V, MI6, from St Albans, 1943

St James's, St James's Street: HQ MI5 (town office, country office Blenheim Palace) 1940

St Paul's: Faraday Building: GPO Main Trunk Switching Centre (used for secret tests)

Shepperton Studios: made dummy aircraft etc. for 'K' bombing decoys

Sloane Square: code-breaking centre for Russian material, 1945

South Kensington, Imperial College: office of Col Wills, CO SOE camouflage dept

South Kensington, 178 Queensgate: used pre-Second World War by Admiralty code-breakers

South Kensington, Natural History Museum: SOE camouflage department workshop; SOE demonstration showroom; and Station XVb SOE exhibitions

Stanmore: Block 'B' of Government offices used for GC&CS Bombes (80) Stanmore, Eastcote
    between Eastcote Road and Lime Grove: Bombes for GC&CS

Stoke Newington: Peto Scott factory made small transmitters used for Meacons

Teddington: Paint Research Station, experiments with camouflage

Tower of London, Combined Services Detailed Interrogation Centre to 1939

Wandsworth: Rediffusion factory made transmitters for Meacons

Wembley: overspill GPO Engineering Branch Research Establishment working with RAF
    No. 80 (Signals) Wing

Westminster, 24 Broadway, HQ of SIS/MI6/'C'

Westminster, Broadway Buildings: first home for GC&CS then to Bletchley Park

Westminster, Broad Sanctuary, 4 Central Buildings, Matthew Parker Street: citadel for govern-
    ment use, possibly SIS

Westminster, 2 Caxton Street: HQ MI8 Signals Unit, then to Devonshire House

Westminster: Jermyn Street, office of Garbo's XX controller (Tomas Harris)

Westminster: 58 St James's Street: HQ XX committee

Westminster, Victoria Embankment, Electra House: HQ Foreign Office Department EH
    (Propaganda to Enemy Countries)

Westminster, Wellington House, Buckingham Gate: War Propaganda Bureau

Woolwich Common: Royal Signals Experimental Establishment

Wormwood Scrubbs: MI5 Registry, Card Index and Transport sections, 1940

Appendix 9

Site Gazetteer

(A list of examples, surviving at time of compilation, not a complete inventory)

Anti-Invasion Defences

London Defence Lines A, B and C

Alexandra Park AT blocks on railway embankment at TQ302905; two Home Guard explosives stores at TQ299905 and 305903

Barkingside Station Lines of AT blocks alongside tracks

Barnes & Kew railway bridges pillboxes and spigot mortar positions

Batchworth AT blocks, Type 22 and two Type 27 pillboxes at TQ074/80–94

Beckenham Type 22 pillbox at TQ367702

Chadwell Heath 50+ AT blocks beside railway at Crow Lane at TQ487877

Cheshunt Type 27, Type 22 pillboxes, and two sets of AT blocks at TL331/3-046/9

Cuffley Three rows of sockets for AT rails and AT blocks on Carbone Hill at TL293039; three pairs of AT blocks with slots for RSJs, and two Type 22 pillboxes, at TL299/304-041/3

Dagenham East *c.*200 large AT cylinders & roadblock at TQ503/5-852; pillbox and more AT cylinders at TQ512850

Epsom Type 24 and two Type 27 pillboxes, AT blocks at Drift Bridge at TQ231601

Epping Type 27 pillboxes at TL434028, 435026, 436016, 434013 & 436021

Epping Forest Traces of AT ditch at TL431006 and 432001

Finchley, Rosemary Avenue, house converted to strongpoint at TQ257903

Hainault and Fairlop Stations AT blocks at TQ45092 and TQ450908

Lee Type 22 pillbox near Dutch House PH, A20 road/rail crossing at TQ413738

Nazeing AT block and fourteen hairpin AT rails at TL382053; crossing point of AT ditch marked by six AT blocks at TL404051

Newbury Park Station 100+ AT blocks at TQ449888

Northaw Pillbox and eight AT blocks on Ridgeway at TL277038

Oxhey Rectangular pillbox under railway bridge at TQ119995

Perry Hill Three Type 27 pillboxes at TL395055, 398052 and 398055

Potters Bar Twenty-five large AT blocks up both sides of railway embankment at TL249024

Putney Bridge Station Pillbox and defended signal box on high-level platform

Shooters Hill Thirteen-sided spigot mortar pedestal at TQ429766 behind police station

Slade Green HAA site defences include two pillboxes at TQ530774 & 532773

Tanfield Stud Long, low machine-gun bunker at TL324050

Turnford Tall pillbox and AT wall and AT blocks at level crossing at TL368052
Wanstead Pillbox at A12 crossing at TQ416884

Vulnerable Points

Airfield Defences

Biggin Hill (Kent) pillbox at TQ 415619
Fairlop (London) FC Construction pillbox at TQ450909
Hornchurch (Essex) BHQ at TQ533840, Type 22 pillboxes at 535840, 536843 and 536848, two
   Tett Turrets at 535842, and others in undergrowth
North Weald (Essex) Type 22 pillbox at TL494046, two FC Construction pillboxes at 487037
   and 495045, thickened hexagonal pillboxes at 489036, 492500 & 495041
Radlett Allan Williams turret at TL157048
Redhill BHQ at TQ303482, two pillboxes at 296484 and 296482
Stapleford Tawney Type 22 pillbox at TQ491975, thickened pillbox at TQ499974

Nodal Points, Depots etc.

Enfield Lock ROF Type 24 pillbox at TQ377998; guard post at approx. TQ378993
North Weald Mobilisation Centre Two Allan Williams turrets at TL505039 & 506039
Purfleet AA Magazine Guard posts at TQ549791 and 550790
South Mimms AT obstacle at TL218015
Woolwich Gallions Reach: mine-watching post at TQ 450805
Woolwich Tripcock Ness: mine-watching post/pillbox at TQ455810

Air Defence

Chadwell Heath Second World War HAA site at TQ488897, eight 4.5in guns +
Cheshunt Albury Farm, Second World War HAA site at TL350017/353016, unarmed
Chigwell Second World War Barrage Balloon depot at TQ439935
Edmonton Firs Lane, Second World War HAA site, four 3.7in (mobile) TQ 325937
Enfield Donkey Lane, Second World War HAA site, unarmed, TQ341973
Enfield Chase Side, Second World War HAA site, four 4.5in TQ306973
Fort Halstead experimental centre for weapons development, in former London Mobilisation
   Centre at TQ501597; currently (2012) scheduled for closure
Goffs Oak Burnt/Poyndon Farms, HAA site, four 3in (mobile) TL321021, TL320020
Herne Hill Velodrome: barrage balloon storage
Honor Oak One Tree Hill, First World War AA gun position at TQ354743
Kensington 206 Brompton Road AAOR in TA drill hall, ex-underground station
Kenwood House HQ of First World War AA defences at TQ271874
Kidbrooke Second World War Barrage Balloon depot at TQ409753
Knockholt ROC Cold War underground post at TQ473614
Lippitts Hill Second World War HAA site and 1950s AAOR at TQ496971
Monkhams Hill First/Second World War AA gun position at TL386024
Mudchute Park Second World War AA site on Isle of Dogs at TQ382788

Purfleet First World War Blockhouse with AA pom-pom at TQ538793; and Second World War London District AA magazines at TQ549789

Romford Colliers Row Lane: Mobilisation Store at TQ500900/1

Ruislip Manor Second World War AA Tower at TQ099869

Slade Green Second World War HAA site TQ530770

Theobalds Park Gunsite Farm, HAA site at TQ334006

Theobalds Park RA barracks for AA personnel

Waltham Abbey Second World War AA Tower at TL370022

Watford (Herts) 1961 ROC sector control centre at Cassiobury Drive at TQ094978

Munitions Production
and Logistical Support

Powder Works: 1600–1850

Bedfont, on the River Crane: 1609
Stratford's Three Mills and St Thomas Mills: early seventeenth-century
Tolworth: 1560
Southwark: 1630
Tottenham and Walthamstow: 1656
Wandsworth: late 1600s
Enfield Mill at Enfield Lock: 1653
Hackney and Clapton: 1652
North Feltham: 1668
Aldgate, the Worshipful Company of Gunmakers' Proof House: 1657 Stepney, 46–50
    Commercial Road: c.1757
Gunmakers' Proof House rebuilt 1826
Balham: 1701
Hounslow: 1757
Wimbledon: late eighteenth century
Hyde Park Magazine: 1805 by James Wyatt, architect to the Board of Ordnance

Munitions Production and Logistical Support: First World War

Acton: Alliance Aeroplane Coy (Waring and Gillow) formed at Acton airfield
Beckton: Gaslight and Coke Co., chemical works
Blackheath: ASC No. 2 Reserve HT Depot, 1915
Bow, Old Ford Road: Connaught Works London Small Arms Company 1867–1919
Bromley-by-Bow: J&W Nicholson's Three Mills Distillery, acetone production
Colindale: Airco aircraft factory
Cricklewood: new Handley Page aircraft factory, 1916
Enfield Lock: National Small Arms Factory, weapons production
Deptford: ASC No.1 Reserve HT Depot, 1914 (to Park Royal)
Deptford: ASC Light Railways & Crane Detachment (985th Coy)
Deptford: ASC Supply Reserve Depot
Feltham: Hanworth Park built as AAP, then Whitehead Aviation from 1915
Finchley: National Balloon Factory in Bohemia Ltd (cinema company) works, 1918

Fulham, Hurlingham Avenue: W.E. Blake Explosives Loading Co., filling factory

Fulham, Stevenage Road: Trench Warfare Department, National Filling Factory No. 27

Greenford, Perivale: National Filling Factory No. 28; gas shells

Greenford Chemical Co.: explosives factory

Grove Park (SE12): ASC No. 1 MT Reserve Depot, 1914; later nucleus of Lee ASC Reception & Training Area (sites in Camberwell, Catford, Eltham and Sydenham)

Hackney Wick, White Post Lane/Wallis Road: Donald Bagley Phoenix Chemical Works, HM Factory, TNT plant

Hayes: Fairey aircraft factory making floatplanes, 1914–18

Hayes: nationalised aero-engine factory, 1917

Hayes: National Emergency Filling Factory No. 7, explosives factory

Hendon: Grahame-White aircraft factory

Holborn, Short's Gardens, Drury Lane: ASC Home MT Depot, 1915 (included sub-depots at Camden, Carlow Street, Gray's Inn Road and Cressy Road)

Holborn, Newton Street: No. 36 Local Auxiliary MT Coy ASC, 1916–18

Holland Park: hostels for 250 Queen Mary's Auxiliary Army Corps (606 Coy ASC)

Islington: ASC Reserve HT Depot, 1914

Kensington Barracks: War Cabinet and Army car pool

Kidbrooke: RAF Stores Depot, 1917

Kilburn: R. Cattle Ltd/Central Aircraft Co.: aircraft component production

Kingsbury, Church Road/Kingsbury Road: Kingsbury Aviation Co. aircraft and vehicles

Kingsbury: Handley Page aircraft factory

Ladbroke Grove: Clement Talbot Ltd (Rolls-Royce) to Ministry of Munitions, 1918

Lee: ASC MT Depot 1917 (Eltham, Kelsey Manor, Shortlands, Norwood, Sydenham)

Lower Edmonton, Balham Road: Snowden Fibre Machining Co. Ltd, cotton waste

Millwall: Vacuum Oil Co Ltd: oil distillery, mineral jelly

Osterley Park: ASC reserve MT depot; sites in Hownslow, Isleworth, Twickenham Park Royal (TQ193828 pre-First World War flying field) ASC No. 1 Reserve HT Depot

Perivale, Willesden Lane, Park Royal: National Filling Factory No. 3, explosives

Pimlico, Grosvenor Road: HQ London General Omnibus Company

Regent's Park: ASC Army Postal Services (620 MT Coy) also Mount Pleasant

Richmond, Townshend Road, drill hall: Whitehead Aviation until 1915

Shepherds Bush, 176–78 Holland Park Avenue: HQ 606 Coy ASC transport for Ministry of Munitions and Aircraft Department

Shepherds Bush, Goldhawk Road, bus garage: workshops & stores ASC 606 Coy

Silvertown, Crescent/Venesta Wharves: Brunner Mond & Co, explosives/TNT plant

Southall: London Explosives Co., explosives/TNT plant

Southwark, Sumner Street: National Emergency Filling Factory No. 8, explosives

Stratford: Admiralty Filling Station

Sudbury, Wembley: Motor Radiator Manufacturing Co. Ltd, nationalised 1918

Waltham Abbey: munitions production

Westminster, 64 Whitehall Court: HQ ASC Forage Dept and Women's Forage Corps

Woolwich Arsenal: experimental work with gas shells; artillery/weapons production

Munitions Production and Logistical Support in the Second World War

Acton: Napier aero-engine factory

Acton: Alliance hangar used by MAP for Mosquito parts for de Havilland

Acton: LPTE workshops assembling Halifaxes

Barking Creek: site for construction of Mulberry Harbour Phoenix Caissons

Bow: Chisenhale Works made veneers for warplanes from 1942

Canning Town: Albright & Wilson (chemicals) shell-filling plant

Charlton, Harden's Manor Way: Siemens factory working on PLUTO

City, Smithfield Market: Pykrete (ice/wood-pulp mix) developed in freezer laboratory

Colindale, Stag Lane: de Havilland aero-engine factory

Cricklewood: Handley Page factory building Halifax bombers

Croydon, Prospect Way: Redwing Aircraft, evacuated to North Watford

Dawley, Bourne Avenue: ROF manufacturing SAA

Earls Court, LPTE workshops: parts for tanks; 500 Handley Page Halifaxes; aircraft components made in subway between Underground station and Exhibition Hall

East Acton: Hawker works building Hurricanes and Tornadoes

Elstree, Aldenham Aero Club: Fairfield Aviation aircraft repair facility for MAP

Feltham (Hanworth Park): British Aircraft Manufacturing Co. Ltd/Rollasons

Fulham, 22 Bagleys Lane: Fuel Oil Technical Laboratory, rocket engine research, 1941

Grays: site for construction of Mulberry Harbour Phoenix Caissons

Great West Road: Packard's marine engines factory

Greenwich: G.A. Harvey produced 3in UP Projectors, 40 per cent of total ordered, 1940

Hampton: Thorneycroft's built MGBs, MLs and MTBs

Hayes: Fairey Aviation factory test-flying from Heathrow and Heston

Heathrow: set up by Fairey in 1929, requisitioned by the Air Ministry in 1942

Heston: Fairey aircraft factory, 1944–45

Heston: Heston Aircraft Co. part of Civilian Repair Organisation

High Holborn (181), WC1: Educational Supply Company, Esavian hangar doors

Kensington, Natural History Museum: camouflage workshop

Kensington, Trevor Square: photographic and make-up camouflage workshop

Kidbrooke: RAF No. 1 MU civilian-manned repair depot

Mayfair, Grosvenor Hotel: RN laboratory developing Mulberry Harbour

North Acton, Gorst Road & Sunbeam Road: 691st US Army Ordnance Depot

Ruislip: RAF No. 4 MU civilian-manned repair depot

Ruislip: RAF Air Ammunition Park, No. 64 MU, 1942

Ruislip LTPE depot: BSA manufacturing Oerlikon LAA guns

Selsdon High Street: Boulton and Paul aircraft factory

Teddington, National Physical Laboratory: development of Mulberry Harbour

Teddington: Paint Research Station, work on camouflage and non-reflective paints

Teddington: Toughs boatyard built MGBs and MTBs

Thornton Heath, Bensham Lane: Redwing aircraft factory

Tottenham Court Road: parachute factory in Heal's furniture shop

Waltham Abbey: munitions production

Walthamstow: Wrighton's (furniture) building Mosquitoes

Wanstead/Gants Hill: Plessey's aircraft components factory in Central Line tunnels

Watford, Odhams printworks: Redwing Aircraft evacuated from Croydon
West Drayton: ORLIT concrete huts
Woolwich Arsenal: development, testing and manufacture of new weapons
Woolwich: Principal Royal Naval magazine
Woolwich: Mulberry Harbour pontoons fitted out
Woolwich: Siemens Bros. & Co., development of PLUTO cables
Woolwich, Dupree Road: Johnson & Phillips pipe-handling equipment for PLUTO
Yeading: ROF manufactured small arms ammunition

Military Hospitals and Welfare 1642–2000

Military Hospitals: 1642–1914

Caterham Guards Depot, military hospital, 1875
Greenwich: Infirmary (1763–68), later Dreadnought Seamen's Hospital, closed 1869
Hounslow Cavalry Barracks, military hospital, 1861
Regent's Park Cavalry Barracks, military hospital, 1877–9
Savoy Hospital, Strand (former palace) military hospital 1642–79
Westminster, Caxton Street, St Ermin's Court Hotel: RAMC Medical School, 1902–5
Westminster, Millbank: RAMC Medical School, 1905
Westminster, Millbank: Queen Alexandra's Military Hospital, 1905–77
Westminster, Rochester Row: Grenadier Guards' Hospital, 1859; now RMP Depot
Woolwich, Woolwich New Road: Royal Ordnance Hospital c.1780
Woolwich, Frances Street: Red Barracks, Royal Marine Infirmary, 1860
Woolwich: Royal Herbert Hospital, 1865

Military Hospitals: First World War

Bloomsbury, Queen Square: National Hospital for the Paralysed and Epileptic
Bloomsbury: University College Hospital, twenty beds for military heart cases
Camberwell: 1st London General Hospital RAMC
Chelsea: 2nd London General Hospital RAMC
Chelsea, Duke of York's HQ: offices 1st, 2nd and 4th London General Hospitals RAMC
Chelsea, Duke of York's HQ: 1st and 2nd London Clearing Hospitals RAMC
Chelsea, Duke of York's HQ: 1st and 2nd London Sanitary Companies RAMC
City: Charterhouse Military Hospital (limbless)
Croydon: Addington Palace War Hospital (typhoid) with hutted camp of 1000 beds
Dartford, Orchard Infectious Diseases Hospital, became military convalescent hospital
Denmark Hill: 4th London General Hospital RAMC
Denmark Hill: Maudsley Neurological Hospital (Maudsley Memorial Hospital)
Edmonton, Silver St, Millfield House: Special Military Surgical Hospital, 1915
Epsom: Horton County of London War Hospital (London County Asylum)
Epsom: Manor County of London War Hospital (London County Asylum)
Epsom, Woodcote Park: military convalescent hospital
Ewell: Ewell County of London War Hospital (The Ewell Colony)
Finchley, King Edward's Hall: VAD hospital
Hampstead: military hospital (only RFC cases, 1917)

Hampstead, Egremont, Lyndhurst Gardens: Artists' Rifles auxiliary VAD hospital, 1915

Ingatestone, Fryerning Hall: Convalescent Hospital

Holborn, 3 Henry Street: HQ and offices of the 3rd London General Hospital, RAMC

Kensington, 10 Palace Green: specialist neurological hospital for officers

Lambeth, St Thomas's Hospital, 5th London General Hospital, RAMC

Latchmere, Ham Common: private mental hospital for shell-shocked officers

Maida Vale: The Hospital for Epilepsy and Paralysis

Marylebone, Welbeck Street: West End Hospital for Diseases of the Nervous System

Marylebone, Westmoreland Street: Hospital for Diseases of the Heart (military beds)

Napsbury War Hospital (Middlesex County Asylum)

Paddington Military Hospital (limbless)

Piccadilly, Arlington Street, temporary hospital in home of Duke of Rutland

Purfleet Military Hospital

Regent's Park, Great Portland Street: Royal National Orthopaedic Hospital

Richmond Park: South African Red Cross Hospital

Roehampton: Queen Mary's Convalescent Hospital (limbless)

Romford Military Hospital

Shepherds Bush Military Orthopaedic Hospital

Sidcup: Queen Mary's Hospital, set up 1917 for plastic surgery on war-wounded

Surbiton, 60–62 Claremont Road: Home Counties Clearing Hospital, RAMC

Tooting Grove: VD hospital

Wandsworth Common, Royal Victoria Patriotic Building: 3rd London General Hospital RAMC

Wandsworth: Springfield War Hospital (Middlesex County Asylum)

Warlingham: Enteric Depot and VD hospital

Westminster, Londonderry House, Park Lane: temporary hospital

Westminster, Millbank: Queen Alexandra's Military Hospital, 1905–77

Westminster: Rochester Row Military Hospital

Woldingham: Enteric Depot in former army camp

Woolwich: Royal Herbert Military Hospital

Military Hospitals: 1918–39

Finchley: RAF Officers' Hospital, 1918

Finchley: RAF Hospital, Princess Mary's RAF Nursing Service permanent staff, 1927

Hampstead, Heath Street: Queen Mary's House, military maternity home, 1922

Uxbridge: Southern Area RAF Medical HQ, 1919

Uxbridge: RAF Officers' Hospital, 1925

Westminster, Millbank: Queen Alexandra's Military Hospital, 1905–77

Woolwich: Royal Herbert Military Hospital

Military Hospitals and Welfare: Second World War

Aldenham, Church Farm: Red Cross Convalescent Home/Auxiliary Hospital

Banstead, Zachary Merton: Red Cross Convalescent Home/Auxiliary Hospital

Beckenham: freeze-drying plant trialled Army Blood Transfusion Service

Colindale Hospital evacuated to Kinmel Park (Clwyd)

Esher, Claygate, Ruxley Towers: HQ NAAFI

Holborn: 11 Kingsway, Awdry/Imperial House: RAF Central Medical Establishment

Kingston Hill Place: Red Cross Convalescent Home/Auxiliary Hospital

Leatherhead: North Street, YMCA Red Triangle Services Club

Mayfair, 9 North Audley Street (Audley House), 14 Duke Street and 7 Grosvenor Square: US Army UK Base Medical Section

Mayfair, 70 South Audley Street, 53 and 54 Mount Street, 76 Cadogan Place and 8 Upper Grosvenor Street: HQ US Command, UK Base medical, dental and dispensary supplies and services

Mayfair, Mount Street: HQ 303rd US Army Station Hospital

Northwood: US Army Hospital

St James's, The Mall, Clarence House: HQ Red Cross and St John's Ambulance

Shenley Military Hospital

Sidcup: Queen Mary's Hospital, burns unit with plastic surgery specialism

Sundridge, Coombe Bank: Red Cross Convalescent Home/Auxiliary Hospital

Swanley, Parkwood: Red Cross Convalescent Home/Auxiliary Hospital

Uxbridge: RAF Central Dental Laboratory

Victoria, Hatherley Street and St George's Square: 150th US Army Station Hospital

Westminster, Millbank: Queen Alexandra's Military Hospital, 1905–77

Woolwich: Royal Herbert Military Hospital

Bibliography

Abrahams, B. *et al.*, 'Hanworth' in *Airfield Review* 61 (1992)

Abrahams, B., 'AIRCO' in *Airfield Review* 63 (1993)

—, 'The Fields of Hendon' in *Airfield Review* 105 (2004)

Alcock, L. and King, D.J.C., 'Ringworks in England and Wales' in A.J. Taylor (ed.), *Chateau Gaillard European Castle Studies: No. 3: Conference Report in German, French and English* (1969)

Anderson, I., 'Radlett Airfield History & Handley Page' in *Airfield Review* 115 (2007)

Bird, S.L., *Stepney: Profile of a London Borough from the Outbreak of the First World War to the Festival of Britain 1914–1951* (Newcastle-on-Tyne, 2011)

Birdsall, M. and Plisko, D., *An Insider's Travel Guide to 150 Spy Sites in London* (Leeds, 2009)

Brook, R., *The Story of Eltham Palace* (London, 1960)

Brooks, A., *London at War* (Barnsley, 2011)

Brooks, R., 'The Lullingstone Decoy' in *Airfield Review* 130 (2011)

Brown, R.A., Colvin, H.M. and Taylor, A.J., *The History of the King's Works: The Middle Ages*, 3 vols, (London HMSO, 1963)

Campbell, D., *War Plan UK* (London, 1982)

Catton, J., *Purfleet Garrison Historical References/Notes* (Thurrock Museum, 1996)

Cobb, P., personal communications and notes in *Aldis & Loopholes* (1975–2005)

Cocroft, W., *Dangerous Energy* (English Heritage, 2000)

Cocroft, W. and Thomas, R., *Cold War 1946–89* (English Heritage, 2003)

Connor, J.E., *Abandoned Stations on London's Underground* (Colchester, 2000)

Davis, P., 'Crenellated Town Houses in Medieval England' in N. Guy (ed.) *Castle Studies Group Journal* 24 (2010/11)

Dawson, G., 'Saxon defences of Southwark' in *London Archaeologist* 13.1 (2011)

Dean, J., *Statistical analysis of Licences to Crenellate*; in N. Guy (ed.), *Castle Studies Group Journal*, 24 (2010/11)

Dobinson, C., *Twentieth Century Fortifications in England: Vol II Anti-invasion defences of WWII* (York: CBA, 1996)

—, *Twentieth Century Fortifications in England: Vol V Operation Overlord* (York: CBA, 1996)

—, *Fields of Deception* (London: EH & Methuen, 2000)

—, *AA Command* (London: EH & Methuen, 2001)

Douet, J., *British Barracks 1600–1914* (Norwich: HMSO, 1998)

Emery, P., 'Fulham Palace moat revealed' in *London Archaeologist* 13.1 (2011)

Evans, D., *Building the Steam Navy: Dockyards, Technology and the Creation of the Victorian Battle Fleet 1830–1906* (Conway Maritime Press: London, 2004)

Faulkner, N. and Durrani, N., *In search of the Zeppelin War: The Archaeology of the First Blitz* (The History Press: Stroud, 2008)

Filler, M., 'Our New Tower in London' in *The New York Review of Books* 27.iii (2010)

Flint, P., *RAF Kenley: the story of the Royal Air Force Station 1917–1974* (Terence Dalton: Lavenham, 1985)

Flintham, D., *London in the Civil War: Civil War Defences of London and Tower Hamlets* (Partizan Press: Leigh-on-Sea, 2008)

—, 'A Tale of Two Forts – London's Hyde Park and St George's Fields Forts' in *FORT* 38 (2010)

Foot, W., *Beaches, fields, streets and hills: the anti-invasion landscapes of England, 1940*, CBA Research Report 144 (Council for British Archaeology: York, 2006)

Foynes, J.P., *The Battle of the East Coast 1939–1945* (published by the author, 1994)

Francis, P., *British Military Airfield Architecture: From Airships to the Jet Age* (Patrick Stephens Ltd: Yeovil, 1996)

Francis, P. and Crisp, G., *Military Command & Control Organisation* (EH on CD, 2008)

Francis, P., *Airfield Defences* (AiX ARG: Ware, 2010)

Goodwin, J., *Military Signals from the South Coast: From Fire Beacons to the railway Telegraph* (Middleton Press: Midhurst, 2000)

Grimes, W.F., 'Excavations in the City of London' in' R.L.S. Bruce-Mitford (ed.), *Recent Archaeological Excavations in Britain* (London, 1956)

Halpenny, B.B., *Action Stations 8: Greater London* (Patrick Stephens Ltd: Yeovil, 1984/1993)

Harwood, B., *Chivalry & Command: 500 Years of Horse Guards* (Osprey: Oxford 2006)

Hutchings, T. and Corley, D., 'Brooklands Aerodrome 1907–39' and 'Brooklands Aerodrome 1939–2006' in *Airfield Review* 107 (2005) and 110 (2006)

Inwood, S., *A History of London* (Macmillan: London, 1998)

James, Brig. E., *British Regiments 1914–18* (Heathfield, 1978)

Keevill, G., *Medieval Palaces: an Archaeology* (The History Press: Stroud, 2000)

Leete, J., *Under Fire, Britain's Fire Service at War* (The History Press: Stroud, 2008)

Litchfield, N., *The Territorial Artillery 1908–88: Their Lineage, Uniforms and Badges* (N.E.H. Litchfield: Nottingham, 1992)

Masters, R., *The Royal Arsenal, Woolwich in Old Photographs* (The History Press: Stroud, 1995 and 2004)

McCamley, N., *Cold War Secret Nuclear Bunkers: The Passive Defence of the Western World During the Cold War* (Pen & Sword: Barnsley, 2002)

Marren, P., *Battles of the Dark Ages* (Pen & Sword: Barnsley, 2006)

Morris, J. (revised S. Macready), *Londinium, London in the Roman Empire* (Pan: London, 1982 & 1998)

Newsome, S., Millward, J. and Cocroft, W., 'Repository Woods, Woolwich; An Archaeological Survey of the Military Repository Training Grounds' (English Heritage: 2009)

O'Brien, H., *Queen Emma and the Vikings: The Woman Who Shaped the Events of 1066* (Bloomsbury: London, 2005)

Osborne M., 'Purfleet Rifle Range' (RSPB Survey Report) (Oxford Archaeology, 2000)

—, *Defending Britain, Twentieth Century Military Structures in the Landscape* (The History Press: Stroud, 2004)

—, *Always Ready, the Drill Halls of Britain's Volunteer Forces* (Partizan Press: Leigh-on-Sea, 2006)

—, *20th Century Defences in Britain – the London area: London Within the M25, Berkshire, Buckinghamshire, Hertfordshire and Oxfordshire* (Concrete Publications: Market Deeping, 2006)

Owen, J., *Danger UXB: The Heroic Story of the WWII Bomb Disposal Teams* (Abacus: London, 2010)

Peerless, G., 'A History of Elstree Aerodrome' in *Airfield Review* 90 (2001)

Perring, D., 'London: A city made for shopping or killing?' in *British Archaeology* 122 (January/February 2012)

Pidgeon, G., *The Secret Wireless War* (*c.*2003)

Pile, Gen. Sir F., *Ack-Ack: Britains' Defence Against Air Attack During the Second World War* (George G. Harrop & Co.: London, 1949)

Price, A., *Blitz on Britain 1939–45* (London, 1976)

Public Record Office, *Camp 020, MI5 & the Nazi spies* (Richmond, 2000)

Rawlinson, A., *The Defence of London* (London, Melrose, 1923)

RCHME, *Pillbox at Merchant Taylors' School; Request Survey* (London, 1995)

Reed, J., 'London's Wartime Headquarters' in *After the Battle,* 37 (1982)

Roberts, Sir H. and Godfrey, W., *Survey of London Volume 22: Bankside* (London, 1950)

Rude, G., *Hanoverian London* (London, 1971 and Stroud, 2003)

Salter, M., *The Castles of Kent* (Folly: Malvern, 2000)

—, *The Castles of Surrey* (Folly: Malvern, 2001)

Schofield, J., *The Building of London* (British Museum Press: London, 1984 & 1993)

Shackel, M., 'Banstead Forts' in *Loopholes* 33 (2005), 34 (2005), and pers. com.

Shaw, S., 'Langley Aircraft Factory and Airfield' in *Airfield Review* 87 (2000)

Sheppard, F., *LONDON: A history* (Oxford, 2000)

Sinclair, W.B., 'The Black Heath' text of lecture delivered 5/5/1955 in *Journal of the London Society* 328, (June 1955)

Smith, V., 'The defences of London during the English Civil War' in *FORT* 25 (1997)

—, 'The London Mobilisation Centres' in *London Archaeologist* (1975)

—, 'The Fortification of London during the Civil War' (Kent Defence Research Group – a *RAVELIN* Special, 1983)

—, *Defending London's River* (North Kent Books: Rochester, 1985)

—, 'Chatham & London; the Changing Face of English Fortification, 1870–1918' in *Post Mediaeval Archaeology* 19 (1985)

Tamplin, J., *The Lambeth & Southwark Volunteers* (Trustees of the Regimental Historical Fund: London, 1965)

Thurley, S., *The Royal Palaces of Tudor England*: *Architecture and Court Life, 1460–1547,* (Yale University Press: London, 1993)

'Two men in a trench' TV series/book (programme in series 2 on RAF Hornchurch)

Wallace, M., *The King's Troop: Royal Horse Artillery* (Kenilworth Press: London, 1984)

Waller, M., *London 1945* (John Murray: London, 2004)

Walling, J., *The Internment and Treatment of German Nationals during the First World War* (Riparian: Grimsby, 2005)

Ward, K., 'RAF Northolt' in *Airfield Review* 111 (2006)

Watson, B., 'Suffolk Place: Southwark's forgotten Tudor royal palace' in *London Archaeologist* 13.1 (2011)

Wills, H., 'British Invasion Defences' in *After the Battle* 14 (1976)

—, *Pillboxes a study of UK defences 1940* (Leo Cooper: London, 1985)

Winser, J., *The D-Day Ships. Neptune: the Greatest Amphibious Operation in History* (World Ship Society: Kendal, 1994)

Wood, D., *Attack Warning Red: Royal Observer Corps and the Defence of Britain 1925 to 1992* (Carmichael & Sweet: Portsmouth, 1976 & 1992)

Ziegler, P., *London at War 1939–1945* (Pimlico: London, 1995)

Absolutely indispensable, are the original London (2) and Middlesex (1) volumes, and the seven updated Greater London volumes of Nikolaus Pevsner's *Buildings of England* series, for details of individual buildings (Harmondsworth (Penguin) & New Haven & London (Yale UP) 1952–2005).

The National Archives at Kew holds some documentation relating to the pre-Sealion Second World War period. WO 166/1159 contains London Area Operation Instructions, giving details of troops defending London, their bases, and plans for their emergency deployment; procedures and measures for countering invasion during the period May 1940 to autumn 1941 and the final, developed London Defence Plan. Amendments and appendices provide a commentary on the effectiveness and development of these plans.

WO 199/617 focuses on the area around Whitehall, describing defence measures and the emergency procedures to be followed in the event of either a raid on London, or a fully developed invasion. This file contains a plan of the New Government Offices, now the Treasury, whose basement was adapted for the Cabinet War Rooms.

WO 199/624 covers the defence of the Thames in the run-up to the expected invasion, containing a detailed map of the defences ashore and on moored vessels.

The volumes produced by Dr Colin Dobinson for CBA during the Defence of Britain Project and packed with information and references. They are available through Local Authority Heritage, Environment and Archive Offices.

Information on defence sites can be found at the following websites:
www.gatehouse-gazetteer.info (Philip Davis's county lists of mediaeval fortified sites)
www.britarch.ac.uk/projects/dob (Defence of Britain Project)
www.pillboxesuk.co.uk (Ian Sanders' pillbox website)
www.pillbox-study-group.org.uk (Pillbox Study Group)
www.airfieldresearchgroup.org.uk (Airfield Research Group)

Index

Page references in **bold** indicate illustrations.

Acton 147, 151, 178, 186, 230

Air Raid Precautions/Civil Defence 152-3, 188-90, 206

Aldermanbury 19

Alexandra Palace 11, 139, 165, 171, 189, 220

Anti-invasion defences 105-7, 120, 154-72, **157**, **159**, **163**, 165, 170, 172

Bank of England 82, 83, 98, 140

Banstead 66, 162, **163**

Barking Creek 13, 164

Barnet 48, 66, 100, 158, 187, 198, 224, 237

Battersea 103, 128, 131, 158, 183, 220, 223

Baynards Castle 25, 28, 30, 43, 59, 60, 215

Beacons 66, 88

Beddington, Carew Manor 54, 59, 72

Bentley Priory/Stanmore 145-6, 147, 155, 156, 184-5, 186, 198, 204, 210, 230, 235, 238

Bermondsey 45, 56

Bexley 65, 201

Biggin Hill 124, 126, 140, 141, **142**, 143, **144**, 146, 151, **152**, 155, 171, 175, 176, 187, 188, **192**, 193, **209**, 210, 230

Blackfriars 31, 33, 37, 43, 158

Blackheath 14, 48, 49, 57, 66, 70, 122, 127, 131, 135, 220, 223

Blackwall 65, 77, 108, 156

Bomb Disposal 137, 181, 190, 208

Bow 56, 109, 113, **165**, 166, 216

Brentford 22, 68, 197, 200, 211

Bridewell 60

British Army

    City of London Yeomanry [Roughriders] 103, 147

    Coldstream Guards 73, 173, 198, 221

    1st County of London Yeomanry [Middlesex Hussars] 91, 147, 148

    2nd County of London Yeomanry [Westminster Dragoons] 104, 147

    3rd County of London Yeomanry [Sharpshooters] 103, 147, 148, 207

    East Surrey Regiment 92, 95, 103, 127, 128-9, 158, 221

    Engineer Volunteer Corps 99, 103

    Essex Regiment 128, 169, 174, 208

    Essex Yeomanry 91, 127

    GHQ Liaison Regiment [Phantom] 221

Grenadier Guards 169

Hertfordshire Yeomanry 100, 127

Honourable Artillery Company 66, 82, 100, 101, **101**, 127, 130, 147, 173

Household Cavalry/Life Guards/Blues & Royals 73, 83, 93, 101, 169, 207, 221-2

19th Hussars 126

Inns of Court Regiment 66, 100, 103, 130, 147

Irish Guards 171

Kent Yeomanry 100, 147, 207

King Edwards Horse 127, 147

Kings Royal Rifle Corps 98, 128, 130, 207

London Balloon Company 100

London Regiment 100, 127, 130, 131, 149, 185, 208, 223

Machine Gun Corps 127

Middlesex Regiment 98, 127, 129, 131, 148, 158, 169, 173, 221

19th Middlesex Rifle Volunteers [Bloomsbury Rifles] 102

20th Middlesex Rifle Volunteers [Artists Rifles] 11, 102, **102**, 130, 138

23rd Middlesex Rifle Volunteers [Royal Fusiliers] 103

Queens Own Royal West Kent Regiment 127

Queens Royal Irish Hussars 222

Queens Royal West Surrey Regiment 100, 101, 127, 128, 150, 185, 207

Rifle Brigade 98, 127, 207

Royal Army Education Corps 222

Royal Army Medical Corps 116, **117**, 137

Royal Army Ordnance Corps 150

Royal Army Service Corps 104, 122, 133, 135, 136, 150, **151**, 171, 200, 221

Royal Artillery 85, 93, 96, 148, 149, 150, 165, 171, 182, 207, 221, 222

Royal Electrical & Mechanical Engineers 200

Royal Engineers 85, 158, 103, **103**, 112, 139, 208

Royal Fusiliers 94, 98, 127, 129, 130, 131, 147, 207, 222

Royal Signals 222

Royal Tank Regiment 170, 221

Special Air Service 137, 221, 222

Surrey Yeomanry 127, 148, 149

Volunteer Light Horse units 99-100, 102

Welsh Guards 127, 198
Yeomen of the Guard 59
Bromley 54-5, 100, 127, 147, 149, 164, 181, 186, 204
Brompton Road AAOR 150, 203, 226
Brooklands **162**, 184, 186, 195, 210, 211, 230
Buckingham Palace 93, 123, 198
Burlington House 11, 102, 132
Bushey 19, 130, 189, 221, 230
Bushy Park, Teddington 199, 201, 210, 230

Caterham **96**, 96, 116, 153, 198, 207, 210, 220, 221, 222
Charterhouse 42
Chelsea 14, 19, 41, 69, 76, 93, 116, 122, 137, **137**, 147, 186, 207, 213, 220, 221, 222, 223
Chessington 28, 89, 161, 215
Chingford 124, 126, 131, 155, 156, 230
Chislehurst Caves 134, 188
Civil War defences 68, **68**, 69-70, **70**
Colindale 116, 133, 195, 230-1
Crayford 108, 134, **135**, 135, 138, 164, 172
Cricklewood 116, 132, 181, 195, 230, 231
Cripplegate 15, **16**, 17, 20, 21, 33, 39, 40
Croydon 31, 35, 52, 72, 85, 126, 132, 133, 140, **144**, 144, 171, 176, 179, 190, 191, 200, 219, 224, 231
Crystal Palace 11, 122, 131, 156, 164, 200, 204

Denham 126, 195, 201, 231
Deptford 65, 76, **77**, 77, **78**, 78, 108, **110**, 110, 122, 220
Drayton Manor **64**, 65
Drill halls 101-4, **148**, **149**, **150**, 149-50, 181, 197, 207, 208, **209**, 223-4

Edgware **148**, 224
Elstree **196**, 197, 198, 204, 221, 231, 237
Eltham 48-9, **49**, 54, 65, 136, **138**, 200, 222
Enfield 55, 59, 155
Enfield Lock Small Arms Factory 91, 98, 107, 113, 114, **114**, 135, 178, **179**, 182, 183
Epping 14, 131, 159, 206
Epsom 129, 138, 161, 163, 181, 200, 206, 220
Erith 12, 65, 122, 133, 164
Esher 52, **53**, 54, 161
Ewell 138, 149, **150**, 206, 224
Eynsford 21, 26-7, **27**, 215

Fairlop/Hainault Farm 122, 124, **125**, 126, 140, 146, 158, 159, 175, 176, 193, 231
Feltham/Hanworth Park 80, 126, 133, 146, 173, 221, 231
Finchley 121, 133, 140, 151, 165, 224
Fort Halstead 112, 183, 211
Fulham 20, 36, 52, 63, 133, 166

Greenwich 22, 48, 49-50, 59, 60, 72, **79**, 131, 135, 210
Grims Ditch/Dyke 19
Grove Park [SE] 126, 136, **136**, 220, 224

Hackney Marshes/Olympic site 12, 14, 134, 155, 165, **165**
Ham/Latchmere 132, 138, 202, 211, 232, 237
Hampton Court 60, 61, 62, 74, **75**
Harringay 100, 200, 221
Harrow/Headstone Manor 19, 52, **53**, 130, 186, 206
Hatton House 134, **134**
Heathrow 89, 173, 195, 204, 214, 232
Hendon 116, 124, **125**, 131, 132, 133, 138, **139**, **141**, 141, 175, 198, 232
Heston 144, **145**, **149**, 173, 195, 224, 232
Home Guard/LDV 164, 165, 168, 169, 170, 178, 180-1, 183, 203
Honor Oak Park 124, **124**
Honourable East India Company 77, 104, 108
Hornchurch/Suttons Farm 124, 140, 141, **143**, 144, 155, 174-5, **178**, 178, 187, 232
Hospital of St John 35, 36, 37, 42, **42**, 45, 56, 60
Hounslow 85, 86, 89, 92, **94**, 95, 115, 116, 118, 126, 131, 134, 136, 158, 186, 198, 199, **199**, 201, 207, 211, 219, 221, 232, 238
Hurst Park 129, 220
Hyde Park 69, 83, 86, **87**, 88, 98, 100, 104, 123, 132, 140, 184, 188, 207, 219

Ilford 13, 17
Isleworth 50, 136

Joyce Green 126, 232

Kempton 11, 34, 35, 129, 220
Kenley 126, 141, 151, 155, 171, 173, 176, 184, 198, 233
Kennington 35, 50-1, 91
Kensington **75**, 76, 99, 122, 136, 146, 149, 181, 202, 220, 223
Kenwood House 83, 121, 124, 220
Keston 13, 171, 214
Kidbrooke 131, 140, 185, 197, 210
Kingston-upon-Thames 13, 35, 36, 52, 72, **95**, 95, 118, 132, 133, 150, 156, 158, 161, 195, 198, 200, 207, 210, 224, 233
Knightsbridge Barracks 83, 84, 85, 90, 93, 169, 207, 219, 221

Lambeth 35, 47, 52, **52**, 65, 78, 82, 107, 108, 123, 137, **212**, 213
Langley 181, 183, 195, 233
Leavesden 195, 211, 233
Lippitts Hill 148, 182, 203, 206, 221
London Bridge 14, 21, 22, 33, 47, 48, 66, 77, 170
London Colney 126, 161, 197, 233
London Docks 79, **80**, 106, 158, 166, 193-4
London Mobilisation Centres 106-7, 176, 183
London Walls and Gates **16**, 17, **18**, 25, 31-3, **32**, 37, 39, **40**, 57-8, 72
Lords Cricket Ground 11, 131, 191, 235
Loughton 13
Lullingstone 27, **64**, 65, 187
Lundenwic 19, 20

Mediaeval moated sites 36-7, 46, 54-6, 216-18
Militia 66, 76-7, 82, 83, 92, 96, **97**, 98, 148, 236
Mill Hill Barracks 96, 155, 158, 164, 183, 198, 199, 200, 205, 207, 220, 221
Montfichet 25, 28, 30, 31, 215

New Scotland Yard 123, 128, **129**
Nonsuch 46, 59, 60-1
Northolt 54, 131, 141, **142**, 155, 172, 176, 187, 204, 233
North Weald [Bassett] 106, 124, 126, 140, 141, 155, 173, 175, **176**, **177**, 182, 193, 206, 233

Oatlands 59, 60-1
Olympia 11, 139
Osterley Park 136, 180
Otford 59, 63, **63**

Peasants' Revolt 39, 47
Perivale 131, 133, 158
Pillboxes 120, **157**, 159-62, **160**, **161**, **162**, **163**, **175**, 175-6, **176**, **178**, **179**, **180**, 182
Police force 83, 90, 120, 205-6
Powder mills 80, 86, 107
Purfleet 86, 88, 104-5, 107, 115-6, **119**, 120, 124, 129, **129**, 169, 178, **182**, 183, 220
Putney 88, 122, 147, 164, **166**, 166

Radlett **177**, 183, 195, 210, 211, 233-4
Redhill 146, 155, 175, 191, **192**, 193, 204, 234
Regents Park and Barracks 92, 93, 103, 121, 136, 198, 219, 221, 222
Richmond-upon-Thames/Sheen 13, 48, 51, 58, 104, 122, 130, 132, 133, 151, 158, 164, 184, 206, 221
Rickmansworth 52, 54, 59, 60, 63, 185, 221
Roehampton 131, 172, 200
Romford 85, 130, 158, 219, 220, 224
Rotherhithe 51, 158
Royal Air Force 140-6, 173, 174, 185, 186, 191-3, 197-8, 201, 227
Royal Air Force Regiment 173, 176, 185
Royal Flying Corps 100, 122, 131, 138
Royal Marines 121, 169
Royal Naval Air Service 120, 121, 122, 131,
Royal Navy 77, 82, 90, 107-9, 110, 120, 136, 140, 153, 169, 171, 190, 193, 226
Royal Observer Corps 122, 146-7, 186-7, 203-5, **204**, **205**
Royal Ordnance Factories 178-9, 197
Ruislip [Manor] **26**, 27, 140, 156, 184, **184**, 197, 210, 215

St Georges Barracks, Trafalgar Square 92, 103
St James's **61**, 62, 83, 92, 156, 202, 219
St John's Wood 92, 93, 103, 150, 219, 221, 222, 234-5
St Pauls 20, 34, 41, 48, 56, 72, 189, 191, 195, 205
Salisbury Hall 65, 195, **196**, 234

Sandown Park 11, 221
Shepherds Bush 136, 220
Sidcup 138
Somerset House 11, 73, **128**, 128, 223
South Mimms 28, 180, 215
Southwark 12, 20, 21, 23, 31, 35, 45-6, **45**, 47, 66, 83, 84, 133, 223
Special Operations Executive 199, 237-8
Stapleford Tawney 146, 173, **174**, 175, **175**, 191, 193, 234
Steelyard 34, 41, 216
Strand/Savoy 36, 38, 44-5, 47, 48, 75-6
Stratford 80, 133

Territorial Army 146, 147-9, 197, 207, 211
Territorial Force 100, 127-8
Thames river patrols 153, 154, 169, 181
Tottenham 22, 80, 148, 224
Tower Hamlets 11, 76, 82, 99
Tower of London 11, 18-19, 21, **25**, 25-6, 28-30, **29**, **33**, 38-9, 57, **57**, **58**, 67, 70, **71**, 73-4, **74**, 89, 91, 92, 93, **94**, 127, 166-7, 190, 219, 222
Trained Bands 68, 69, 71, 76, 83

Uxbridge 84, 91, **97**, 126, 131, 140, 145, 146, 147, 151, 155, 156, **161**, 198, 210, 234, 235

Volunteer forces 11, 83-84, 91, 98-9, 99-100, 130-1, 136
Volunteer Training Corps 130, 153

Waltham Abbey 56, 59-60, 86, 114, **115**, 123, **123**, 133, 135, 178, 183, 184, 187, 197
Walthamstow 80, 133, 211
Wandsworth/Clapham 80, 118, 121, 128, 137, 166, 202, 220
Wapping 65
Watford 132, 133, 147, 161, 186, 204,
Wellington Barracks 92, **93**, 169, 190, 198, 207, 221, 222
Wembley 137, 165, 166, 184, 194, 239
Westminster 14, 17, 23, 34, 35, 43-4, 48, 66, 68, 69, 83, 118, 136, 167, 181, **212**, 213, 219, 222, 223, 228, 239
White City 127, 139, 198
Whitehall 34, 35, 44, 59, 62-3, 69, 73, **86**, 86, **87**, 91, **109**, 121, 145, 167, **168**, 168-9, 180, 190-1, 201, 219, 220, 221, 222, 225
Wickham Court 55, **55**
Wimbledon 98, 128, 130, 131, 164, 200, 203, 214
Woldingham 129, 131, 199, **200**, 220
Woolwich 56, 65, 72, 77, 78, **78**, 80, 81, 85-6, **85**, 86, 88, 96, 104, **104**, 106, 107, **107**, **111**, **112**, 110-12, **113**, **117**, **121**, 127, 133, 134, 135, 138, 147, 150, 164, **170**, 172, 178, 190, 194, 197, 200, 211, 219, 220, 221, 222
Wormwood Scrubs 126, 131, 239